Sebastian Lohsse | Reiner Schulze
Dirk Staudenmayer (Eds.)

Private Law and the Data Act

Münster Colloquia on EU Law and the Digital Economy VIII

HART

Nomos

The Deutsche Nationalbibliothek lists this publication in the Deutsche Nationalbibliografie; detailed bibliographic data are available on the Internet at http://dnb.d-nb.de

ISBN:	HB (Nomos)	978-3-7560-1892-5
	ePDF (Nomos)	978-3-7489-4784-4

British Library Cataloguing-in-Publication Data
A catalogue record for this book is available from the British Library.

ISBN:	HB (Hart)	978-1-5099-8516-6

Library of Congress Cataloging-in-Publication Data
Lohsse, Sebastian | Schulze, Reiner | Staudenmayer, Dirk
Private Law and the Data Act
Münster Colloquia on EU Law and the Digital Economy VIII
Sebastian Lohsse | Reiner Schulze | Dirk Staudenmayer (Eds.)
256 pp.
Includes bibliographic references.

ISBN	978-1-5099-8516-6	(hardcover Hart)

Online-Version
Nomos eLibrary

1st Edition 2024

Table of Contents

Preface

With the Data Act the eighth Münster Colloquium "Private Law and the Data Act" on 11/12 January 2024 focused on a new EU legal act, which came into force on precisely this date. The act represents a milestone in the emerging law of the European data economy. Presentations and panel contributions from academia, politics and business explored the significance of this new piece of legislation for European private law and for the further development of the data economy in the Union.

Hopefully, the contributions published in this volume, based on the fruitful discussions of the conference, may provide inspiration for the interpretation and application of the Data Act in legal practice as well as for the development of the legal doctrine and private law of the digital economy.

The editors would like to thank the authors of this volume and the staff of Nomos Verlag for their extraordinary efforts to enable the timely publication of the conference contributions. The editors are also grateful to the student assistants Kim von Göldel and Yannik Tasei for their outstanding commitment in organizing the eighth Münster Colloquium and in preparing this volume.

June 2024

Sebastian Lohsse

Reiner Schulze

Dirk Staudenmayer

An Introduction

The Data Act – a Cornerstone for the European Data Economy

*Sebastian Lohsse/Reiner Schulze/Dirk Staudenmayer**

The Data Act[1] came into force on the first day of the eighth Münster Colloquium dedicated to 'Private Law and the Data Act'. The key reasons to choose this legislation as a topic of the 'Münster Colloquia on EU Law and the Digital Economy' were that the Data Act is both a cornerstone for the European data economy and an important deliverable towards a European Digital Private Law.

I. The Data Act – regulating contracts in the data economy

1. The central question of the data economy

For the data economy to flourish, private law has to find an answer to the question of who has access to data and under what conditions can data be used commercially.[2] This question is so central for, among other reasons, the emerging dependency in the data economy between the 'data-haves' and the 'data-have-nots', resulting from the growing significance of data as factor of production. It has been said that in the 21st century data is set to replace land and materials as the most important factor of production.[3] Yet even if data should not replace the classical factors of production, it

---

* Sebastian Lohsse and Reiner Schulze are Professors of Law, Centre for European Private Law, University of Münster. Dirk Staudenmayer was as Head of Unit in the Directorate General Justice and Consumers of the European Commission closely involved in the elaboration and negotiation of the private law part of the Data Act; he is also Honorary Professor at the University of Münster. This contribution only reflects the personal opinions of the authors and does not bind in any way the European Commission.

1 Regulation 2017/2394 of 13 December 2023 on harmonised rules on fair access to and use of data (Data Act), OJ L 1/71 of 22.12.2023. Recitals and Articles without indication of the source stem from the Data Act.

2 Cf. Rec. 4 sentence 1. According to *Harari* (21 Lessons for the 21st Century, 2018, p. 97) it could be the most important political question of our time how to regulate the use of data.

3 *Harari* (fn. 2), p. 94.

will at least be an important additional factor. It will become the blood in the veins of the data economy.[4] In particular, the rise and roll-out of the Internet of Things (IoT) allow smart products[5] to collect data.[6] The fast and ever-increasing mass of data[7] leads among other things to a datafication of business processes and data-based business models. Even more than at present, future innovative business models will therefore need data. Dependency is thus created, when a business needs data of another business for developing or running its own innovative business model, but does not have access to this data.

Two features of data are particularly relevant in this context. Data is a non-rivalrous resource, which means that the use of data by one market player does not limit the availability, the usability, nor the value of the same data for use by other market players.[8] While this potentially would allow for easy sharing of data, data is at the same time also an excludable resource. In other words, it is by no means automatically available for use by anyone as its use can be easily restricted.[9]

This can be probably best explained with an example, using a predictive maintenance business model.[10] A car driver might be informed on his screen by the IoT-capable sensors in his tyres that the profile of the rear tyres is lower than 1.6 mm[11] and that these tyres should thus be replaced as soon as possible. Together with this message, the digital display in the car could inform the consumer that the costs for replacing two tyres in the recommended garage, which happens to be a car dealer accredited by the car producer, would be 298.99 € and allow the consumer to make an appointment with that garage directly. In addition, the display might advise the consumer not only to replace the rear tyres but all four tyres which could be done at the same garage for the promotional price of 448.99 €.

4 *Lohsse/Schulze/Staudenmayer*, Trading Data in the Digital Economy: Legal Concepts and Tools, p. 15.
5 As regards the importance of smart products in the IoT, see *Lohsse/Schulze/Staudenmayer*, 'Smart Products' – A Focal Point for Legal Developments in the Digital Economy, in: Lohsse/Schulze/Staudenmayer (eds.), Smart Products, 2022, p. 13 et seq.
6 Cf. Rec. 1 sentence 2. The Data Act regulates the so-called connected products (Art. 2 (5)). Cf. also Rec. 14.
7 On this phenomenon called 'big data' cf. for instance *Mayer-Schönberger/Cukier*, Big Data, 2013.
8 Cf. Rec. 1 sentence 4.
9 Cf. Rec. 20 sentence 3.
10 Cf. Rec. 16 sentence 1; Rec. 20 sentence 2.
11 Minimum profile for instance in Germany according to § 36 para (3) sentence 3 Straßenverkehrszulassungsordnung.

If not only the car producer but also independent after-sales companies have access to the same data, the latter could at the same time inform the car owner that the same operation of replacing two or four tyres at an independent garage would cost 248.99 € or 395.99 € respectively. In addition, not only the independent after-sales sector but also the tyre producer and the car owner's car insurance company would be potentially interested in access to this data in order, for example, to improve their tyres or to offer the consumer an insurance policy tailor-made to the driving style of the car owner. The issue is of the same importance in relation to non-personal data. For instance, data access would be decisive for the question of whether a jet engine producer, a plane producer or an independent third party could have access to the jet engine sensor data from the party which factually or contractually controls the data, in order to offer predictive maintenance services to the airline.

2. Data sharing through contracts

The main reasons why the Data Act is a cornerstone for the European data economy is that it provides two key elements towards answering the question of who has access to data and under what conditions.[12] The first is a right to access, use and share co-generated data. According to the second element the modalities how such data access, use and sharing must be done are elaborated through contracts.

a) The right to data access and use

Art. 4 (1) grants the user of a purchased or rented connected product or of a related service a data access right.[13] This access right concerns data[14] which the data holder can access based on a contract and without disproportion-

12 As to first ideas, preceding the proposal for a Data Act, how a regulatory approach answering this question could be designed see *Staudenmayer*, Towards a European Private Law of the Digital Economy? – Trends, in: Janssen/Schulte-Nölke (eds.), Researches in European Private Law and Beyond – Contributions in Honour of Reiner Schulze's Seventieth Birthday, 2020, p. 83 et seq., in particular p. 86 et seq.

13 Only if the user wants this access (Art. 4 (1) 2, Rec. 21 sentence 9), in which case this access should be automatic (Rec. 21 sentence 10).

14 As well as the relevant metadata necessary to interpret and use the data (Art. 4 (1) 1; 2 (2); Rec. 15 sentence 11).

ate effort going beyond a simple operation.[15] The data should be accessible to the user without undue delay, of the same quality as is available to the data holder, easily, securely, free of charge, in a comprehensive, structured, commonly used and machine-readable format and, where relevant and technically feasible, continuously and in real-time. The Data Act takes the requirement of the structured, commonly used, and machine-readable format over from Art. 20 (1) GDPR. Access to the data is granted free of charge because the user has a contractual (sales, rent or service contract) right to the respective product or services. In addition, without the use of the product or service by the user, the data would not be generated.[16]

The user can use the accessed data for any lawful purpose and, above all, can pass it on to third parties.[17] Art. 5 (1) creates a right of the user to request the data holder to make the data available to a third party with the same features as to the user.

While the modalities of the data access, use and sharing are elaborated through contracts, the Data Act clarifies that the data holder cannot prevent access by simply refusing to conclude such contract; such right can be directly invoked in court.[18]

b) Contracts as tools for data access, use and sharing

The Data Act presumes[19] the existence of different contracts and regulates[20] them, albeit to a different extent.

When the relevant parties use co-generated IoT data, there are as a matter of principle relationships between three different parties, i.e. the data holder, the user and the third-party data recipient. For that reason, there are three different contracts between the parties containing the conditions for data access, use and sharing, and constituting for non-personal data the

15 Art. 2 (17); Rec. 20 sentences 5, 6.
16 Rec. 17 sentence 1; Rec. 18 sentences 3, 4.
17 Rec. 30 sentence 1, 2; Rec. 35 sentence 1.
18 Rec. 42 sentence 6, 7.
19 Thus *Hennemann/Steinrötter,* Der Data Act – Neue Instrumente, alte Friktionen, strukturelle Weichenstellungen, NJW 2024, p. 6, are correct in stating that the legislator “thinks”in contractual relationships.
20 Rec. 9 confirms that national contract law remains applicable, unless otherwise regulated in the Data Act.

legal base thereof. In many instances, the Data Act refers to the contracts between the different parties.[21]

In addition, there are as a matter of principle between data holder and user three different contractual relationships (which can be regrouped into one single contract): the sales, rent or leasing contract for a connected product, the consent according to Art. 6 (1) a) GDPR[22] and the contract on the modalities of data sharing and use. The seller or lessor in a sale, rent or leasing contract of a connected product can be identical with the data holder, but this does not have to be the case. In the above-mentioned predictive maintenance example, the producer is likely to be the data holder while the accredited car dealer acts as the seller. In such cases, the contract between the data holder and the user is concluded with the seller acting as the intermediary.

Finally, there could be a so-called "related service" as part of the sales, rent or leasing contract on a connected product[23] or as an independent services contract[24]. Such a contract could be concluded with the data holder, e.g. the producer,[25] or any third party[26]. The definition of a related service[27] in Art. 2 (5), Rec. 17 is inspired by the regulation of goods with digital elements in the Sale of Goods Directive (SGD) (and the Digital Content Directive [DCD]).[28] However, the Data Act has a broader scope and covers

---

21 As regards contracts between data holder and user s. Art. 2 (13); 3 (2) (d), (3) (a) - (c), (i); 3 (3) (i); 4 (2), (6) 2, (14); 5 (2); 6 (2) (c); Rec. 15 sentence 12; 20 sentence 5; 25; 26; 27 sentence 2; 28; 31 sentence 4; 37; 38 sentence 9, between user and data recipient Art. 6 (1); Rec. 23 sentence 3; 25 sentence 8; 10; 33 sentences 5 – 7; 38 sentence 9 and between data holder and data recipient Art. 5 (1) 2, (8), (9) 2; 8 et seq.; Rec. 26; 40 sentence 14; 40; 42 – 45; 48; 52.

22 The GDPR presumes that the consent is not just simply a unilateral declaration but is given in the context of a contract. In its Rec. 42 it presumes that the Unfair Contract Terms Directive applies to a declaration of consent pre-formulated by the controller, which is only possible if there is a B2C contract.

23 Rec. 17 sentences 4, 5.

24 Rec. 17 sentence 7.

25 Rec. 6 sentence 1.

26 Rec. 17 sentence 8.

27 Beyond the definition, Art. 2 (6) follows Rec. 21 sentence 8 DCD, 14 sentence 3 SGD stipulating that the time of the connection of the related service with the product is not decisive. Rec. 17 sentence 9 takes over the presumption of Art. 3 (3) 3 SGD, 3 (4) 2 DCD that in case of doubt the related service is provided as part of the contract. Rec. 17 sentence 5 uses wording from Art. 7 (1) d) SGD, 8 (1) b) DCD.

28 Art. 2 (5) b); 3 (3) sentence 2 SGD and Art. 2 (3); 3 (4) sentence 1 DCD. See *Staudenmayer*, in: Schulze/Staudenmayer (eds.), EU Digital Law, 1st ed. 2020, Art. 3 DCD, para. 73 et seq.

more data. Not only services, the absence of which would prevent the product to perform their functions, are included, but also those services whose absence would prevent the product to perform any of its functions, i.e. even an auxiliary one.

c) Balanced contracts

While still emphasising the principle of contractual freedom,[29] the Data Act introduces principles to guide contractual design and negotiation in order to ensure that passing on data by the data holder to a third-party data recipient upon the request of the user is dealt with in balanced contracts.[30]

Art. 8 (1) obliges data holders to share data with data recipients at fair, reasonable and non-discriminatory conditions and in a transparent way.

For the application of these principles, which are also the basis for the model contract clauses to be recommended by the Commission, the Data Act provides only rather rudimentary help. It fleshes out the principle of fairness, with reference to the unfair contract terms control in Art. 13. The reasonableness principle relates to the compensation when sharing data. The reasonable compensation called for by Art. 9 (1) shall provide a balance between the objective of the Data Act to achieve more data sharing and still providing an economic incentive for the data holder to continue to collect data.[31] Art. 9 (2), (3), Rec. 47 explains this in a bit more detail and Art. 9 (5) obliges the Commission to submit guidelines. If, however, the data recipient is an SME, Art. 9 (4) caps the compensation to the costs incurred to make the data available.[32]

The principle of non-discrimination does not prohibit unequal treatment which is justified by objective reasons.[33]

The transparency principle is manifested in the disclosure obligations in Art. 8 (3) 2, 9 (7) as regards non-discrimination and the calculation basis for the reasonable compensation.

---

29 Rec. 43.
30 Art. 5 (1) 2; 8 et seq.
31 Rec. 46.
32 See also Rec. 49.
33 Art. 8 III 1; Rec. 45 sentence 2.

The potential of the Data Act for promoting data sharing is increased through its 'future-oriented' effect.[34] While the rules on the modalities of data sharing in Art. 8 et seq. apply directly to the right to data access, use and sharing as regards co-generated data, they shall also apply to future data sharing rights still to be created in sectoral EU law.[35] The underlying idea is that future sectoral rules containing data access and sharing rights should refer to the Data Act as far as modalities are concerned. In effect, thus, the principles of the Data Act and the model contract terms to be recommended by the Commission would constitute a blueprint for future sectoral data access and sharing rights. It remains however to be seen whether this approach, which does not bind the *lex posterior* legislator, will be implemented in forthcoming proposals of the Commission and the adopted legal acts.

Finally, in Art. 13, the Data Act submits both contracts between data holder and data recipient on co-generated data[36] and all other contracts with a data access and use element, to an unfair contract terms control (see II.2.b).

II. The Data Act – an important deliverable towards a European Digital Private Law

The Data Act is part of a larger context, i.e. the adaptation of EU private law to the needs of the digital economy. This process is taking place in three waves.[37] The first wave began at the end of the nineties and amended EU private law for the purpose of promoting electronic commerce and adapting consumer protection tools. At present, we are in the second wave. This second wave is partially a reaction to a new generation of digital products enabled through new technologies. These new products – digital content and digital services as well as smart products – are now regulated by the

34 Its importance is also underlined by *Podszun/Pfeiffer*, Datenzugang nach dem EU Data Act: Der Entwurf der Europäischen Kommission, GRUR (Gewerblicher Rechtsschutz und Urheberrecht) 2022, p. 956.

35 Art. 12 (1); Rec. 6 sentence 4; 42 sentence 1. As regards the margin foreseen in Art. 44 (2), Rec. 115 and Art. 9 (6), Rec. 50 cf. *Staudenmayer*, Privatrechtsregeln für Datenzugangsrechte – Der Verordnungsschlag der Europäischen Kommission zum Datengesetz, EuZW 2022, p. 1039.

36 Art. 8 (1), (2), Rec. 44.

37 Cf. Staudenmayer (ed.), Europäisches Digitales Zivilrecht, 2024 (to appear), §§ 2 and 25.

Digital Content Directive and the Sale of Goods Directive. The other trend of this present phase is the response to emerging dependencies in the digital economy, in particular[38] that between the 'data-haves' and 'data-have-nots'. The prime example of the latter trend in the second phase is the Data Act. The third wave, which is likely to principally regulate the means by which private law should deal with autonomously acting AI, has already begun. The Commission proposals for an AI Liability Directive and for the review of the Product Liability Directive are the first elements of this third wave.[39]

1. Coherent adaptation

The adaptations by the Data Act to private law, in particular contract law,[40] are part and parcel of the digitalisation of EU private law. The Data Act therefore endeavours to insert itself in this larger development in a coherent way.

The Data Act regulates data obtained using smart products and services. It is thus important that the Data Act is consistent with the regulation of digital content, digital services and smart products in the Digital Content Directive and the Sale of Goods Directive,[41] i.e. the other strand of this second wave of digitalisation of EU private law. In this context, in regulating

38 The other dependency is the one between platform providers and their customers. Cf. for an explanation of private law acts dealing with the dependencies in the platform economy Staudenmayer (fn. 37), § 17. For a detailed commentary cf. Schulze/Staudenmayer (eds.), EU Digital Law, 2nd edition 2024 (to appear).

39 COM 2022 (496) final and COM 2022 (495) final v. 28. 9. 2022. On the challenges of AI for tort law cf. *Lohsse/Schulze/Staudenmayer*, Liability for AI – Opening a new chapter of adapting European private law to the digital transition, in: Lohsse/Schulze/Staudenmayer (eds.), Liability for AI, 2023, p. 7.

40 Rec. 5 sentences 4 and 5.

41 For an explanation of both Directives in the context of European Digital Private Law cf. *Staudenmayer*, The Directives on Digital Contracts: First Steps Towards the Private Law of the Digital Economy, ERPL 2020, p. 219. For a detailed commentary cf. Schulze/Staudenmayer (fn. 28).

related services[42] the Data Act primarily borrows from the rules of the Digital Content Directive and the Sale of Goods Directive.[43]

In addition, the Commission and the EU-legislator use the Common European Sales Law (CESL)[44] as a "quarry ", from which they take building blocks for proposals and legal acts. The Commission had attempted with the CESL to create directly applicable European private law through optional harmonisation in form of an alternative sales law.[45] As such optional harmonisation would have created a competition of CESL with national legal orders and influenced national contract law, the CESL did not find the necessary majority in Council. The Commission withdrew the proposal[46] after the adoption of the Digital Content Directive and the Sale of Goods Directive, because both Directives had fully harmonised remedies for goods (including smart products) as well as digital content and services.

The Digital Content Directive and the Sale of Goods Directive had already taken over the CESL wording multiple times in their texts.[47] The Data Act continues this trend: It takes over the design and much of the wording of the terms concerning the control of unfair contract terms in Chapter 8 CESL.

2. Private law relevant regulatory approaches

When regulating data access, use and sharing at the EU[48] level, the Data Act strengthens existing trends in the digitalisation of European private law or introduces new private law-relevant regulatory tools.

---

42 In addition, the "clear and comprehensible manner" in Art. 3 (2), (3), in which pre-contractual information has to be given, stems from Art. 5 (1), 6 (2) Consumer Rights Directive. Rec. 24 sentence 6 takes over the substance of the definition of durable medium in Art. 2 (10) Consumer Rights Directive as well as other consumer contract law directives, for example Art. 2 (13) Digital Content Directive and 2 (11) Sale of Goods Directive.

43 I.2.b).

44 Proposal of 11.10.2011 for a Regulation on a Common European Sales Law, COM (2011) 635 final.

45 For an introduction cf. *Staudenmayer*, Proposal for a Regulation on a Common European Sales Law – Textbook, 2011, p. VII et seq. For details cf. Schulze (ed.), Common European Sales Law, 2012.

46 OJ C 321/40 of 29. 9 2020.

47 See *Staudenmayer* (fn. 41), p. 223 et seq.

48 Cf. *Hennemann/Steinrötter* (fn. 19).

a) Inclusion of personal data in the scope

One of the main achievements of the Data Act in the digitalisation of private law and the development of the private law of the data economy is to make a decisive step towards the introduction of the missing contract law dimension of the GDPR[49]. The Data Act achieves this with the use of two distinctions. Besides the obvious distinction between personal and non-personal data, the Data Act for the first time makes use of the distinction between the legal base and the modalities of the data use.[50]

The Data Act covers personal data as object of the contract on the modalities of data access, use and sharing. Art. 1 (2) and Rec. 35 sentence 6 confirm explicitly the application of the Data Act to personal and non-personal[51] data. This approach does not run counter to the GDPR; rather, the Data Act complements the GDPR.[52] According to Rec. 35 sentence 6 the right of the user to access data and share data with a data recipient is independent of the legal base for processing personal data. Of course, the Data Act still upholds the principle according to which, for personal data, that legal base must be in Art. 6 GDPR.[53] The Data Act however adds the contract law dimension, which designs the modalities of access to, use and sharing of personal data.[54]

For non-personal data the distinction between the legal base and the modalities of the data use is not relevant. The legal base for processing, access and sharing of non-personal data is the contract;[55] such contract also regulates the modalities of the use of non-personal data.[56]

The Data Act therefore makes a decisive step forward in a discussion, which began with the Digital Content Directive and until now slowed down the development of the law of the data economy[57]. This Directive included personal data in its scope. While it was clear that personal data

49 See *Staudenmayer* (fn. 41), p. 234.

50 Rec. 4 sentence 1 at the end.

51 The fact that Rec. 26, 33 sentence 4 speak about non-personal data and Rec. 25 sentence 10 mentions B2B contracts, does not mean that the Data Act only applies to these, but that the Data Act sees here considerable economic potential.

52 Art. 1 (5); Rec. 6 sentence 3; 25; 35 sentences 1, 2 and 5.

53 Rec. 6 sentences 5 – 7; 34 sentences 2, 6, 7; 33 sentences 5, 6; Art. 4 (7); 5 (7).

54 Rec. 25 sentence 8; 35 sentences 8 f.; 37.

55 Art. 4 (13) 1; Rec. 25 sentences 2, 8, 10; 26; 33 sentences 5, 7.

56 Cf. Art. 4 (14); Rec. 26 sentences 7 – 9; 31 sentence 4; 35 sentences 8, 9; 37.

57 *Hennemann/Steinrötter* (fn. 19) p. 5 speak of the “Gordian Knot of data economy law”.

constitutes the contractual counter-performance of digital content or digital services, the legislator had avoided wording to that extent.[58] However, already with the Modernisation Directive[59] which adapted the Consumer Rights Directive to the Digital Content Directive, the legislator no longer followed this "He-Who-Must-Not-Be-Named' approach"[60]. Rather, it was recognised that data can be the object of consumer contracts.[61] In the legislative process on the Data Act an unequivocal clarification was discussed but still avoided. As with the Digital Content Directive,[62] the legislator made an effort to pay tribute to stressing the application of the GDPR.[63] The reason was that, as when negotiating the Digital Content Directive, there were two camps in the EP[64] and in Council. Those who considered personal data as a tradeable commodity did not want to endanger the timely adoption of the Data Act by provoking the opinionated supporters of data protection. For this reason, the Data Act is based on the distinction between the GDPR as the legal base for processing personal data and the regulation of the conditions of data use in a contract. The approach offers a constructive and pragmatic model, which, simultaneously, serves the important objective of data protection while allowing for the regulation of contracts having as their object personal data.

b) Unfair contract terms control

With the introduction of an unfair contract terms control, the EU legislator goes beyond existing rudimentary rules in this regard in B2B contracts. The Data Act does not only create an unfairness control for a specific

---

58 On this discussion in the Digital Content Directive s. *Staudenmayer*, in: Schulze/Staudenmayer (fn. 28), Art. 3 DCD, para. 46 et seq.

59 Directive 2019/2161, OJ L 328/7 of 18.12.2019.

60 *Staudenmayer*, in: Schulze/Staudenmayer (fn. 28), Art. 3 DCD, para. 55, by way of analogy with the avoidance of the name of Lord Voldemort in J. K. Rowling's Harry Potter novels and referring to Elise Poillot in a conference of the European Law Academy in Trier on 28.4.2022. *Sattler*, Informationelle Privatautonomie, 2022, p. 3 et seq. speaks of 'anticipatory political correctness'.

61 *Staudenmayer*, in: Schulze/Staudenmayer (fn. 28), Art. 3 DCD, para. 65.

62 *Staudenmayer*, ibid, para. 54.

63 For the private law relevant part of the Data Act s. Rec. 7 – 8; 20; 24; 31; 34 – 35; 40; 42; 45; 94; Art. 1 (5); 4 (7); 5 (7), (8); 6 (2) (b).

64 Among the four involved EP committees, the Civil Liberties, Justice and Home Affairs Committee, responsible for data protection, was prominent in this regard.

problem area, i.e. late payments (Art. 1 (2), 7 (1) Late Payments Directive[65]) or prohibits certain specific clauses in a rather narrowly circumscribed sector[66]. Rather, the legislator uses the instrument of an unfair contract terms control to tackle emerging dependencies within the data economy.[67] Chapter IV of the Data Act covers almost all[68] contract clauses concerning access to, and the use of, data or liability and remedies for the breach or the termination of data related obligations. It also covers such clauses in all possible contracts, i.e. not only contracts with the primary objective of data sharing, but also data sharing elements for instance in a sales or services contract or in a cloud contract. This goes far beyond existing precedents in EU private law and is a new dimension in the process of digitalising European private law. The importance, which the legislator attributed to this regulatory instrument to achieve balanced contracts,[69] is demonstrated not only in its substantive but also in its personal scope. In contrast to the original Commission proposal, the legislator extended the scope of the unfair contract terms control to contracts between all companies and did not limit it to contracts with SMEs.[70]

The unfair contract terms control of the Data Act uses tools which are already well-known in national and EU law, i.e. a general clause, a 'black' list with per se unfair clauses and a 'grey' list with clauses where the unfairness is presumed. Details are explained in the contribution of Hennemann and elsewhere[71].

65 Directive 2011/7, OJ L 48/1 of 23.2.2011.

66 Directive 2019/633 on unfair trading practices in business-to-business relationships in the agricultural and food supply chain, OJ L 111/59 of 25.4.2019, Art. 3.

67 As to first ideas, preceding the proposal for a Data Act, how such regulatory solution could be designed s. *Staudenmayer* (fn. 12), p. 83 et seq., in particular p. 88 et seq.

68 Except concerning the traditional (s. Art. 4 (2) Unfair Contract Terms Directive, Art. 80 (2) CESL) exception excluding the main subject matter of the contract and the price, Art. 13 (8).

69 Rec. 5 sentence 4, 58 sentence 1.

70 Art. 13 (1), Rec. 58 sentence 2. The Unfair Contract Terms Directive would apply to B2C contracts (Art. 1 (9), Rec. 9, 28).

71 As to the sources of these tools, their advantages and disadvantages, content, scope and consequences s. *Staudenmayer* (fn. 35), p. 597 et seq. (as regards the Commission proposal; the relevant provisions were practically unchanged in the final version of the Data Act).

c) The new instrument of model contract clauses

The direct purpose of these model contract clauses is to help contracting parties, in particular SMEs for which legal advice costs for design and negotiation of contracts can be a burden,[72] and in doing so, to lower transaction costs. A more indirect purpose is to achieve balanced contracts for data access, use and sharing[73] and data processing services[74].

The model contract clauses which the Commission should recommend according to Art. 41, are a significant novelty of the Data Act. It is the first time in European private law that the EU legislator uses this tool. The use of this tool is part of an overall policy development in data sharing over recent years.

In the 2017 Data Economy Communication and the accompanying Commission Staff Working Document[75] the Commission explained the problem of the lack of data sharing and put forward some objectives as well as options when launching a public consultation process. In the light of its results, the Commission took a careful approach, based on freedom of contract and leaving the question of whether, and if so how, to share data to be resolved contractually. Thus, the subsequent 2018 Data Sharing Communication[76] focused on promoting voluntary data sharing. It put forward principles like transparency, shared value creation, respecting each other's commercial interest, ensuring undistorted competition and minimising data lock-in. The Commission Staff Working Document accompanying the Communication contained guidance on sharing private sector data.[77]

In the Data Strategy[78] the Commission still, as a matter of principle, favoured the approach of voluntary data sharing. Only where there was an established market failure, which could not be solved through competition law, was a sector specific data access right 'under fair, transparent, reason-

72 Art. 41; Rec. 111 sentence 2; 42 sentence 4.
73 Art. 41, Rec. 111 sentence 3.
74 Rec. 96 sentence 2.
75 Communication "Building a European Data Economy" of 10.1.2017, COM (2017) 9 final, p. 11 et seq. and Staff Working Document "on the free flow of data and emerging issues of the Data Economy" SWD (2017) 2 final p. 30 et seq.
76 Commission Communication "Towards a Common European Data Space" of 25.4.2018, COM (2018) 232 final, p. 10.
77 Guidance on sharing private sector data in the European data economy, SWD (2018) 125 final p. 5 – 8.
78 Commission Communication "A European strategy for data" of 19.2.2020, COM (2020) 66 final.

able, proportionate and/or non-discriminatory conditions' considered.[79] The idea of such a data access right goes back to the Data Economy Communication which already mentioned an access right under FRAND (Fair, Reasonable And Non-Discriminatory)[80] conditions as an option.[81]

The results of the consultation on the Commission Data Strategy made it clear that the approach of the Data Sharing Communication, which only relied upon voluntary data sharing, had not sufficiently improved the situation. 75% of participating businesses, in particular SMEs, were still experiencing difficulties with access to data.[82] The weakness of the guidance accompanying the Data Sharing Communication was that it was addressed those data-holders who are willing to share data and upon reasonable conditions. An approach, which restricts itself to promoting voluntary data sharing, falls short of providing an incentive to data holders who are not inclined to share data or only on conditions which are prohibitive or highly restrictive.

It was thus necessary to go beyond the exclusive promotion of voluntary data sharing and couple that approach with the introduction of mandatory rules. In this context, the use of the regulatory tool of model contract clauses, which was already one of the options put forward in the Data Economy Communication,[83] is a leftover of the policy approach giving preference to voluntary data sharing. The Data Act emphasises the principle of contractual freedom and that parties should remain free, within its

79 Ibid, p. 13.

80 Beside competition law, FRAND principles are used in a number of different regulatory approaches. See Data Economy Communication SWD (fn. 75), p. 38, the more comprehensive overview in *Heim/Nikolic*, A FRAND Regime for Dominant Digital Platforms, jipitec 2019, p. 41 et seq. and the case of the REACH Regulation 1907/2006 of 18.12.2006 concerning the Registration, Evaluation, Authorisation and Restriction of Chemicals, OJ L 304/1, 30.12.2006, in more detail in *Drexl*, Designing Competitive Markets for Industrial Data – Between Propertisation and Access, jipitec 2017, p. 289 et seq. While the underlying reasoning of the use of the FRAND approach differs, the regulatory use cases share the idea that because of a public policy need identified access to data is granted and use also the same broad features of its content. Therefore, as regards an access right based along FRAND principles, cf. *Drexl*, p. 290 et seq. taking the example of REACH as a model; *Crémer/De Montjoye/Schweitzer*, Competition Law in the Digital Era, 2019, p. 97, 109 and *Heim/Nikolic*, p. 53, 55 (albeit for platforms).

81 Fn. 75, Communication, p. 13 and SWD, p. 36 et seq.

82 Impact assessment of the proposal for the Data Act, SWD (2022) 34 final, of 23.2.2022, p. 8.

83 Fn. 75, Communication, p. 12 and SWD, p. 31.

framework, to negotiate the precise conditions for making data available in their contracts.[84] While pursuing the objective of leaving the contractual parties a significant margin to design their own contract terms, the model contract terms are the regulatory tool to steer the contractual design in the right direction.[85]

The model contract terms to be recommended by the European Commission are also to intended to assist with two restrictions which the Data Act imposes on its own scope. Firstly, Rec. 9 confirms that national contract law remains applicable, unless otherwise regulated in the Data Act. The Data Act interposes itself into national contract law only to the extent necessary. More importantly, the Data Act is largely a principle-based legislation. However, this is at odds with the legal nature of the Data Act as a directly applicable regulation. On the one hand, the parties must apply the Data Act directly, but on the other hand the Data Act does not give the parties the necessary details for the direct application in practice. If the Data Act had been a Directive, it could have relied on the details being regulated through national implementation provisions. This not being possible, the model contract terms are an attempt of the EU legislator to overcome this dilemma. Therefore, the model contract terms to be recommended by the European Commission are fulfilling a purpose which is *de facto* comparable to national transposition rules. They demonstrate how the legislator would like to see the Data Act to be applied in practice in order to ensure that contracts for data access, use and sharing and data processing services[86] are balanced.

This purpose is also manifested by the fact that the EU legislator set the European Commission a deadline for putting forward the model contract terms, which coincides with the date of application of the Data Act.[87] By making sure that the model contract terms are available, when the Data Act needs to be applied, the EU legislator confirms their role as 'implementing soft law' of the Data Act.

Finally, Rec. 55 explicitly recognises this aspect of the model contract terms by requiring that the dispute settlement bodies in proceedings according to Art. 10[88] should take into account the model contract terms.

84 Rec. 43.
85 Cf. Rec. 111 sentence 3.
86 Cf. Rec. 96 sentence 2.
87 Art. 41, 50 sub-para. 2.
88 Cf. *Staudenmayer* (fn. 35), p. 1042 et seq.

Beyond this expressly anticipated use by the dispute settlement bodies and the help for negotiating parties mentioned by Rec. 62 sentence 5, one can also expect that national courts will use the model contract terms recommended by the European Commission when applying the unfair contract terms control. When applying the general clause of Art. 13 (3), courts according to Recital 62 sentence 4 have the negative examples of the 'grey' and 'black' list as benchmarks for what is unfair. Beyond these examples, it will be difficult for courts to use the other traditional tool when applying a general clause, i.e. to refer to dispositive law[89] to establish what the legislator envisaged to be a balanced contract. The problem is likely to be that there is no dispositive national law for contracts for data access, use and sharing. Art. 13 (2) will not help, as there is no such dispositive EU law either. This gap can only be closed – at least de facto and for the time being – by the model contract terms recommended by the European Commission.

The importance given by the EU-legislator to the regulatory tool of model contract terms is demonstrated by the extension of their scope by the legislator, when compared to the Commission proposal[90]. According to Art. 41, model contract terms shall be recommended not only for data access and use in general. The legislator specifies certain content to be included, i.e. the reasonable compensation according to Art. 8 et seq. and the protection of trade secrets according to Art. 4 (5), 5 (9)[91]. In addition, standard contract terms for cloud-computing shall also be recommended.

It remains to be seen, whether, and to what extent, the model contract terms to be recommended by the Commission will be taken up by the market or whether in the longer-term, default contract rules law[92] may be needed.[93]

---

89 See the ECJ for the Unfair Contract Terms Directive in its judgment Banco Primus C-421/14, ECLI EU:C:2017:60, para. 59. See for data contracts already the Commission Staff Working Document SWD (2017) 2 final, p. 32, accompanying the Commission Communication "Building a European Data Economy" v. 10.1.2017, COM (2017) 9 final. Cf. also *Jansen*, in: Jansen/Zimmermann (eds.), Commentaries of European Contract Laws, 2018, Art 6:201, para. 13; *Heiderhoff*, Europäisches Privatrecht, 5th ed. 2020, para. 404, 167.

90 Art. 34 COM (2022) 68 final.

91 See also Rec. 31 sentences 3 – 4.

92 S. the Data Economy Communication (fn. 75), p. 12 and the Staff Working Document (fn. 75), p. 31 et seq.

93 Cf. *Lohsse/Schulze/Staudenmayer* (fn. 4), p. 20.

d) The use of the 'good faith' principle and the binding nature of the Data Act rules

In the second wave of adaptation of EU private law to the needs of the digital economy, the Data Act responds to emerging dependencies in the digital economy, i.e. the imbalance of bargaining power between the 'data-haves' and 'data-have-nots' as well as between cloud providers and cloud customers. For this purpose, it uses two regulatory tools traditionally used in contract law in situations of negotiation imbalance, the principle of 'good faith' and the binding nature of its rules.

In European private law, the principle of 'good faith'[94] plays an important horizontal role in B2C contracts. It is used as a criterion in the general clause for the control of unfair contract terms[95] and unfair commercial practices[96]. It is qualified by the legislator as "requirement"[97] or as "general principle"[98] and by the ECJ as "principle of civil law"[99]. In contrast, in B2B contracts, its use so far was less important. It was used for the first time in the Commercial Agents Directive.[100] Interestingly, in this B2B contractual relationship, the principle of 'good faith' is clearly used in its function as a standard of conduct.[101] In addition, it is also used in minor cases of unfair contract terms control.[102] In these latter cases, the principle of 'good faith' is drafted in its formula as 'good faith and fair dealing'.[103] This wording stems

94 For the legal history basis and the comparative situation s. *Jansen* (fn. 89), Art 1:201, paras. 14 et seq., 25 et seq.

95 Art. 3 (1), Rec. 16 Unfair Contract Terms Directive.

96 Art. 2 h) Unfair Commercial Practices Directive.

97 Rec. 16 Unfair Contract Terms Directive.

98 Art. 2 h) Unfair Commercial Practices Directive.

99 In the Messner case C-489/07, EU:C:2009:502, para. 26.

100 Art. 3 (1), 4 (1) Directive 86/653, OJ L 382/17 of 31.12.1986.

101 As to the two ways of using „good faith", see *Jansen* (fn. 89), Art 1:201, para 4 et seq.

102 Art. 7 (1) a), Rec. 28 Late Payments Directive and Art. 1 (1) a), Rec. 1 of Directive 2019/633 on unfair trading practices in business-to-business relationships in the agricultural and food supply chain.

103 As inspiration was taken the Late Payments Directive, which in turn inspired the Directive 2019/633 on unfair trading practices in business-to-business relationships in the agricultural and food supply chain, from the DCFR (von Bar/Clive (eds.) Principles, Definitions and Model Rules of European Private Law – Draft Common Frame of Reference (DCFR), Full Edition, Sellier 2009). Rec. 28 Late Payments Directive is the only case in the EU acquis where the DCFR is quoted as a source.

from its use as standard of conduct in PECL[104], the Unidroit principles[105] and the DCFR[106], from which it found its way also into CESL. In CESL, 'good faith', also qualified as a "general principle",[107] is used mainly (other than in some specific cases) as a general standard of conduct[108] and in its function as benchmark within the unfair contract terms control both for B2C[109] and B2B[110].

As already explained, the Data Act largely takes over the design and wording of the unfair contract terms control chapter of CESL, including the use of the good faith principle (described as 'good faith and fair dealing', as used in CESL). In addition to its role in the unfair contract terms control, the Data Act also introduces this principle in its function as a standard of conduct. Art. 27 and Rec. 97 contain a duty of the contractual parties[111] of a data processing service contract to cooperate in good faith in order to make the switching process successful. This provision, albeit seemingly focussing on a technical point, is a noteworthy point for the development of European private law. It is only the second time, since the Commercial Agents Directive, that such a contractual standard of conduct provision has been introduced. According to Recital 2 and relevant ECJ case law[112], one main purpose of this Directive is to protect commercial agents in their (contractual) relationship with their principals. The reason for this protection is that agents are in a situation of economic dependency. Chapter VI of the Data Act deals with switching as one important aspect of the contract between cloud providers and cloud customers. The situation of dependency, which characterises such contracts, can often lead to a situation of lock-in for customers who want to switch often.[113] Consistent with

104 *Lando/Beale*, Principles of European Contract Law, Parts I and II, 2000, Art. 1:201.
105 UNIDROIT Principles of International Commercial Contracts, 4th ed. 2016, Art. 1.7. Cf. also Art. 7 (1) CISG.
106 III.-1:103 (Fn. 104).
107 Rec. 31.
108 Art. 2.
109 Art. 83 (1).
110 Art. 86 (1) b).
111 Extended also to certain third parties, s. Rec. 85 sentence 3 and 4.
112 See for instance judgments Bellone C-215/97, ECLI EU:C:1998:189, para. 13; Ingmar C-381/98, ECLI EU:C:2000:605, para. 20 et seq.; Chevassus C-19/07, ECLI EU:C:2008:23, para. 22 and in particular in the contractual relationship of the commercial agent with the principal Honyvem Informazioni Commerciali, C-465/04, ECLI EU:C:2006:199, para. 19; Semen C-348/07, ECLI EU:C:2009:195, para. 14.
113 Cf. Rec. 78 sentence 2.

its use in the Commercial Agents Directive, the Data Act thus uses 'good faith' as standard of conduct for these contracts in order to regulate, at least on one important aspect, this situation of dependency. As all customers of data processing services are in the same situation, that use of 'good faith' as standard of conduct applies both to B2B and in B2C contracts[114].

To avoid that the stronger party uses a situation of dependency to waive the contractual rights granted to the other contractual party, the Data Act also uses the binding nature of its rules as a regulatory tool. While the use of mandatory law is the norm in European private law for the B2C relationship, there are only a few cases where B2B rules have a binding character.

For contracts on accessing, using and sharing co-generated IoT, the Data Act designs the rights as mandatory. Art. 7 (2), 8 (2) 2nd alt. and 12 (2) make the rules of Chapters II and III of the Data Act binding. While the wording is inspired by the relevant CESL standard clause making an article or a chapter binding[115], a party with stronger bargaining power can always make changes which are more favourable to the other party. As in Art. 81 CESL, the unfair contract terms control is made a mandatory provision in Art. 13 (9).

Chapter VI on switching does not contain a provision equivalent to Art. 7 (2), 8 (2) 2nd alt., 12 (2) or 13 (9). Art. 23 (1) 2nd sentence and Rec. 79 sentence 2, combined with Art. 40 (1) have a different approach, but probably come to the same result, while leaving Member States a margin of flexibility as to the effect of a violation of the Chapter VI rules.

When private law rules are designed as mandatory, that does not necessarily mean that they are also internationally binding, i.e. "overriding mandatory provisions" according to Art. 9 Rome I Regulation.[116] In contrast to Art. 1 (2) Platform-Regulation[117] or Art. 1 (2) DMA[118], the Data Act does not contain a clause which makes it internationally binding. The former Regulations address the systematically greater market power of platforms, especially so-called "gatekeepers", which are mostly situated outside the EU, and thus another dependency of the digital economy. The Data Act

114 Art. 2 (30).

115 As to the CESL approach on this s. *Staudenmayer* (fn. 41), p. XVII.

116 Regulation 593/2008, OJ L 177/6 of 4.7.2008.

117 Regulation 2019/150 on promoting fairness and transparency for business users of online intermediation services, OJ L 186/57 of 11.7.2019.

118 Regulation 2022/1925 on contestable and fair markets in the digital sector (Digital Markets Act), OJ L 265/1 of 12.10.2022.

remains more in a tradition of private international law to be restrictive when imposing internationally binding EU rules on other legal orders. It is possible that the ECJ may use the dependency argument to come to the result, as with the *Ingmar* case related to the Commercial Agents Directive[119], that the rules are also internationally binding. However, given that the argumentation of the ECJ in the *Ingmar* judgment was rather short and has not been followed since, this would remain to be seen.

III. Research challenges and focal topics

Against this background, three topics deserve particular attention, both in terms of understanding the terminology and regulatory instruments of the Data Act and in terms of the tasks that will arise when the act is applied in practice: (1) the mandatory data sharing in the triangle between data holder, user and data recipient; (2) the voluntary data sharing on a bilateral basis; and (3) the regime for cloud contracts. These three topics formed the focus of the colloquium from which this volume emerged and accordingly determine its structure. For each of them, the general regulatory objectives of the Data Act, as outlined in the beginning, are dealt with in more detail.

1. Mandatory data sharing in the triangle between data holder, user and data recipient

a) Data sharing between private autonomy and mandatory law

As a basic structure of the data economy, the triangle between data holder, user and data recipient describes in abstract terms the relation between three main actors with regard to the data-sharing mechanism[120] regulated by the Data Act. In the Data Act, this structure is already expressed by the definitions of the 'data holder" (Art. 2 no. 13), the 'user' of a connected product or related service (Art. 2 no. 12, 5 and 6) and a third party to whom the data holder makes data available (Art. 2 no. 14). The role of these three actors and their relationship to each other has been given legal form by the definitions and rules of the Data Act. By doing so, this legal act has changed

119 Ingmar (fn. 112), para. 20 et seq.
120 *Zech*, Data Access Rights as Property Rights, in this volume.

the use of data on the basis of a *de-facto* control into a de-iure control[121] and in this respect has led to a "juridification" of this area.

In this legal framework, the triangle of data holder, user and data recipient is primarily based on a contractual approach. As rightly emphasised, this is not only reflected in the fact that Chapters II to IV and VI of the Data Act presuppose or require contracts between the actors involved. Rather, the legislator has also generally "thought" the provisions of data holder and user within this framework on the basis of contractual relations.[122] This "contractualization"[123] reflects the fact that the legal relations between the actors in consideration are primarily governed by contracts and should continue to be governed in this way under the Data Act. Private autonomy thus retains a prominent role in this field. However, within the scope of the contract-based regime, the Data Act not only provides for the drawing up of model contractual terms to support the parties in the drafting of contracts within the framework of private autonomy.[124] Rather, it also binds and limits private autonomy in the design of contracts by the parties through, not least, a series of mandatory provisions concerning the rights and obligations in the triangle of data holder, user and data recipient with regard to accessing, using and sharing data. This legal model of mandatory data sharing not only requires an analysis of the interaction of mandatory law and private autonomy on the part of the contracting parties within the scope of the Data Act. Rather, it also raises the challenge of rethinking the role and content of model contractual terms specifically with regard to this interaction in mandatory data sharing.[125]

b) Contract law and property rights

The Data Acts focus on contract law raises the question of how this legislative perspective relates to the approaches in legal doctrine that attempt to determine the characteristics of rights relating to data – and therefore also the legal position of the data holder and the user – with recourse to

121 See above I.1, I.2 and *Staudenmayer*, Der Data Act im Gefüge des europäischen digitalen Privatrechts, NJW 2024, point 13.

122 *Hennemann/Steinrötter* (fn. 19) and cf. Rec. 21.

123 Ibid, point 33.

124 II.2.c).

125 A more in-depth look at this challenge from *Wendehorst*, Model Contractual Terms for Mandatory Data Sharing: Challenges and Considerations, in this volume.

the concept of property rights. In view of the controversial discourse in legal doctrine on the character of rights in data matters[126], it could even be asked whether the "contractualisation" in the Data Act is to be regarded as a general rejection of the understanding of data access rights as property rights on the part of European legislators – with relevance possibly even beyond this legal act. Such an assessment would lead to consider whether a purely contractual view in this area of data sharing would in principle correspond more to the non-rivalrous characteristics of data and whether such an approach would also be favorable for European law because of the problems arising from the differences between the national concepts of property rights, which are hard to reconcile.

A detailed examination of the legal position of the actors involved in data sharing may however lead to not entirely denying the relevance of the theory of property rights for the legal description of data and access to data in particular with reference to the contractual orientation of the Data Act. The primary contractual orientation of the Data Act may not completely rule out the possibility that an exclusionary effect is attributed to the legal position of the user not only in relation to the data holder, but also vis-à-vis third parties and in this sense has similarities with the model of a property right as its shown in more detail in an article in this volume, particularly with reference to the provision on trade secrets.[127] In this respect, the legal position of the user under the Data Act may cover not only the right to use and the right to transfer but also the exclusion against third parties. In addition, some elements of co-ownership could perhaps even be recognisable in the Data Act, especially insofar as data holder and user must ensure the protection of trade secrets.[128]

From these starting points, further discussion on data sharing may need to consider in more detail the relation between contractual rights and obligations on the one hand and property rights on the other hand. This may not only be of significant relevance for the legal position of the actors in the matters governed by the Data Act, but also for future EU legislative measures on data trading, access to data and related matters. As one of the next steps in the development of EU law in this regard, it is also

---

126 See for many others *Hugenholtz*, Data Property in the System of Intellectual Property Law: Welcome Guest or Misfit?, in: Lohsse/Schulze/Staudenmayer (eds.), Trading Data in the Digital Economy: Legal Concepts and Tools, 2017, p. 57.

127 *Zech* (fn. 120), ch. III.

128 *Zech* (fn. 120), ch. IV.

possible that the planned model contractual terms[129] may, at least implicitly, provide more insight into the legal nature of the rights and obligations of the parties in data sharing by specifying the more precise shape that such rights and obligations should take in the contracts based on the Data Act. Beyond this, however, the extent for conceptual clarification and further development in legislative practice may be limited at European level taking into account different national legal traditions concerning the concept of property rights and their relation to contract law. It is therefore likely that further preparatory work by legal doctrine and more intensive exchange among European lawyers will be necessary to achieve a consistent set of contractual and property rights in European Private Law for the digital age.

c) From consumers to users?

The conceptual focus of the Data Act on the legal position of the user in his relation to the data holder and the data recipient further raises the question of how this new perspective relates to the traditional protection of the consumer, which has so far played a prominent role in European private law and in particular in EU contract law. This relation between user rights and consumer protection needs to be reconsidered in two directions in particular: on the one hand, the question arises as to whether – in view of the challenges of the digital age – the concept of the user is better suited to taking on some of the protective functions traditionally associated with consumer protection. Possibly, in this regard, a user-orientation can not only complement the concept of the consumer, but in some areas of the emerging private law of the digital age it may even replace it. On the other hand, it also remains to be considered whether the Data Act's broad definition of the user can sufficiently take into account the specific protection needs of consumers as users of IoT devices or whether additional provisions are necessary in order to guarantee a high standard of protection for consumers in this area.

In the first respect, for example, it must be taken into account that when a contract is concluded "machine to machine" it is often almost impossible to identify the status of a party that is a user of a connected product in the

129 See above II.2.c).

IoT as a consumer or business.[130] For this and other reasons, it has been proposed on various occasions, for instance, to extend protective provisions (such as those contained in the Digital Content Directive in favour of consumers with regard to the obligation to update digital content and services) to other users of the Internet, be it small and medium-sized enterprises or to all customers in general.[131] It should also be taken into consideration that primarily standardised contracts are concluded on the Internet (in contrast to individually negotiated contracts as the "classic" model in contract law) and that digitalisation has therefore further increased the relevance of general terms and conditions in the practice of contracting not only in B2C relationships, but also in the B2B area.[132] With such standardised contracts, an inequality between the parties can arise in particular if one party concludes a large number of contracts of the type in question, while for the other party it is a one-off or at least not a frequent transaction. In these cases, the transaction effort for the individual conclusion of the contract is much less for one party than for the other, with the consequence that the contract is often determined unilaterally by the former – irrespective of whether the other party is a consumer or whether it is a business that does not often conclude a transaction of this type.

Against this background, the European legislator has increasingly recognised, particularly with regard to contracting on the Internet, that mandatory legal standards for the control of standardised contracts beyond consumer law may be appropriate. Important measures along this path were the provisions for general terms and conditions in B2B contracts in the

130 *Spindler/Stein*, Die endgültige Richtlinie über Verträge über digitale Inhalte und Dienstleistungen – Anwendungsbereich und grundsätzliche Ansätze, MMR 2019, p. 415 (416).

131 *Schulze*, Die Digitale-Inhalte-Richtlinie – Innovation und Kontinuität im europäischen Vertragsrecht, ZEuP 2019, p. 695 (702); on the extension beyond consumer law in Austria see *De Franceschi/Schulze*, Harmonizing Digital Contract Law – an Introduction, in: De Franceschi/Schulze (eds.), Harmonizing Digital Contract Law, 2023, p. 10 as well as *Wendehorst*, Die Regelungen des VGG zu digitalen Leistungen unter besonderer Berücksichtigung der Aktualisierungspflichten, in: Bydlinski (ed.), Das neue Gewährleistungsrecht, 2022, p. 69 et seqq.

132 *Schulze*, European Private Law in the Digital Age – Developments, Challenges and Prospects, in: Janssen/Lehmann/Schulze (eds.), The Future of European Private Law, 2023, p. 141 and p. 148; *Schulze/Arroyo Vendrell*, Standardisierte Verträge zwischen Privatautonomie und rechtlicher Kontrolle – eine Einführung, in: Kindl/Perales Viscasillas/Arroyo Vendrell (eds.), Standardisierte Verträge - zwischen Privatautonomie und rechtlicher Kontrolle, 2017, p. 11 et seq.

Regulation on Online Intermediation Services[133] and in the Digital Services Act[134]. The Data Act has now taken a further major step in this direction by using unfair contractual terms control as one of its main instruments with regard to both contracts between data holder and data recipient on co-generated data and to all other contracts with a data access and data use element, and by not limiting this control to contracts with small and medium-sized enterprises, but covering contracts between all companies. These and other aspects[135] could indicate that in future European legislation also with a view to other "digital matters" it could be preferable to move from the traditional protection of the "consumer" to a broader protection of those affected when acting on the Internet and that the concept of the "user" could play a decisive role in this.

Nevertheless, it should not be assumed that concepts such as the "user" could render the specific protection requirements associated with the concept of the consumer completely superfluous. Rather, there is much to suggest that even in the area in which the Data Act ensures the legal position of users of connected products, including consumers, in relation to data holders and data recipients, specific rules for the protection of consumers are required. The considerations in this volume, which are dedicated to the question of "How to better serve the consumer" when it comes to IoT data sharing in B2C relationships[136], emphasise a specific need for regulation in the context of Art. 4 (13) in this respect (in particular insofar as "the functionality of products should not be linked to the authorisation to collect and process data that is not necessary for their function"[137]). In addition, they propose, among other things, the inclusion of certain forms of bricking in the Unfair Terms Directive and the establishment of a consumer right to data-collection-free and data-collection-friendly products as supplementary

133 Regulation 2019/1150 on promoting fairness and transparency for business users of online intermediation services, OJ L 186/57 of 11.7.2019.

134 Regulation 2022/3065 on a Single Market for Digital Services and amending Directive 2000/31/EC (Digital Services Act), OJ L 277/1 of 27.10.2022.

135 In more detail see *Schulze*, Quelles limites aux droit de la consummation? – Propos introductifs, in: Mäsch and others (eds.), Quelles limites aux droit de la consummation? (forthcoming); *Schulze*, Digital Vulnerability in European Private Law, in: Crea/De Franceschi (eds.), Digital Vulnerability in European Private Law, ch. IV.3. (forthcoming).

136 *Specht-Riemenschneider/El-Rifaai/Mehnert/Bodemann*, IoT Data Sharing in B2C: How to Better Serve the Consumer, in this volume.

137 *Specht-Riemenschneider/El-Rifaai/Mehnert/Bodemann* (fn. 136), ch. V.

consumer-specific measures alongside the Data Act.[138] These suggestions will not only need to be discussed with regard to possible improvements to the Data Act and its regulatory environment. Rather, they can also provide a template for future regulations in other areas with regard to the task of combining general regulations on data sharing and data trading with specific provisions for the protection of consumers.

2. Voluntary data sharing on a bilateral basis

a) The concept of fairness in voluntary data-sharing

Beyond the above-mentioned regulations regarding mandatory data sharing in the triangle of data holder, user and data recipient, the Data Act aims to promote the conclusion of balanced and fair contracts by the parties also in the context of voluntary bilateral data sharing mainly by using two regulatory instruments: on the one hand the model contractual terms pursuant to Art. 41 and on the other hand the unfair contractual terms control. While the former are a new regulatory instrument below the threshold of mandatory law, intended to assist parties in drafting and negotiating contracts, the unfair contractual terms control as mandatory law has the sanctioning effect that unilaterally imposed contractual terms[139] which do not fulfil its requirements do not bind the other party in accordance with Art. 13 (1).

For both regulatory approaches – the model contractual terms and the unfair contractual terms control – the concept of "fairness" or "unfairness" assumes a central role. Art. 41 refers to fairness as the first characteristic in the trilogy of features of the desired contracts ("contracts with fair, reasonable and non-discriminatory contractual rights and obligations"). In Art. 13 (1), the decisive criterion for a unilaterally imposed contractual term not to be binding is whether it is unfair. What is to be understood as unfairness in this respect is defined by a general clause, a "black list" and a "grey list" in Art. 13 (3) to (5). The concept of "fairness" or "unfairness" therefore deserves particular attention with regard to the regulatory instruments of the Data Act and its future application in practice.

---

138 *Specht-Riemenschneider/El-Rifaai/Mehnert/Bodemann* (fn. 136), ch. IV.2. and 3.

139 For the content and problems of this concept, see *Hennemann*, A Fair Share? – Data Contracts and Unfair Terms Control, in this volume; *Graf von Westfalen*, Der neue Data Act – Eine Kaskade AGB-rechtlicher Verbote im unternehmerischen Verkehr, BB 2024, p. 515 (517).

This volume, thus, pays special attention to this topic, primarily with consideration of how the drafting of model contractual terms can serve as a tool to deal with unfairness.[140] Its evaluation of the unfairness risks arising from market failures in B2B data sharing can be linked to the results of the impact assessment that was submitted with regard to the proposal for the Data Act[141] and in particular to a related study on model contractual terms and fairness control.[142] This risk assessment forms the basis not only for analysing the potential benefits of model contractual terms with regard to the objective of fairness and other objectives such as the reduction of transaction costs, but also for examining different options for the way of application of these model terms in contractual practice. In that respect, this study goes beyond the examination of the existing provisions of the Data Act and may – together with the corresponding study on model contractual provisions for mandatory data sharing[143] – provide valuable input or even starting points for the setting of guidelines in view of the upcoming work to draft the model clauses envisaged in Art. 41.

As far as the understanding of the principle of fairness in respect of the control of contract terms is concerned, the focus must primarily be on the parameters expressed in Art. 13 (3) to (5). Analysing these provisions is thus linked to the question of what the potential characteristics or "dimensions" of fairness with regard to data access and data use might be. The contribution addressing this issue in the present volume[144] does not only refer to the materials used by the European Commission to prepare the most recent legislation.[145] Rather, it also points to the suggestions that may arise from the ongoing work of UNCITRAL in this regard.[146] It thus confirms and substantiates the assumption that the projects to modernise contract law at international and European level can be mutually beneficial in the current phase of adaptation to the changes in the digital age, as has

140 Cf. *Rodríguez de las Heras Ballell*, Drafting Model Contractual Terms for Voluntary B2B Data Sharing: A Tool to Deal with Unfairness, in this volume.

141 *Rodríguez de las Heras Ballell* (fn. 140).

142 *Rodríguez de las Heras Ballell* (fn. 140).

143 *Wendehorst* (fn. 125).

144 *Hennemann* (fn. 19).

145 In particular EU Commission, Guidance on sharing private sector data in the European data economy – "Towards a common European data space", SWD, 2018, 125 final, p. 3.

146 In particular UNCITRAL, Report of the Working Group IV (Electronic Commerce) on the work of its sixty-sixth session (Vienna, 16-20 October 2023), A/CN.9/1162, p. 14.

been shown in the previous phases, for example in the relationship between the UN Convention on Contracts for the International Sale of Goods, the Principles of European Contract Law and the Consumer Sales Directive.[147]

b) The challenges of smart contracts

In addition to the description of new regulatory approaches in the Data Act, it is also worth pointing out that this legislation, despite its relevance for data sharing, has given less consideration to some issues for which a need for future regulation is foreseeable. This includes, for example, the role of smart contracts for data transactions and thus also for data sharing.

Nevertheless, with regard to the role of smart contracts, it must at least be recognised that, despite the unresolved tasks, the Data Act contains some remarkable starting points for the legal structuring of this increasingly important subject matter, albeit from a technical perspective. This includes the definition of the "smart contract", which, in accordance with the prevailing view in the doctrine[148], characterises it as a certain type of software ("a computer program used for the automatic execution of an agreement..."; Art. 2 No. 39) and thus clearly distinguishes it from the "contract" in the legal meaning as a bilateral legal transaction[149]. Moreover, the detailed provisions of Art. 36 on the essential requirements regarding smart contracts for executing data sharing agreements form an important building block for the inclusion of smart contracts in the legal construction of data sharing.

However, the provisions of this Art. 36 directly only concern the computer programs used in connection with the conclusion and execution of contracts and not – or at least not directly – the executed contractual relationships themselves. Both the problems resulting from that as well as the extent to which these problems may be overcome on the basis of other provisions in the Data Act (in particular unfair contract terms control)

147 *Schulze*, Digital Vulnerability in European Private Law, in: Crea/De Franceschi (eds.), Digital Vulnerability in European Private Law, ch. IV.1. (forthcoming).

148 See e.g. *Kaulartz/Heckmann*, Smart Contracts – Anwendungen der Blockchain-Technologie, CR 2016, p. 618 (621, 624); *Kollmann*, Smart Contracts im bürgerlichen Recht – Rechtliche Analyse ausgewählter verbraucherschutzrechtlicher Aspekte, MMR 2024, p. 137 (138).

149 For more details on this see *Borges*, Smart contracts for data transactions and the Data Act, in this volume, ch. 2.

are subject of a detailed examination in this volume[150] It also addresses the extent to which regulations for data transactions may be additionally required in view of the automation of contractual relations through smart contracts. This examination is based firstly on an analysis of the legal processes involved in data transactions (with the distinction between data transfer and its multiple legal bases in the Data Act, such as, on the one hand, the legal obligations to share data under Art. 4 and 5 DA and on the other hand mandating the parties to conclude an agreement on data transfer under Art. 8 DA).[151]Secondly, it undertakes a comprehensive assessment of the challenges arising from the automation of data transactions in general and in particular from the automation of contractual relationship through smart contracts.[152] In this respect, this contribution focusing on the smart contracts may also provide valuable suggestions for the further development of overarching conceptual structures in the field of data law.

As a result of this contribution, it is becoming apparent how incomplete the legal framework for data transactions still is, especially with regard to the automation of such transactions. Unresolved key issues that the Data Act has not addressed include such important aspects as for example the relationship between the contractual provisions and the algorithm that implements them or the responsibility for data quality.[153]

3. Cloud contracts

The dependencies that emerge in the data economy and which the Data Act addresses[154] include, last but not least, aspects of the contractual relationship between cloud providers and cloud customers. The importance of the cloud for data-based and AI-based business models and its arguably oligopolistic market structure lead to off-the-shelf cloud models which are rarely tailored according to the needs of the customers and take-it-or leave contracts[155], leaving little to no margin for negotiation.[156]

150 *Borges* (fn. 149).
151 *Borges* (fn. 149), ch. I.1.
152 *Borges* (fn. 149), ch. II.
153 *Borges* (fn. 149), ch. IV.
154 Rec. 78; 88; 99.
155 A commonality which cloud contracts share with data sharing contracts, cf. Rec. 59.
156 Cf. *Staudenmayer* (fn. 12), 2020, p. 83 et seq.

However, the Data Act does not in a horizontal manner focus on this situation of contractual imbalance. The only such horizontal element to be found is, that the unfair contractual terms control in Art. 13 also applies to the data access and use elements of cloud contracts. Otherwise, the Data Act concentrates on the situation where the cloud customer wants to switch the cloud provider. Thus, it aims at abolishing contractual obstacles for customers[157] and thereby strives to achieve a more competitive market with low entry barriers for providers[158]. Furthermore, the Data Act has chosen to speak about "data processing services" in order to include not only the provision of services on the cloud, but also edge-computing and similar services.[159] However, the Commission's mandate to recommend standard contractual clauses for cloud computing contracts,[160] reflects a certain concentration on these contracts.

Art. 23 (1) 2, 25 et seq. set out the minimum content of the contract regulating the switching of the cloud provider, in particular the rights and obligations of the parties during the switching process as well as information duties and the gradual withdrawal of switching charges. With regard to these provisions, however, a number of questions deserves further attention. A contribution in this volume[161] therefore examines, beside other aspects, the exceptions to the scope of application of the mandatory requirements for contracts on switching and deals with the question how the scope of the term "switching charges" is to be defined. In the latter respect, it shows the reasons that may be brought forward against teleologically reducing the wording of Art. 2 No. 36 to the levying of data egress charges only. In contrast, it argues that a preferable approach is to define the concept of switching charges and, above all, the scope of the gradual withdrawal of switching charges in a negative manner by identifying all charges that the legislator has explicitly or implicitly excluded from the gradual withdrawal of switching charges.

While the Data Act regulates the switching of cloud contracts in an extremely detailed way, other topics of the contract between cloud provider

157 Rec. 79.
158 Rec. 78; 89.
159 Art. 2 (8), Rec. 78 sentence 1, 80 et seq.
160 Art. 41; cf. also Art. 1 (7).
161 *Sattler*, Switching of Providers – Mandatory Requirements, important Exception and their Impact on Standard Contractual Clauses for Cloud Computing, in this volume, ch. III. 2. and 3.

and cloud customer are left to the model contractual terms[162] and to freedom of contract between the parties. Given the arguably oligopolistic market structure and – in the data economy – the increasing dependency of cloud customers on cloud providers offering off-the-shelf cloud models and "take-it-or-leave" contracts both in B2C and B2B relationships, the impact of this approach is dubious.

In view of this fundamental problem and in view of the questions requiring clarification in Chapter VI of the Data Act, it will not be an easy task to draft the standard contractual clauses for cloud computing contracts that stipulate fair, reasonable and non-discriminatory rights and obligations as provided for in Art. 41. This makes it all the more important to consider as early as possible how the standard clauses should be designed in this area. The proposals contained in this volume with regard to such clauses for the switching process in cloud computing[163] may form one of the starting points for this. A broad and intensive discussion of such suggestions with regard to cloud contracts – as well as corresponding considerations with regard to mandatory data sharing[164] and voluntary data sharing[165] in other contractual relationships – may make a helpful contribution to realising the goals of the Data Act in contractual practice, for instance its goal of "facilitating switching between data processing services" (Art. 1 (1) (d)) and its guiding principle for the actions of all parties involved in the switching process to "cooperate in good faith" (Art. 27).

162 See above II.2.c).
163 *Sattler* (fn. 161), ch. IV. 2.
164 *Wendehorst* (fn. 125).
165 *Rodríguez de las Heras Ballell* (fn. 140).

Mandatory Data-Sharing in the Triangle between Data Holder – User – Data Recipient

Data Access Rights as Property Rights

Prof. Dr. Herbert Zech[1]

Property rights theory is still an important and useful analytical framework to understand the mechanism of data sharing. Although, with the advent of the Data Act, the focus has changed from data ownership to data access, the question remains whether and how the future legal framework will facilitate data contracts. This article is based on the premise that functioning data markets are a key aspect for intensifying data use, especially for the training of AI (although, also with data, arguably, as with any good, there is an optimum level and an increase in data use is not an end in itself, only the optimum use of data). Therefore, based on property rights theory, this article examines whether the Data Act has the potential to enable data markets.

The article proceeds (after preliminary remarks on the property rights theory and on the Data Act data sharing mechanism) by analysing first the position of the data holders, second the position of the users, and finally asking the question if the position of both can be seen as a kind of co-ownership or can be contractually treated as such. This bears in mind that also the production of the data is a kind of joint effort, an aspect which is also explicitly stated in Recital 6 of the Data Act.[2]

The article itself and its structure builds on a paper by Martina Eckardt and Wolfgang Kerber.[3] Their paper discusses to which extent different concepts of data governance are realised in the Data Act. First it shows that the Data Act builds, as a starting point, on a data holder-centric concept, assigning the bundle of rights on non-personal IoT data in an IP-like way to the data holders. Second, it shows how the Data Act adds a user-centric

---

1 Chair of Civil Law, Technology Law and IT Law at Humboldt University, Berlin, Director at the Weizenbaum Institute.

2 Recital 6 sentence 1 DA: „Data generation is the result of the actions of at least two actors, in particular the designer or manufacturer of a connected product, who may in many cases also be a provider of related services, and the user of the connected product or related service."

3 Eckardt/Kerber, Property rights theory, bundles of rights on IoT data, and the Data Act (2023).

concept, assigning the bundle of rights on non-personal IoT data to the users (which arguably are the lynchpin of the data markets facilitated by the Data Act). Finally, the article discusses the concept of co-generated data, going beyond exclusivity, as the most suitable concept for IoT data markets (also advocated by other important voices in academic literature[4]).

I. Preliminary Remarks

1. Property Rights

Property rights theory provides a theoretical framework for the legal attribution of goods. By explaining the economic function of such an attribution, i.e. facilitating markets, it provides one potential justification of such rights. The archetype of such an attribution is ownership, comprising the exclusive right to use and to transfer this position. However, even legal ownership comes with restrictions. IP rights still provide for exclusivity but feature broader exceptions and limitations. Although property rights theory defines such rights as a bundle of rights (and privileges) this can be reconciled with the Blackstonian view of things as objects of property. Whether you stress one aspect or the other is „largely a matter of focus“ (Merrill/Smith).[5] So the answer to: "What is ownership? Is there such a thing as ownership in a thing or has it to be understood as nearly a bundle of entitlements to that thing?" is that current legal research sees it as a kind of spectrum.

Characterising the different aspects of the bundle of rights allows the analysis of existing legal rights. As such aspects in relation to things or goods can be differentiated: rights to exclude, use and transfer. These three aspects have been called the „core of property“.[6] An older categorisation, found in property rights theory differentiates *usus* (use), *usus fructus* (enjoyment of fruits of the use), *abusus* (misuse) and *translatio* (transfer).[7] For

4 ALI/ELI Principles for a Data Economy, Data Transactions and Data Rights, As Adopted and Promulgated by The American Law Institute on May 18, 2021 and The European Law Institute on September 1, 2021 (Principles 18–23); Metzger/Schweitzer, Shaping Markets: A Critical Evaluation of the Draft Data Act, ZEuP 2023, 42 (55).

5 Merrill/Smith, Property (2010), p. 6; similar Zech, Information als Schutzgegenstand (2012), p. 100–102.

6 Merrill/Smith, Property (2010), p. 6.

7 Zech, Information als Schutzgegenstand (2012), p. 116.

information goods, like raw data, this can be reinterpreted to access, use, integrity, and transfer.[8] From an economic perspective, information goods are non-rivalrous in their use. Therefore access (which may be exclusive or non-exclusive) replaces possession (which is exclusive).[9] Access enables the use of information. However, exclusivity, use, and transfer remain the core aspects of property.

An important aspect of typical property rights like ownership and IP is that they are „good against the world"[10], they have, legally speaking, an in-rem effect (as opposed to an in-personam effect). Property rights theory is not limited to legal attribution. In contrast, it accepts from an economic point of view any kind of attribution facilitating the contractual exchange of goods as equal. Such an attribution may be legally protected, based on any social guarantee for an expectation or only factually protected.[11] The key aspect is that the attribution must be transferable. Therefore, assignable IP rights qualify as property rights whereas personality rights only contain some aspects of property (allowing for the licensing of personality aspects) but in their core are not property rights.[12] The economic analysis of property rights focuses on their function of facilitating contracts. However, they might have other important economic functions (and hence, from a legal policy point of view, justifications) like incentives to invest. Nevertheless, property rights always focus on goods and their attribution as a basis for trading these goods. To sum it up, the important questions when analysing a legal position are: "Can I exclude others from the use of these goods, can I use the goods myself and finally can I transfer that position?"

A final interesting aspect of property rights is that property law is also seen as a basis for corporate law (alongside contract law).[13] Whereas corporations are based on multilateral contracts, their functioning in the mar-

8 Zech, Information als Schutzgegenstand (2012), p. 117–129; Zech, Information as Property, JIPITEC 2015, 192 (195).

9 Zech, Information as Property, JIPITEC 2015, 192 (195); Zech, Data as a tradeable commodity, in: De Franceschi (eds.), New Features of European Contract Law – Towards a Digital Single Market, Intersentia, Cambridge (2016), p. 51 (56).

10 Merrill/Smith, Property (2010), p. 9.

11 Barzel/Allen, Economic Analysis of Property Rights, 3rd ed. (2023), p. 15–19; cf. Merrill/Smith, Property (2010), p. 2.

12 Sattler, Autonomy or Heteronomy – Proposal for a Two-Tier Interpretation of Art. 6 GDPR in: Lohsse/Schulze/Staudenmayer (eds.), Data as Counter-Performance – Contract Law 2.0 (2020), 225 (244s.: "personal data can be traded, but not transferred").

13 Hansmann/Kraakman, Property, Contract, and Verification: The Numerus Clausus Problem and the Divisibility of Rights, 31 J. Leg. Stud. 373 (2002); Armour/Whincop,

kets can only be explained with the additional in-rem effects of property rights regarding their assets.

2. The Data Act data sharing mechanism

Before beginning with the detailed analysis of the positions of the data holder and the user, the data sharing mechanism provided by the Data Act (especially Articles 4 and 5) shall be briefly introduced. The mechanism mainly concerns a triangle between data holders, users and data recipients (defined in Article 2(13), (12) and (14) respectively). The Data Act stipulates an accessibility obligation (Article 3 DA) and an access right (Article 4 DA), making available product data and related service data to the user of the connected product or related service (cf. Article 1(1)(a) DA) and a sharing right (Art. 5 DA), making available data by data holders to data recipients (cf. Article 1(1)(b) DA). According to Article 4(1) DA, data holders shall make certain data accessible to the user (access right). According to Article 5(1) DA the data holder shall, upon request by a user, make certain data available to a third party without undue delay (sharing right). Article 5(1) DA explicitly states that this shall be done in accordance with Articles 8 (agreement between data holder and third party) and 9 (compensation based on this agreement) but free of charge to the user.

Regarding the legal policy functions of these rules, Recital 2 DA states „an optimal allocation of data for the benefit of society" as the aim of the data sharing mechanism. Recital 32 DA refers to the overarching aim of this optimized data use: „not only to foster the development of new, innovative connected products or related services, stimulate innovation on aftermarkets, but also to stimulate the development of entirely novel services making use of the data concerned, including based on data from a variety of connected products or related services." On the other Hand, Recital 32 DA also shows the conflict with welfare-relevant interests of the data holders: „At the same time, this Regulation aims to avoid undermining the investment incentives for the type of connected product from which the data are obtained...". As a consequence, the Data Act tries to strike a tricky balance between a better allocation and, consequently, a better use of data on the one hand, and avoiding disincentives for the data holders

---

The Proprietary Foundations of Corporate Law, 27 Oxf. J. Leg. Stud. 429 (2007). cf. Armour/Hansmann/Kraakman/Pargendler in: Kraakman et al. (eds.), The Anatomy of Corporate Law, 3rd ed. (2017), 1, 5–6.

(for whom constructing new IoT-devices might become unattractive) on the other hand.

II. The position of the data holder

The position of the data holder shows two important aspects: de facto control of the data, arguably linked with trade secret protection, and the requirement of a contract with the user.

1. De facto control of the data

The Data Act, as a starting point, acknowledges the data holders' control over "their" data. Data holders are allowed to keep their de facto control over the data, although with the important exception of Article 3 DA (obligation to make product data and related service data accessible to the user). They are even allowed to use technical protection methods, Article 11(1) DA.

2. Trade secret protection

Arguably, data holders also enjoy trade secret protection. Articles 4 and 5 DA may even be seen as a model for compulsory licences in trade secrets, where complex rules try to maintain the trade secret while at the same time granting access to certain entitled parties.

The key requirement for trade secret protection is that the data can be qualified as information in the sense of Article 2(1) Trade Secrets Directive (TSD).[14] In addition, the information must be secret (lit. a), have commercial value because it is secret (lit. b), and subject to reasonable steps to keep it secret (lit. c). Among these requirements, arguably only commercial value may be interpreted in a way allowing the restriction of protection for raw data.

---

14 Aplin, Trading Data in the Digital Economy: Trade Secrets Perspective, in: Lohsse/Schulze/Staudenmayer (eds.), Trading Data in the Digital Economy: Legal Concepts and Tools (2017), 59, 65–66; Zech, A legal framework for a data economy in the European Digital Single Market: rights to use data, 11 JIPLP (2016) 460, 465; Zech, Data as a tradeable commodity, in: De Franceschi (ed.), New Features of European Contract Law – Towards a Digital Single Market (2016), 51, 62–62.

Information in the sense of Article 2(1) TSD must be understood as semantic information (meaning it is demarcated on the semantic level).[15] This, however, does not rule out the protection of data sets or even a single datum. Trade secret protection has an effect on any embodiment of the protected information, meaning any representation by code (on the syntactic level) or physical embodiment on a data carrier (on the structural level). Data in the sense of the Data Act is a digital representation of information. According to Article 2(1) DA „'data' means any digital representation of acts, facts or information and any compilation of such acts, facts or information, including in the form of sound, visual or audio-visual recording". Recital 15 DA distinguishes data in raw form (source or primary data), pre-processed data and information inferred or derived from such data. All of them are information in the sense of the Trade Secrets Directive. Although in the Data Act the data sharing mechanism only encompasses data in raw form and pre-processed data and the term information is only mentioned with the information inferred from such data this does not change the assessment of the term information in the Trade Secrets Directive.

The remaining valve is the requirement of a commercial value. It may be argued that single data do not have a significant value. However, the fact that there is an unmet demand for raw data shows that data do have a value, even if only a very small one per single datum. It may also be argued that judging the value from the perspective of the trade secret (data) holder leads to a lack of commercial value. Recital 14 TSD links the commercial value to the harm for the trade secret holder caused by unlawful acquisition.[16] However, even from this perspective, the loss of the possibility to trade the data means a harm for the trade secret holder. To sum it up, regardless of how small the value of a single datum may be, data sets or raw data in general do have a commercial value, although mostly a small one.[17]

Although Recital 16 TSD stresses that the Trades Secrets Directive "should not create any exclusive right to know-how or information protect-

---

15 Zech, Data as a tradeable commodity, in: De Franceschi (ed.), New Features of European Contract Law – Towards a Digital Single Market (2016), 51, 62.

16 Cf. Aplin, Trading Data in the Digital Economy: Trade Secrets Perspective, in: Lohsse/Schulze/Staudenmayer (eds.), Trading Data in the Digital Economy: Legal Concepts and Tools (2017), 59, 65.

17 Aplin, Trading Data in the Digital Economy: Trade Secrets Perspective, in: Lohsse/Schulze/Staudenmayer (eds.), Trading Data in the Digital Economy: Legal Concepts and Tools (2017), 59, 66.

ed as trade secrets" Trade Secret Protection resembles in many aspects IP rights (e.g. regarding enforcement and licensing (from a competition law perspective, TT-BER).[18] Not least it enjoys protection as property under the Charter of Fundamental Rights of the European Union and the European Convention on Human Rights.

The Data Act seems to be ambiguous about whether raw data may be protected as trade secrets. Recital 20 DA seems to deny the existence of exclusive rights in data: „manufacturers are able to determine, through their control of the technical design of the connected products or related services, what data are generated and how they can be accessed, *despite having no legal right to those data*" (emphasis added). This may be explained the qualification of trade secret protection as not being an exclusive right (Article 43 DA ensures that the right for the maker of a database in Article 7 of Directive 96/9/EC does not apply). Recital 31 DA, on the other hand, acknowledges at least the possibility of trade secret protection: „While this Regulation requires data holders to disclose certain data to users, or third parties of a user's choice, even when such data qualify for protection as trade secrets, it should be interpreted in such a manner as to preserve the protection afforded to trade secrets under Directive (EU) 2016/943." This wording seems to leave the question whether trade secret protection for raw data is possible open.

Arguably, trade secret protection is part of the balance between the interests of the data holders and the interests of the parties entitled to access the data. Trade secrets are preserved under the Data Act (meaning that it does not follow an open data approach). This is not only expressed in Recital 13 DA but also in Article 8(6) DA which states that "Unless otherwise provided for in Union law, including Article 4(6) and Article 5(9) of this Regulation, or by national legislation adopted in accordance with Union law, an obligation to make data available to a data recipient shall not oblige the disclosure of trade secrets."

The Data Act contains detailed rules for the preservation of trade secrets in Article 4(6)-(9) DA and Article 5(9)-(12) DA: Trade secrets shall only be disclosed where the data holder and the user take all necessary measures to preserve their confidentiality. Confidentiality agreements between holder and user or holder and recipient are envisaged. In exceptional circum-

18 Cf. Aplin, Trading Data in the Digital Economy: Trade Secrets Perspective, in: Lohsse/Schulze/Staudenmayer (eds.), Trading Data in the Digital Economy: Legal Concepts and Tools (2017), 59, 64: "Trade Secrets Directive precludes rights *in rem*".

stances the holder may refuse. An elaborate dispute settlement mechanism and a right to seek redress are stipulated.

3. Use and transfer: requirement of a contract with the user

While data holders do enjoy factual and even legal (trade secrets) protection, they are not free to do with the data whatever they want. In contrast, Article 4(13) and (14) DA stipulate for non-personal data the need for a contractual agreement with the users if they want to make use of the data or if they want to transfer the data. For personal data, a similar restriction arises from data protection where consent given by the data subject (Article 4(1) GDPR) according to Article 6(1)(a) GDPR arguably serves as the main (but not the only one) potential reason for the lawfulness of processing.[19]

This amounts to a kind of exclusive right for the users relative to the holders (which shall be examined in more detail under III.). Two aspects may be discerned: use and transfer.

Use is addressed in Article 4(13) DA. Article 4(13) DA requires for all readily available non-personal data a contract with the user: "A data holder shall only use any readily available data that is non-personal data on the basis of a contract with the user". This means that the right to use the data is allocated with the user.

Transfer is addressed in two different rules, Article 4(14) DA and Article 8(4) DA. Article 4(14) DA only applies to non-personal product data (data generated by the use of a connected product, Article 2(15) DA): "Data holders shall not make available non-personal product data to third parties for commercial or non-commercial purposes other than the fulfilment of their contract with the user. Where relevant, data holders shall contractually bind third parties not to further share data received from them." This means that the right to transfer non-personal product data is also allocated with the user. A similar rule can be found in Article 8(4) DA: "A data holder shall not make data available to a data recipient, including on an exclusive basis, unless requested to do so by the user under Chapter II." However, this rule arguably applies to all kind of data. As a parallel to Article 4(13) DA, the rule might be understood to be restricted to non-personal data with personal data following GDPR.

As a summary of the position of the data holder, trade secret protection is preserved regarding third parties but the rights to use and transfer data

19 Andreas Sattler, personal communication.

are allocated with the user. The holder keeps the possibility to exclude third parties (meaning parties that are neither user nor data recipients). But the right to use non-personal data is allocated to the user (the right to use personal data according to the GDPR to the data subject). Moreover, the right to transfer is also allocated to the user.

III. The position of the user

Users enjoy (besides being the beneficiaries of the accessibility obligation according to Article 3 DA) the access right according to Article 4 DA and the sharing right according to Article 5 DA. In addition, as was already shown, with respect to the holders the use is assigned to the users which, together with trade secret protection, amounts to an exclusive use right (see at 2.). This position is also transferable (see at 3.).

1. Use/access

Access factually enables the use of the data.[20] The possibility to use is therefore mediated by the right to access. Access is also facilitated by the accessibility obligation in Article 3 DA. The right to access the data is stipulated in Article 4 DA (rights and obligations of users and data holders with regard to access). This right is transferable by virtue of Article 5 (right of the user to share data with third parties). To be precise, the access right is not transferable as such, but another right of the user is created (the sharing right) which entails the access and use by the recipient. This may be the reason why Article 4 DA is not simply entitled "access right" but "rights and obligations of users and data holders with regard to access". The issue of transferability is further analyzed at 3.

The right is non-waivable „to the detriment of the user", Article 7(2) DA, Article 8(2) DA. This seems to follow the scholarly proposal of a non-waivable access right.[21] By allowing contracts which are not to the detriment of the user, arguably the door is open for contractual agreements "selling" the user right back to the data holder (by waiving the right against

20 Zech, Data as a tradeable commodity, in: De Franceschi (ed.), New Features of European Contract Law – Towards a Digital Single Market (2016), 51, 56.

21 Drexl, Data Access and Control in the Era of Connected Devices – Study on Behalf of the European Consumer Organisation BEUC (2018), 156–157.

remuneration in the contract between the data holder and the user), but not for free. In other words, although uncompensated buy-out agreements will not be possible a functioning data market that includes data holders on the demand side is feasible.

2. Exclusivity

The mechanism of Article 4(13)(14) DA and Article 8(4) DA, allocating the right of use and transfer within the relationship between data holder and user to the user was already examined (see at II.3). In addition, and this is important to stress, trade secrets protection steps in. To the extent trade secret protection for raw data is accepted, this protection not only acts for data holders but also for users (and recipients) as soon as they are in control of the data. The user enjoys trade secret protection against the recipient and other third parties. Because both the data holder and the user (and even the data recipient) are persons lawfully controlling the trade secret both (or all) are trade secret holders in the sense of Article 2(2) TSD. The preservation of trade secrecy described at section II.2 not only serves to protect the data holders but, as an automatic effect, also the user, the data recipients, and further recipients. Trade secrecy therefore serves as a kind of tradeable IP right in the Data Act. It must be borne in mind however that trade secrets licenses are not genuine licensing agreements but only agreements to disclose trade secrets to the contracting party which in turn must keep it secret. This means that "licensing" trade secrets still causes higher transaction costs than licensing IP rights.

The preservation of trade secrecy is also reflected in Article 4(14) DA where the second sentence reads: "Where relevant, data holders shall contractually bind third parties not to further share data received from them." The obligation to prevent disclosure by third parties serves the user by upholding trade secrecy. This argument is reinforced by Recital 37 DA: „In order to prevent the exploitation of users, third parties to whom data has been made available at the request of the user should process those data only for the purposes agreed with the user and share them with another third party only with the agreement of the user to such data sharing." In effect, the Data Act envisages a chain of contracts binding recipients and further recipients and thereby upholding trade secrets protection.

3. Transfer

The key question when analysing the user's position is whether the user has a right to transfer (allowing the trading of his or her right). The answer to this question is clearly affirmative. Arguably, it is the key idea of the Data Act that the user may transfer (and trade) the data to whoever he or she likes. Recital 25 DA states: „This Regulation does not prevent users, in the case of business-to-business relations, from making data available to third parties or data holders under any lawful contractual term, including by agreeing to limit or restrict further sharing of such data, or from being compensated proportionately, for example in exchange for waiving their right to use or share such data." At least in business-to-business relations the user may transfer the data (or enable the transfer of the data)

(1) to holders, cf. Article 7(2), 8(2) DA, but not „to the detriment of the user" (see at III.1.);
(2) to third parties (data recipients);
(3) to further third parties (further recipients), cf. Recital 33: „ Upon the agreement with the user, and subject to the provisions of this Regulation, third parties should be able to transfer the data access rights granted by the user to other third parties, including in exchange for compensation." Moreover, according to Recital 33 „data intermediaries ... may support users or third parties", clarifying that data intermediaries may trade the rights to further recipients.

The "data access rights granted by the user" mentioned in Recital 33 refers to the right of the user in Article 5 DA. When the user does not exert the right him- or herself but transfers the right to the data recipient (number 2 of the abovementioned alternatives) a transferable right arises. The position of the data recipient may then be interpreted as "a party acting on behalf of a user" in the sense of Article 5(1) DA. The data recipient then is the "third party" according to Recital 33 transferring the data access rights to "other third parties". The wording of Recital 33 also allows for further transfers. All this, however, is only possible "[u]pon the agreement with the user".

To sum the position of the user up: The user enjoys exclusion not only against the data holder but also against third parties, by virtue of trade secret protection. The user enjoys a right to use, enabled by a right to access. Finally, the position is transferable, or, in the words of property rights theory, the user also enjoys a right to transfer. In essence, the position of the user fulfils all the criteria that constitute the core of property (see at I.1.).

IV. Co-ownership?

The question remains whether in the Data Act also aspects of co-ownership can be found. Property rights theory, in that respect, may serve as an analytical framework for managing shared assets. Co-ownership is distinct from a mere overlap of property rights. It entails a certain degree of joint management of an asset. As an example, §§ 741–758 BGB (German Civil Code) and similar rules in IP law may serve. For data, the ALI-ELI Principles for a Data Economy developed principles for co-generated data (Principles 18–23).[22]

The Data Act arguably does contain some elements of co-ownership. The user profits from exclusivity derived from the data holder's trade secret protection. Both enjoy trade secrecy protection which they must uphold jointly. For a detailed analysis, different aspects of co-ownership may be discerned which can be derived from the "standard models" for co-ownership like co-ownership in tangible assets and in IP. This not only allows to clearly flesh out the effects of the Data Act data sharing mechanism but also to design appropriate contracts and model contracts.

As the core aspects of co-ownership may be mentioned:

(1) Use (both parties should have a use right), cf. § 743(2) BGB: Each party has a right to use as far as the other party's use is not afflicted. Here, the non-rivalrous nature of data use can be taken into account.
(2) Exclusion (against third parties, in that respect, co-ownership is different from open data).
(3) Transfer (including dereliction of the right, which for trade secrets would be the public disclosure of the secret).

Among further aspects of co-ownership may be mentioned (as a non-exhaustive list)

22 ALI/ELI Principles for a Data Economy, Data Transactions and Data Rights, As Adopted and Promulgated by The American Law Institute on May 18, 2021 and The European Law Institute on September 1, 2021 (Principles 18–23); Similar Metzger/Schweitzer, Shaping Markets: A Critical Evaluation of the Draft Data Act, ZEuP 2023, 42 (55).

(4) Integrity, meaning the preservation of the asset.
(5) Management which as the norm is joint management (but can contractually be stipulated otherwise), cf. § 744(1) BGB, and includes safeguarding of the right.
(6) Fruits, meaning the distribution of gains derived from the management of the asset. For example, § 743(1) BGB distributes fruits corresponding to the share in co-ownership. Arguably, this is also the idea of the Data Act, cf. Article 9(1), Recital 47: „may (also) include a margin". The data holder, therefore, should also be entitled to a participation in economic gains, corresponding to his or her merit in generating the data.

V. Final assessment: Data access right(s) as an enabler for data markets and further fields of action

Finally, coming back to the main function of property rights, it may be asked whether the Data Act data sharing mechanism has the potential to enable data markets (cf. Recital 4: "a well-functioning internal market for data"). Regarding the transferable "data access rights" mentioned in Recital 33 this can clearly be answered in the affirmative. The position of the user as a whole is designed in a way to allow trading the resulting access rights to all interested parties, including the data holder him- or herself. This, hopefully, will lead to data markets fostering the use of raw data.

As a legal policy perspective, it is worth mentioning that the aim of arriving at functioning data markets can be helped by acting in two important areas of activity which are also mentioned in the Data Act and which do not require legislative action. The first is supporting data intermediaries (cf. Recital 26, 33) and personal information systems (PIMs). The second is the development of model contracts between data holders and users (cf. Article 41: „non-binding model contractual terms on data access and use") which may even include partnership contracts.

With model contracts, not only the optimum allocation of data but also distributional justice can be addressed (which is also underlying the non-waivability „to the detriment of the user", cf. section III.1). The idea should be to incentivize a co-operative utilization of raw data instead of an adversarial approach. The main function of the Data Act remains the enablement of functioning markets for raw data. The creation of a transferable access right seems to be a step in the right direction. With the development of proper model contractual terms (hopefully fostering co-operative acting on the markets), it might be even helped further.

IoT Data Sharing in B2C: How to Better Serve the Consumer

*Prof. Dr. Louisa Specht-Riemenschneider, Marwan El-Rifaai, Victor Mehnert, Leonard Bodemann**

I. Introduction

The Data Act[1] (DA), which came into force on 11 January 2024, stipulates that data generated during the operation of connected products and related services must be made accessible for data users. Under the meaning of the DA, connected products can be vehicles, household appliances and consumer goods, medical and healthcare products or agricultural and industrial machinery, see Recital 14 DA.[2] For example, a smart refrigerator using odour sensors and visual sensors to independently detect when food is about to spoil, is addressed.[3] The scope of the DA does not cover storage-only media or purely online services. Furthermore, certain products that are primarily intended to display or play content or to record and transmit it, such as personal computers, servers, tablets and smartphones, cameras, webcams, sound recording systems and text scanners, are also not covered by the DA, cf. Recital 15 DA.

Therefore, the DA especially addresses IoT products. They collect a large amount of data, which can be personal and non-personal, depending on the application. For example, the smell of a product in a smart fridge that is about to spoil is not a personal data in itself, but the information that this is happening in a natural person's fridge is related to an identified or identifiable natural person and is, therefore, personal. However, if personal

---

* University of Bonn.

1 Regulation (EU) 2023/2854 of the European Parliament and of the Council of 13 December 2023 on harmonized rules on fair access to and use of data and amending Regulation (EU) 2017/2394 and Directive (EU) 2020/1828 (Data Act).

2 According to Article 2(3) DA, a "related service" is a digital service, including software, which is incorporated in or inter-connected with a product in such a way that its absence would prevent the product from performing one of its functions; however, this is not the focus of this article.

3 E.g., the smart fridge from Copenhagen Collective, see https://nttdata-solutions.com/ch/blog/smart-fridge-wie-ki-innovationen-die-nachhaltigkeit-foerdern-koennen/, last accessed on 3.4.2024.

data is sufficiently anonymised, it is in turn non-personal. The General Data Protection Regulation (GDPR) primarily applies to personal data. It contains comprehensive provisions for processing personal data, some of which entail legal uncertainty, but the material content of which is sufficient to ensure comprehensive protection of data subjects. The DA shall supplement the GDPR in terms of data access and data portability, Art. 1(5)(2) DA. In the event of a conflict the GDPR shall prevail, Art. 1(5)(3) DA. However, legal enforcement is often problematic in the context of the GDPR. In addition to the consumer concerns of data control already regulated in the DA and the GDPR, there are other consumer interests worthy of protection in IoT products that the legislator has not yet sufficiently considered. Therefore, this article focuses on these consumer concerns relating to the use of IoT devices as a whole and builds on the results of an expert workshop conducted by the German Advisory Council on Consumer Affairs (SVRV). The article is based on the following theses:

1. The DA should provide for more robust consumer protection, especially against bricking[4] and the linking of data use and product functionality. A right to data collection-free products should be provided.
2. Consumers' remuneration for disclosing data and possible disincentives to disclose data should be carefully considered. One alternative could be to revisit the data tax discussed in 2018.[5]

II. Course of the Investigation

The article aims to analyse the issues faced by consumers when using IoT products (III.). It then discusses the adequacy of current laws in addressing these problems and identifies the need for legislative action. The article primarily focuses on four problem areas: the right to data access for consumers, bricking, the right to analogue and data collection-free products, and the remuneration of consumers for sharing (non-personal) data (IV.).

---

4 See for a definition of "bricking" below under IV. 2.

5 Vorerst keine Digitalsteuer in Europa, available at https://www.tagesschau.de/wirtschaft/digitalsteuer-107.html, last accessed on 05/04/2024; The failure of the European digital service tax prompted some European countries (particularly Austria, France and the UK) to introduce national regulations, see: Budget 2018: Tech giants face digital service tax, available at https://www.bbc.com/news/business-46023450, last accessed on 05/04/2024.

Finally, the article concludes with specific recommendations for legislative action (V.).

III. Problem Identification

Legal science does not provide a method for understanding the problems that consumers encounter when using IoT devices. Instead, sociological and economic methods have to be applied. Law therefore only comes into consideration at a later stage as one of several solution components of an identified problem. In this respect, quantitative surveys that have already been conducted can be used to identify the problems consumers are facing in the IoT. In addition, the SVRV carried out an expert workshop that was methodologically based on the principal-agent theory[6] and the theory of socio-technical systems.[7]

1. Quantitative Survey

In a survey among the German-speaking resident population aged 16 and over, the question "Why don't you use smart home applications yet?" was mainly answered with IT security concerns and concerns about control over the data generated (fear of misuse of personal data, fear of privacy, I fear hacker attacks, a smart home is scary for me), technical aspects (lack of compatibility, lack of repairability, operation too complicated, solutions not technically mature) and consumer-specific aspects (benefits too low, installation too complex, devices too expensive). This is essentially consistent with the results of the SVRV's expert workshop.

In addition to these broad reasons for the non-use of smart home devices, the SVRV's expert workshop also revealed that there are concerns about the use of IoT overall:

- that the manufacturer can switch off IoT devices at his discretion (bricking)
- that the user may have to conclude a second contract to put the device into operation

6 *Eisenhardt*, Agency Theory: An Assessment and Review (1989), The Academy of Management Review, p. 57 et seqq.

7 *Baur, Markt*, in: *Baur/Korte/Löw/Schroer*, Handbuch Soziologie (2008), p. 273.

- that there is no possibility to use the devices in analogue mode or at least without data collection, which is not necessary for their functionality
- that money is earned with user data without the users participating
- that dark patterns are used, e.g. that the platform design is such that exercising user rights is made more difficult.

2. Expert Workshop

The principal agent theory applied in the SVRV's expert workshop identifies hidden characteristics, hidden actions, and hidden intentions in contractual relationships, each of which is based on a particular form of information asymmetry. Information asymmetry is present in certain performance characteristics, such as hidden traits.[8] The result of such information asymmetry may be that a principal makes an economically inefficient choice between two products offered to him. The principal then decides, for example, based on different costs, not realising that the quality is also different. This subsequent problem is also known as adverse selection.[9] Hidden actions refer to actions of the agent that are unknown to the principal or that the principal cannot judge to the extent that these actions could be harmful.[10] Hidden intentions refer to principal–agent information asymmetry regarding the other party's intentions in the relationship.[11]

However, the principal-agent theory assumes that a fully informed consumer always makes rational decisions in their favor.[12] Even if consumers are well-informed, however, they make irrational decisions.[13] In order to compensate for these deficits of the principal-agent theory, the theory of socio-technical systems is used as a second theoretical basis. The theory of socio-technical systems looks in particular at the external context of

8 *Eisenhardt*, Agency Theory: An Assessment and Review (1989), The Academy of Management Review, p. 57, (59 et seqq).
9 *Eisenhardt*, Agency Theory: An Assessment and Review (1989), The Academy of Management Review, p. 57, (59 et seqq).
10 *Shapiro*, Agency Theory (2005), Annual Review of Sociology, p. 263 (264).
11 Under the heading of information asymmetry: *Shapiro*, Agency Theory (2005), Annual Review of Sociology, p. 263 et seqq.
12 *Eisenhardt*, Agency Theory: An Assessment and Review (1989), The Academy of Management Review, p. 57, (60 et seqq); *Baur, Markt*, in: *Baur/Korte/Löw/Schroer*, Handbuch Soziologie (2008), p. 273.
13 *Baur, Markt*, in: *Baur/Korte/Löw/Schroer*, Handbuch Soziologie (2008), p. 274 et seq.

a contractual relationship.[14] The external context is the necessary social and legal framework for contractual relationships.[15] For example, users of messenger services (e.g. WhatsApp) often do not decide which service offers the highest data protection setting or whether certain functionalities are offered. Instead, decisions are made based on which messaging service is used by the most contacts.

IV. Solutions

IT security law already focuses comprehensively on technical aspects and fears of misuse and data protection law also aims to address the misuse of personal data, e.g. via data protection principles, the rights of data subjects or the options for sanctions and legal action. Control over the use of non-personal data on the other hand is to be ensured by the DA. In this respect, the DA also addresses dark patterns and provides information obligations for data holders.[16] In contrast, the topics of bricking, the right to analogue or data generation-free/data collection-free products and the issue of remuneration have not yet been addressed in regulatory terms or at least not fully. In the following, the regulations of the DA will, therefore, first be examined regarding their suitability for implementing the identified consumer concerns to then discuss the topics of bricking, the right to analogue or data generation-free/data collection-free products and the issue of remuneration.

1. Limited Suitability of the DA for Implementing Consumer Requests[17]

The DA governs the relationship between the data holder and the user of a connected product or related service regarding data access and use. Within the context of the DA, a user is any natural or legal person that owns a connected product or to whom rights to use the connected product have

14 *Baur, Markt*, in: *Baur/Korte/Löw/Schroer*, Handbuch Soziologie (2008), p. 281.
15 *Baur, Markt*, in: *Baur/Korte/Löw/Schroer*, Handbuch Soziologie (2008), p. 273, 281 et seq.
16 See under IV. 1. b) for information obligations and under IV. 1. d) for dark patterns.
17 This part of the article on the DA has already been partially published in German in: *Specht-Riemenschneider*, Der Entwurf des Data Act (2022), Multimedia und Recht-Beilage, p. 809.

been temporarily transferred by contract or that receives related services, Art. 2(12) DA. This means that a consumer can also be considered a user per Art. 2(23) DA. The DA, thus, addresses the consumer's request for data control. However, the DA only realises this data control of the consumer on paper, because too little is asked about which protective measures are necessary to provide the consumer with actual control instruments. This is also because the DA only differentiates between the various users in question in individual aspects (e.g. in Art. 6(2)(h) DA) when structuring its regulations; essentially, it provides standardised regulations for data access for natural persons acting privately and commercially as well as for legal entities. These regulations can be found in Chapter 2 of the DA. The data holder's obligations towards the data user essentially include ensuring data accessibility by default in Art. 3(1) DA, according to which connected products must be designed and manufactured and related services designed and provided in such a way that product data and related service data are provided easily, securely, free of charge, in a comprehensive, structured, commonly used and machine-readable format and, where relevant and technically feasible, directly accessible to the user by default. Pre-contractual information obligations are also standardised under Art. 3(2) and (3) DA, whereby the obligations are differentiated according to whether a contract is concluded for using a connected product. In addition, the data access right of the user is standardised under Art. 4(1) DA, which also includes the possibility of requesting the transfer of data directly to a third party, Art. 5(1) DA. This does not include gatekeepers under Art. 3 Digital Markets Act (DMA)[18], Art. 5(3) DA. The data holder may use non-personal data solely based on a contract under Art. 4(13) DA. Data processing prohibitions on third parties are also regulated in Art. 6 DA and a de minimis rule for micro and small enterprises, Art. 7 DA.[19] The DA also contains interoperability regulations in Chapter 8; however, these are not the focus of this article.

18 Regulation (EU) 2022/1925 of the European Parliament and of the Council of 14 September 2022 on contestable and fair markets in the digital sector and amending Directives (EU) 2019/1937 and (EU) 2020/1828 (Digital Markets Act).

19 *Specht-Riemenschneider*, Der Entwurf des Data Act (2022), Multimedia und Recht-Beilage, p. 809 (812).

The following considerations interfere with effective consumer protection in the DA:

- First, according to Art. 3 DA, the data must be made accessible in the technical-factual sphere of control of the manufacturer and not in the technical-factual sphere of control of the user
- Data access under Art. 3 DA can be implemented as a mere in-situ right[20]
- There are no design regulations, such as button solutions that allow users to easily exercise their rights
- Data access according to Art. 3 DA does not include derived data. Derived data is data that is generated as the outcome of additional investments into assigning values or insights from the data, Recital 15 p. 13. This includes, in particular, data obtained through sensor fusion, Recital 15, p. 14.
- The information requirements contained in Art. 3(2) and (3) DA do not meet the needs of consumers. Under Art. 3(2) DA, no information is provided as to whether a second contract may be required to make the product functional, nor that this contract may not be free of charge, but that the user may have to pay a fee or "pay" with "his" data. There is also no information about the fact that the manufacturer or even the seller can 'brick' the product, nor about whether the user can also use the product offline as long as the data collection is not required to fulfil the main function of the connected product. Finally, no information is provided as to whether and, if so, to what extent, money is earned with the user's data.
- Under Art. 4(6) DA, trade secrets shall only be disclosed 'if all necessary measures prior to the disclosure to preserve their confidentiality regarding third parties'. It is the data holder or, where they are not the same person, the trade secret holder who identifies the data protected as trade secrets, including in the relevant metadata. He or she shall then agree with the user proportionate technical and organisational measures necessary to preserve the confidentiality of the shared data. The data holder also initially assesses which measures are appropriate, who can provide the user with standard contractual clauses or confidentiality agreements, the application of technical standards, strict access protocols or even codes of conduct, without these being subject to specific regulatory restrictions.

---

20 See under IV. 1. a) bb).

- If the user is a natural person, the contract between the user and the data holder is not subject to any adequate consumer protection requirements and thus only ensures private autonomy in theory.

In detail:

a) Data Accessibility by Design

The DA applies to the design and manufacturing of connected products and related services. Art. 3 DA is not explicitly aimed at manufacturers. Nevertheless, the entire life cycle is taken into account.[21] In the following, we will explain the purpose of Art. 3 DA and how data accessibility could be structured, as well as which categories of data are covered.

aa) Ensuring the Possibility of Control over Data

According to Art. 3(1) DA, products must be designed and manufactured and related services designed and provided in such a way that product data and related service data are, by design, easily, securely, free of charge, in a comprehensive, structured, commonly used and machine-readable format and, where relevant and technically feasible, directly accessible to the user.[22] This is also referred to as "data accessibility by design".[23] Data accessibility can be realised, for example, through user interfaces.[24] Whether data access is requested however depends on the user, who bears the burden of action in this respect.[25] The user receives data access not by default, but is forced

---

21 *Hennemann/Steinrötter*, Der Data Act (2024), Neue Juristische Wochenschrift, p. 1 (3); *Metzger/Schweitzer*, Shaping Markets: A Critical Evaluation of the Draft Data Act (2023), Zeitschrift für Europäisches Privatrecht, p. 42 (52).

22 *Specht-Riemenschneider*, Der Entwurf des Data Act (2022), Multimedia und Recht-Beilage, p. 809 (815).

23 *Steinrötter*, Verhältnis von Data Act und DS-GVO, Zugleich ein Beitrag zur Konkurrenzlehre im Rahmen der EU-Digitalgesetzgebung (2023), Gewerblicher Rechtsschutz und Urheberrecht, p. 216 (220).

24 *Specht-Riemenschneider*, Der Entwurf des Data Act (2022), Multimedia und Recht-Beilage, p. 809 (815).

25 *Specht-Riemenschneider*, Der Entwurf des Data Act (2022), Multimedia und Recht-Beilage, p. 809, (815 et seqq); Article 25 GDPR; *Steinrötter*, Verhältnis von Data Act und DS-GVO, Zugleich ein Beitrag zur Konkurrenzlehre im Rahmen der EU-Digitalgesetzgebung (2023), Gewerblicher Rechtsschutz und Urheberrecht, p. 216 (220).

to take appropriate measures.[26] The situation would only be different, if the data, in addition to being stored in the technical-factual sphere of control of the manufacturer, were also stored automatically at least in storage media that are under the users' control, e.g. in a user-controlled cloud storage location, or in a neutral technical-factual sphere of control, e.g. with a data trustee.[27] In this respect, the DA standardises "data accessibility by default", but in fact, this does not mean a technical-factual assignment of the data to the user, but to the manufacturer.[28] The technical-factual dominance of the manufacturer is the principle that is only broken where the user makes use of his right to access the data.[29] The DA therefore does not guarantee control over the data generated during the operation of IoT products, but merely the possibility of control.

bb) In Situ Right

In addition, the data does not necessarily have to be transmitted to the user, but data access can be designed as a mere in situ right. In situ data access does not give the user the technical-factual sovereignty over the data. This remains with the data holder. An in situ right is merely a right to read data.[30] Recital 22 DA states that data access can be granted, for example, by providing data access directly from on-device data storage or from a remote server to which the data are communicated. The server can be the

---

26 *Specht-Riemenschneider*, Der Entwurf des Data Act (2022), Multimedia und Recht-Beilage, p. 809 (815).

27 *Specht-Riemenschneider*, Der Entwurf des Data Act (2022), Multimedia und Recht-Beilage, p. 809 (815).

28 Insofar as no access to the data is included, this does not break the control of the data owner. In addition, the *status quo* that the manufacturer initially has (exclusive) technical-factual control over the generated data may even be strengthened (see also: *Podszun/Pfeifer*, Datenzugang nach dem EU Data Act: Der Entwurf der Europäischen Kommission (2022), Gewerblicher Rechtsschutz und Urheberrecht, p. 953 (957); *Specht-Riemenschneider*, Data Act – Auf dem (Holz-)Weg zu mehr Dateninnovation? (2022), Zeitschrift für Rechtspolitik, p. 137 (138); *Kerber*, Governance of IoT Data: Why the EU Data Act Will not Fulfill It's Objectives (2023), Gewerblicher Rechtsschutz und Urheberrecht Internationaler Teil, p. 120 (123 et seq.); but see *Schmidt-Kessel*, Heraus- und Weitergabe von IoT-Gerätedaten (2024), Multimedia und Recht-Beilage, p. 75 (78).

29 *Specht-Riemenschneider*, Der Entwurf des Data Act (2022), Multimedia und Recht-Beilage, p. 809 (815).

30 *Steinrötter*, Verhältnis von Data Act und DS-GVO (2023), Gewerblicher Rechtsschutz und Urheberrecht, p. 216 (220).

manufacturer's own local server capacities or those of a third party or a cloud service provider, cf. Recital 22 DA.

According to Recital 24 and Art. 3(2) and (3) DA, information must be provided regarding the possibility of exercising user rights, including information on how the data can be stored or retrieved or how it can be accessed. However, there are no design regulations, such as button solutions for the easy exercise of user rights. This also hinders actual data control.

cc) Categories of Data Collected

According to Art. 3(1) DA, the product data, and the related service data have to be made directly accessible to the user. Product data is data generated by the use of a connected product that the manufacturer designed to be retrievable, via an electronic communications service, physical connection or on-device access, by a user, data holder or a third party, including, where relevant, the manufacturer, Art. 2(15) DA. Related service data is data representing the digitisation of user actions or of events related to the connected product, recorded intentionally by the user or generated as a by-product of the user's action during the provision of a related service by the provider, Art. 2(16) DA. It should include all data generated by the connected product as a result of use, as well as data automatically generated by sensors and data recorded by embedded applications, Recital 15 DA. This data should also include data generated in an inactive state, for example when the product is in stand-by mode, Recital 15. Derived data should not be included. The benchmark is whether further investment was necessary to obtain the data or information, Recital 15 p. 13. These investments should be protected.

b) Pre-contractual Information Obligations, Art. 3(2) and (3) DA

The SVRV's expert workshop based on principal-agent theory and the theory of socio-technical systems showed that there is a lack of information for users.[31] Consumers want information on whether a product is smart, what data is collected and passed on, who the data recipients are, and what purpose the data transfer serves. Information about software updates

31 See above under III.

is also desired. The GDPR contains numerous information obligations for personal data.[32]

Art. 3(2) and (3) of the DA establish information obligations for some of the identified consumer concerns, but they prove to be unsuitable for the majority.

- Under Art. 3(2)(a)-(d) DA, at a minimum, the following information must be provided before concluding a contract for the purchase, rent or lease of a connected product:
- the type, format, and estimated volume of product data that the connected product is capable of generating
- information on whether the connected product can generate data continuously and in real-time;
- whether the connected product is capable of storing data on-device or on a remote server, including, where applicable, the intended duration of retention
- information on how the user can access, retrieve, or, where relevant, erase the data, including the technical means to do so, as well as the relevant terms of use and quality of service.

Further information obligations apply before the conclusion of a contract to provide a related service, under Art. 3(3)(a)-(i) DA. A related service is a digital other than an electronic communications service, including software, which is connected with the product at the time of the purchase, rent or lease in such a way that its absence would prevent the connected product from performing one or more of its functions, or which is subsequently connected to the product by the manufacturer or a third party to add to, update or adapt the functions of the connected product, Art. 2(6) DA. The related services may themselves generate data that have value for the user, irrespective of the data collection capabilities of the connected product to which they are connected, per Recital 17 p. 6 of the DA. This refers to services that are able to transmit commands to the connected product, which in turn may have an impact on its action or behaviour,

32 In particular, Art. 13 GDPR should be mentioned, which imposes the obligation on the controller to inform about the identity and the contact details of the controller, the purposes of the processing for which the personal data are intended as well as the legal basis for the processing, where applicable the legitimate interests pursued by the controller or by a third party and the recipients or categories of recipients of the personal data, if any.

Recital 17 p. 2 DA. The following information must be provided in a clear and comprehensible manner following Art. 3(3)(a)-(i) DA:

- the nature, estimated volume, and collection frequency of product data that the prospective data holder is expected to obtain and, where relevant, the arrangements for the user to access or retrieve such data, including the prospective data holder's data storage arrangements and the duration of retention
- the nature and estimated volume of the related service data to be generated, as well as the arrangements for the user to access or retrieve such data, including the prospective data holder's data storage arrangements and the duration of retention
- whether the prospective data holder expects to use readily available data itself and the purposes for which those data are to be used, and whether it intends to allow one or more third parties to use the data for purposes agreed upon with the user
- the identity of the prospective data holder, such as its trading name and the geographical address at which it is established and, where applicable, of other data processing parties
- the means of communication which make it possible to contact the prospective data holder quickly and communicate with that data holder efficiently;
- how the user can request that the data are shared with a third party and, where applicable, end the data sharing
- the user's right to lodge a complaint alleging an infringement of any of the provisions of this Chapter with the competent authority designated pursuant to Article 37;
- whether a prospective data holder is the holder of trade secrets contained in the data that is accessible from the connected product or generated during the provision of a related service, and, where the prospective data holder is not the trade secret holder, the identity of the trade secret holder;
- the duration of the contract between the user and the prospective data holder, as well as the arrangements for terminating such a contract.

The consumer is therefore informed that the product is smart (that it can collect data), Art. 3(2)(a) and (b) DA, and as to which third parties the data is transferred and for what purposes, Art. 3(3)(c) DA (although this obligation towards the contractual partner of a connected product is missing in Art. 3(2) DA). The fact that software updates may be required and where these can be obtained must be communicated under Art. 8(2) of the Digital Content Directive (DCD).[33] However, Art. 3(2) DA does not state whether a second contract is required to make the product functional, nor whether this contract is free of charge, but that the user may have to pay a fee or 'pay' with 'his or her' data. Art. 3(2) DA also does not state that the manufacturer or even the seller can brick the product or whether the user can also use the product offline as long as the data collection is not required to fulfil the main function of the connected product (i.e. the cooling function in the case of the smart fridge). Finally, no information is provided as to whether and, if so, to what extent, money is earned with the user's data.

c) Right of Access to Data, Art. 4 DA

Insofar as the user cannot already access the data directly from the product under Art. 3 DA, the data holder shall provide the user with readily available data without delay, simply, securely, free of charge, in a comprehensive, common and machine-readable format and, where relevant and technically feasible, in the same quality as for the data holder continuously and in real-time, upon simple request by electronic means, insofar as this is technically feasible, Art. 4(1) DA.[34]

aa) Categories of Data Collected

Readily available data are product data and related service data that a data holder lawfully obtains or can lawfully obtain from the connected product or related service, without disproportionate effort going beyond a simple operation, under Art. 2(17) DA. It is not explicitly regulated by the DA under which circumstances the data holder may lawfully obtain data from the connected product or related service.[35] In addition to statutory access rights, the DA's system often relies on contractual arrangements between

---

33 Directive (EU) 2019/770 of the European Parliament and of the Council of 20 May 2019 on certain aspects concerning contracts for the supply of digital content and digital services [2019] OJ L 136/1.

34 *Specht-Riemenschneider*, Der Entwurf des Data Act (2022), Multimedia und Recht-Beilage, p. 809 (815).

35 *Specht-Riemenschneider*, Der Entwurf des Data Act (2022), Multimedia und Recht-Beilage, p. 809 (815).

the parties involved.[36] It is clarified in Recital 25 DA that freedom of contract is still guaranteed. It expressly clarifies that contractual freedom is guaranteed in data law. This means that compliance with any contractual agreements and the GDPR requirements are particularly important.[37] This includes both data intentionally recorded by the user and data generated as a by-product of user actions, such as diagnostic data, as well as data generated without any user action, e.g. when the product is in standby mode and data are recorded while the product is switched off, per Recital 15 p. 5, 7 of the DA. What matters is that the data are generated by a device in the user's possession, without the specific use being relevant and without the user contributing to data generation that goes beyond possession.[38] Weather data recorded during the operation of a connected vehicle, for example, are therefore also covered by the data access claim.[39]

The data access right under Art. 4 DA does not apply to derived data, per Recital 15 DA. However, derived data also contain a user reference, so a data access claim relating to them could be justified, especially given the DA's objective of ensuring the fair distribution of the added value from data, per Recital 5 and Recital 15 DA.[40] Since the user has created 'more' added value in this case, restricted use of derived data in the sense of a fair distribution of added value would be conceivable.[41]

---

36 *Hennemann/Steinrötter*, Der Data Act, Neue Instrumente, alte Friktionen, strukturelle Weichenstellungen (2024), Neue Juristische Wochenschrift, p. 1 (6).

37 *Specht-Riemenschneider*, Der Entwurf des Data Act (2022), Multimedia und Recht-Beilage, p. 809 (815).

38 See: *Bomhard/Merkle*, Der Entwurf eines EU Data Acts, Neue Spielregeln für die Data Economy (2022), Recht Digital, p. 168 (171).

39 *Specht-Riemenschneider*, Der Entwurf des Data Act (2022), Multimedia und Recht-Beilage, p. 809 (815).

40 *Specht-Riemenschneider*, Der Entwurf des Data Act (2022), Multimedia und Recht-Beilage, p. 809 (815); cf. contra: *Leistner/Antoine*, IPR and the use of open data and data sharing initiatives by public and private actors, p. 16, available at: https://www.europarl.europa.eu/RegData/etudes/STUD/2022/732266/IPOL_STU(2022)732266_EN.pdf, last accessed on 04/04/2024.

41 *Specht-Riemenschneider*, Der Entwurf des Data Act (2022), Multimedia und Recht-Beilage, p. 809 (815); cf. *Drexl/Banda/Gonzalez Otero/ Hoffmann/Kim/Kulhari/Moscon/Richter/Wiedemann*, Position Statement of the Max Planck Institute for Innovation and Competition of 25 May 2022 on the Commission's Proposal of 23 February 2022 for a Regulation on harmonised rules on fair access to and use of data (Data Act), para. 25 et seq., available at: https://papers.ssrn.com/sol3/papers.cfm?abstract_id=4136484; last accessed on 04/04/2024; *Hennemann/Steinrötter*, Der Data Act, Neue Instrumente, alte Friktionen, strukturelle Weichenstellungen (2024), Neue Juristische Wochenschrift, p. 1 (3).

bb) Requirements of the Data Access Claim

The prerequisite for the data access claim is the simple user request, which is not subject to any further requirements.[42] In particular, no specific formal or deadline requirements are to be met.[43] The data access claim also requires that the user cannot access the data directly from the product, Art. 3 DA.[44] Design specifications, e.g. a button solution for exercising user rights, are also missing here.

cc) Organisation of Data Access

For users and data holders, the question of whether the user's right to data access is a right to data portability, i.e. the data must actually be transferred to the user and the data holder may even have to delete the data when exercising the right to data access or whether the right of access can also be designed as a mere in-situ right, i.e. it is limited to the user viewing the data at the data holder's premises and, if necessary, processing it on the data holder's servers, which is likely to be of considerable importance.[45] Recital 22 of the DA clearly favours such an in-situ right.[46] However, Recital 22 of the DA is linked to the design of connected products and, thus, according to the wording, rather to Art. 3(1) DA.[47] The phrasings of Article 4 and 5 DA imply that users have the right to access and obtain copies of their data.[48] This would also be more compatible with the character of the

42 *Specht-Riemenschneider*, Der Entwurf des Data Act (2022), Multimedia und Recht-Beilage, p. 809 (815).
43 *Specht-Riemenschneider*, Der Entwurf des Data Act (2022), Multimedia und Recht-Beilage, p. 809 (815).
44 On the relationship between Art. 3 DA and Art. 4 DA, see *Specht-Riemenschneider*, Der Entwurf des Data Act (2022), Multimedia und Recht-Beilage, p. 809 (815).
45 *Kerber*, Governance of IoT Data: Why the EU Data Act Will not Fulfill It's Objectives (2023), Gewerblicher Rechtsschutz und Urheberrecht Internationaler Teil, p. 120 (123 et seq.).
46 See above under: IV. 1. a) bb).
47 Irrespective of the fact that recitals are not part of directly applicable law, only "[...] connected products *may* be designed [...]" is mentioned.
48 *Podszun/Pfeifer*, Datenzugang nach dem EU Data Act: Der Entwurf der Europäischen Kommission (2022), Gewerblicher Rechtsschutz und Urheberrecht, p. 953 (957).

regulation as a supplement to Art. 20 GDPR than a mere in-situ right.[49] However, the matter remains inconclusive and will ultimately require a decision from the European Court of Justice (ECJ). This also applies to the right to data access in favor of third parties under Art. 5 GDPR.

dd) Limitations of the Data Access Claim

The user's right to data access is subject to the limits of the GDPR, i.e. any data access must be compatible with the GDPR's requirements.[50] Data access under Art. 4(1) of the GDPR and the right to data portability under Art. 20(1) of the GDPR should complement each other, Art. 1(5)(2) DA and cf. Recital 35 DA. Restrictions also arise from Art. 4(2) DA if data access would undermine legally defined security requirements of the connected product, as well as from Art. 4(6)-(8) DA if the data concerned are subject to trade secret protection. Under Art. 4(6) DA, trade secrets are only disclosed "where the data holder and the user take all necessary measures prior to the disclosure to preserve their confidentiality in particular regarding third parties". The data holder determines whether the data are a trade secret and agrees with the user on 'proportionate technical and organisational measures necessary to preserve the confidentiality of the shared data, in particular in relation to third parties, such as model contractual terms, confidentiality agreements, strict access protocols, technical standards and the application of codes of conduct'. The only viable option is to regulate the general terms and conditions, which may not benefit the consumer much due to the non-typical nature of the underlying agreement. If the consumer does not agree to the specified regulation, the data holder can refuse or suspend access to the data, see Art. 4(7) DA. Although the user can challenge the decision per Art. 4(9) DA, it is known that such ex-post control options are generally only very rarely utilised by consumers due to limited time capacities, limited knowledge and limited financial resources.[51] Ex-ante control mechanisms be better, e.g. specific regulations on terms

49 *Steinrötter*, Verhältnis von Data Act und DS-GVO, Zugleich ein Beitrag zur Konkurrenzlehre im Rahmen der EU-Digitalgesetzgebung (2023), Gewerblicher Rechtsschutz und Urheberrecht, p. 216 (222).

50 On the similar relationship between the GDPR and the DGA, cf. *Specht-Riemenschneider*, in: *Specht/Hennemann* (eds.) Data Governance Act (1st edn., 2023), Art. 1 para. 40 et seqq.

51 *Kaesling/Knapp*, Umsetzung der urheberrechtlichen Verantwortlichkeit von Upload-Plattformen, Gestaltung eines nutzerzentrierten Anreizschemas (2021), Multimedia

and conditions or mandatory laws. However, the DA does not include any provisions for such ex-ante control mechanisms.

ee) Right of the Data Holder to Use the Data on a Contractual Basis, Art. 4 (13) DA

Art. 4(13) DA is essential for controlling data in connected products, according to which the data holder may use available data solely based on a contract with the user. This may initially appear to be a high hurdle and, particularly in comparison with the requirements of the data protection law, it is notable that the processing of personal data under Art. 6 and 9 of the GDPR is subject to lower requirements because consent is only one of several legal bases for processing personal data.[52] A comparison with the processing authorisation under data protection law according to Art. 6(1)(b) GDPR would fall short because of Art. 6(1)(b) GDPR, which permits processing that is necessary for the performance of a contract, which is something completely different from processing based on a contractual agreement with which the user consents to the processing. The standard of comparison must therefore be Art. 6(1)(a) GDPR. However, just like consent under data protection laws, the contractual agreement required in Art. 4(13) of the GDPR is a hurdle that is all too easy to overcome and only ensures formal, but not material, self-determination. This is because the contract between the user and the data holder is not subject to any adequate consumer protection requirements, at least if the user is a natural person. It is not uncommon for this agreement to be a contract for goods with digital elements within the meaning of Section 327(3) of the German Civil Code (BGB) or for goods with "dispensable" digital products following Section 327(2) BGB. Sections 327 et seq. BGB do not, however, provide any protective mechanisms that would guarantee the user the necessary self-determination when making their declaration under Art. 4(13) DA. According to the DA, the Unfair Terms Directive should apply to this contract (see Recital 26 DA), but the specific restrictions required for these contracts

und Recht, p. 11 (14); *Penney*, Privacy and Legal Automation: The DMCA as a Case Study (2019), Stanford Technology Law Review, p. 412 (451).

52 *Hennemann/Steinrötter*, Data Act – Fundament des neuen EU-Datenwirtschaftsrechts? (2022), Neue Juristische Wochenschrift, p. 1481 (1483); *Bomhard/Merkle*, Der Entwurf eines EU Data Acts, Neue Spielregeln für die Data Economy (2022), Recht Digital, p. 168 (174).

cannot be found in the current law on general terms and conditions. For example, the data owner can conclude comprehensive buy-out contracts with the user which authorise him to pass on the data to third parties for a fee. Although contractual clauses that give the data holder the right to use data should be transparent to the user, there is no restriction on the purposes of use, Recital 25 DA. Making consent under Art. 4(13) more granular and anchoring corresponding information obligations alone would not solve this problem, as it is well known from consumer behaviour research that information does not necessarily contribute to better decision-making by the consumer; on the contrary, from an individually determinable amount of information, the absorption of information decreases or even stops completely.[53] In the area of general terms and conditions and data protection declarations, this is also known as the clicking without reading phenomenon,[54] which can be attributed to various market failures.

In addition, the data holder can link the conclusion of the contractual agreement with the user to the functionality of the product, at least within the scope of what is permissible under general terms and conditions law, as there is no prohibition on linking the use of data to the functionality of the product. This means that provisions that allow the data owner to render the product inoperable if the user cancels the contractual agreement (so-called bricking) are also possible. Although the German Federal Court of Justice (BGH) has declared this type of specific provisions in general terms and conditions to be invalid under German law, European law is interpreted autonomously, which is why the BGH's decision does not affect the contractual agreement under Art. 4(13) DA. However, even if such a clause were also inadmissible according to an autonomous interpretation of the Clauses Directive under EU law, it would still be technically possible for the data owner to break the product and only restore its functionality if the consumer continues the contractual agreement under Art. 4(13) DA. Whether this is permissible would have to be clarified by the consumer through lengthy legal proceedings. It would, therefore, be more useful to

---

53 *Alemanno/Sibony*, Nudge and the Law: A European Perspective (2015) p. 329 et seqq.; *Hacker*, Verhaltensökonomik und Normativität (2017), Studien zum Privatrecht, p. 117 et seqq.; *Schmölke*, Grenzen der Selbstbindung im Privatrecht (2014), p. 180 et seq.; *Zamir/Teichman*, Behavioral Law and Economics (2018), p. 285.

54 *Khong*, The Clicking Without Reading Problem (undated), published at: https://papers.sioe.org/paper/551.html; last accessed on 22/06/22; "click and forget": *Hennemann/Steinrötter*, Data Act – Fundament des neuen EU-Datenwirtschaftsrechts? (2022), Neue Juristische Wochenschrift, p. 1481 (1483).

have an ex-ante ban on bricking and corresponding sanctions for noncompliance.

d) Dark Patterns

Dark patterns are design techniques that push or deceive consumers into decisions that have negative consequences for them, Recital 38 p. 6 DA. They are at least partially prohibited by the DA. For example, data holders may not unreasonably impede the exercise of choices or rights by the user under Art. 4 DA, including by offering the user choices in a non-neutral manner or by undermining or impairing the user's autonomy, freedom of choice or freedom of decision through the structure, design, function or operation of a digital user interface or part thereof, see Art. 4(4) DA. The same obligation also applies to third parties who receive data under Art. 5 DA and must agree to the processing conditions and purposes with the user under Art. 6(2)(a) DA. The digital interface's designer (data holder or third party) should also not use dark patterns, Recital 38 p. 5 of the DA. However, there is no corresponding prohibition of dark patterns in Art. 3 DA.

2. Bricking

Bricking is the IoT trader's ability to remotely monitor consumers and automatically downgrade the IoT product, discontinue the service, remove functionalities, determine the lifespan of the product and even deactivate it.[55]

The practice of bricking IoT products is not only relevant regarding the DA (see above) but can also collide with the regulations on general terms and conditions as well as the Digital Content Directive which is implemented in German consumer law by Sections 327a et seq. of the BGB. In particular, clauses in End User License Agreements, sales contracts or other contracts that enable manufacturers or sellers of IoT products to remotely downgrade or deactivate product functions could violate the provisions of the Council Directive 93/13/EEC of 5 April 1993 on unfair

55 *Tusikov*, Regulation through "Bricking": Private Ordering in the "Internet of Things" (2019), Internet Policy Review, 8 (2), p. 4 et seq.

terms in consumer contracts (Unfair Terms Directive)[56] (Sections 305 et seq. BGB). Further, bricking could lead to a lack of conformity of the IoT product with the contract between the consumer and the seller of the IoT product or a third party providing digital goods or services. In that case, consumers are entitled to remedies under the DCD and/or the Sale of Goods Directive (SGD.)[57]

Whether and where legislative improvements are necessary to better protect consumers from bricking can, therefore, only be assessed after a detailed analysis of the current legal situation, which will be carried out in the following. Four things are important to highlight:

1. The various purposes of bricking must be clearly distinguished. The functionality of a device can be restricted or cancelled for reasons that are provided for in the contract (default of payment, other breaches of contract) or that are unilaterally specified by the manufacturer (e.g. planned obsolescence). Whether bricking is legally permissible for a specific purpose is ultimately a question of contractual agreements and, therefore, subject to the legality of general terms and conditions in mass contracts.
2. If the possibility of bricking has already been created at the time the digital product has been supplied by an if/else link (e.g. smart car, where the driving function is only provided within the borders of the country, but not abroad), this must be treated differently in legal terms than the bricking of a product that takes place after the digital product has been supplied, e.g. by installing a kill update (e.g. if the functions of the operating system of a smartphone are affected by an update to the detriment of the consumer or if cloud access is simply blocked or deactivated).
3. The DCD and the SGD differentiate between three different types of contracts: Contracts for "pure" digital products (e.g. cloud services), contracts for digital products that are incorporated in or inter-connected with a good in such a way that the absence of the digital product does not prevent the good from functioning (e.g. a navigation software in a

56 Council Directive 93/13/EEC of 5 April 1993 on unfair terms in consumer contracts [1993] OJ L 95/29.

57 Council Directive (EU) 2019/771 of the European Parliament and the Council of 20 May 2019 on certain aspects concerning contracts for the sale of goods, amending Regulation (EU)
2017/2394 and Directive 2009/22/EC, and repealing Directive 1999/44/EC [2019] OJ L 136/28.

car) and contracts for goods with digital elements (e.g. the operating system of a smartphone). Bricking can lead to a lack of conformity with the contract in all three cases – but different rules apply.[58]

4. Ultimately, it is important to consider the provision period of the digital product or the goods with dispensable or indispensable digital products on the one hand and the period of the necessary updates to be provided on the other. If the digital product or the goods with digital products are to be provided in a one-off exchange relationship, this is to be assessed differently in legal terms than the continuous provision of the digital product.

In this context, the section below explains the differences between the various types of contracts (a.). It also explains how bricking affects consumer remedies in each scenario (b.)

a) Digital products and Goods with Digital Elements

Digital products are digital content and digital services. Under the legal definition in Section 327(2)(1) BGB[59], digital content means data which are produced and supplied in digital form. Digital services can take two different forms according to Section 327(2)(2) BGB[60]. A digital service can be a service that allows the consumer to create, process, store or access data in digital form or a service that allows the sharing of or any other interaction with data in digital form uploaded or created by the consumer or other users of that service. In the IoT however, digital products are often incorporated in or inter-connected with digital products. In that case, Section 327a(2) BGB[61] states that Sections 327 et seq. BGB generally apply to these contracts. However, according to Section 327a(3) BGB they do not apply, if the absence of the digital product prevents the good from performing its functions (goods with digital elements). Rather, these contracts are regulated by Sections 475b et seq. BGB[62].

It is therefore important to assess if the digital product incorporated in or inter-connected with the tangible IoT device is essential for the whole IoT system to function.

58 *Bernzen/Specht-Riemenschneider,* Erman BGB (17th edn., 2023), § 327e para. 17 with further references.
59 National implementation of Art. 2(1) DCD.
60 National implementation of Art. 2(1) DCD.
61 National implementation of Art. 3(6) DCD.
62 National implementation of Art. 6, 7 and 8 SGD.

It is therefore important to assess if the digital product incorporated in or inter-connected with the tangible IoT device is essential for the whole IoT system to function. It is important that "the digital product makes the goods digital in the first place and gives them a significant character.[63] This is not to be determined subjectively based on the contractual agreement, but rather abstractly and objectively, according to the functions of the goods that can be expected, regardless of a possible agreement between the parties.[64] There are two scenarios in which a digital product imparts defining characteristics to goods: First, if the digital product enables the core functions of the goods, e.g., software that makes a smartphone functional or a car roadworthy. Second, if the digital product characterises the goods independently of their core function to such an extent that they would have a completely different character without the digital product.[65] For example, a smart fridge can fulfil a cooling function even without the software for personalised shopping, but it is precisely the software that makes it smart. According to this approach, the smart fridge, for example, would also be considered a product with digital elements.

b) Bricking of Goods with Digital Elements

The conformity of goods with digital elements is regulated by Section 475b(2) BGB[66]. Goods with digital elements are (in the terminology of the BGB) free from defects if they fulfil the subjective requirements, the objective requirements, the assembly requirements and the installation requirements at the time of delivery and concerning an update obligation also during a certain period according to Section 475b(3)(2) BGB and Section 475b(4)(2) BGB.

63 *Mayer/Möllnitz*, Gewährleistung für „smarte" Produkte nach Umsetzung der Digitale Inhalte- und Warenkauf-Richtlinien (2021), Recht Digital, 333 (334); see also *Bernzen/Specht-Riemenschneider*, Erman BGB (17th edn., 2023), § 327a para 27.

64 See: *Dubovitskaya*, Kauf von Waren mit digitalen Elementen – Fortschritt und Rechtsunsicherheit im Verbrauchsgüterkaufrecht (2022), Multimedia und Recht, 3 (4); *Mayer/Möllnitz,* Recht Digital 2021, 333 (338).

65 Cf., MüKoBGB/*Metzger* (9th edn., 2022), § 327a para. 12.

66 National implementation of Art. 5 SGD.

aa) Requirements at the Time of Delivery

According to Section 475b(3)(1) BGB[67], the good with digital elements must fulfil the requirements of Section 434(2) BGB. Therefore, if a particular quality, features or a certain intended use is contractually agreed upon, the good with digital elements must comply with this agreement. Therefore, if it is agreed that a car should also be roadworthy outside the national borders, an if/else link that restricts the roadworthiness to certain territories would violate the subjective requirements.[68] Moreover, products with digital elements must generally meet the objective requirements under Section 475b(4) BGB[69]. The key consideration here is what a consumer could reasonably expect. Therefore, even if there is no agreement on roadworthiness outside the Member State borders, the car is defective if it is usually expected to be roadworthy outside borders.

(1) Subjective Requirements

However, it is also possible to deviate from these objective requirements under certain conditions through a contractual agreement, cf. Section 476(1)(2) BGB[70]. Negative quality agreements are those in which the subject matter of the contract should not have a certain quality and thus fall short of the legal quality standard of objective quality.[71] Technical protective measures that restrict the roadworthiness to certain areas cause the subject matter of the contract to fall short of the objective quality[72] and must, therefore, be agreed within the limits of Section 476(1)(2) of the

67 National implementation of Art. 6(a)-(c) SGD.

68 On the inadequacy of technical protective measures, see *Schmidt-Kessel*, Verträge über digitale Inhalte – Einordnung und Verbraucherschutz (2014), Kommunikation & Recht, 475 (482); *Grützmacher*, Endlich angekommen im digitalen Zeitalter!? (2013), Zeitschrift für geistiges Eigentum, 46 (79); *Ganzhorn*, Rechtliche Betrachtung des Vertriebs und der Weitergabe digitaler Güter (2015), p. 330.

69 National implementation of Art. 7(3) SGD.

70 National implementation of Art. 21 SGD.

71 MüKoBGB/*Westermann* (8th edn., 2019), § 434 para. 23.

72 *Mackenrodt*, Technologie statt Vertrag? (2015), p. 284 et seq.; see already: *Specht*, Mark-Oliver Mackenrodt: Technologie statt Vertrag? (2016), Zeitschrift für geistiges Eigentum, 484 (485 et seq.) and: *Specht*, Beschränkung der Verkehrsfähigkeit digitaler Güter durch technische Schutzmaßnahmen (2016), Zeitschrift für geistiges Eigentum, 289 (297 et seq.); *Specht*, Diktat der Technik (2019), p. 278 et seq.

BGB so that the subject matter of the contract with the technical protective measure. Such a negative quality agreement is also possible in general terms and conditions,[73] however, it must remain within the limits of what is permissible under Sections 307 et seq. BGB. Copyright case law on technical protection measures could be utilised here.[74] A disproportionate technical protection measure under the principles of the *Nintendo* decision[75] must, if agreed upon, constitute an unreasonable disadvantage within the meaning of Section 307(2)(1) BGB.[76] If it is not agreed upon, its installation constitutes an implied quality agreement that is not effective under Section 476(1)(2) BGB. The BGH recently declared an invalid clause that authorised a bank to suspend its obligation to provide services and prevent the battery of a car from being recharged in connection with the rental of batteries for purchased and leased vehicles. The central argument was that the use of the vehicle and therefore the car battery was of considerable interest for the daily life of the consumer.[77] If the negative quality agreement is ineffective, no quality has been subjectively agreed upon, meaning the product can fall short of the objective requirements. It must then fulfil the objective requirements.

(2) Objective Requirements

The good with digital elements must also be fit for the purposes for which goods of the same type would normally be used and have a quality that is customary for items of the same type and that the buyer can reasonably expect. The decisive factor here is the expectations of a reasonable average buyer at the time the contract is concluded, whereby a comparison

---

73 Beck-OGK BGB/*Faust* (69th edn.), § 476 para. 28.

74 See: *Specht*, Mark-Oliver Mackenrodt: Technologie statt Vertrag? (2016), Zeitschrift für geistiges Eigentum, 484 (485 et seq.) and: *Specht*, Beschränkung der Verkehrsfähigkeit digitaler Güter durch technische Schutzmaßnahmen (2016), Zeitschrift für geistiges Eigentum, 289 (297 et seq.); that not every use of technical means constitutes a defect was already established by the BGH in its judgement of 25.03.1987 – VIII ZR 43/86, NJW 1987, 2004, 2005 – Programmsperre II.

75 ECJ, judgement of 23 January 2014 – C-355/11, ECLI:EU:C:2014:25, Europäische Zeitschrift für Wirtschaftsrecht, 2014, 304.

76 See: *Ganzhorn*, Rechtliche Betrachtung des Vertriebs und der Weitergabe digitaler Güter (2015), p. 331.

77 BGH, judgement of. 26.10.2022 – XII ZR 89/21 para. 29; see *Beurskens*, Akkusperre aus der Ferne (2023), Recht Digital, 1 (4).

with other items of the same type is required.[78] Restricting the driving function of an electric car to domestic borders is unlikely to correspond to the expectations of a reasonable average buyer. Therefore, the vehicle is unsuitable for normal use in cases of such a driving area restriction. If the goods with indispensable digital elements do not fulfil the objective requirements, the consumer is entitled to remedies under Section 439 BGB. This is also not contradicted by Section 442 BGB, according to which warranty rights for defects are excluded if the buyer has knowledge or grossly negligent ignorance of the defectiveness of the subject matter of the contract. This knowledge or grossly negligent ignorance can generally be obtained through a negative quality agreement. However, remedies are not excluded according to Section 442 BGB if the knowledge is obtained within the framework of an invalid contractual agreement,[79] e.g. one that does not fulfil the requirements of Section 476(1)(2) BGB. However, behaviour cannot be an abuse of rights if it merely contradicts an invalid agreement. Section 442 BGB does not typically apply in the case of contractual agreements, but rather when such an agreement does not exist because the buyer, but not the seller, is aware of the defect.[80]

(a) Defect due to Bricking after Delivery of the Goods with Digital Elements

Section 475b (3)(2) BGB[81] expands the subjective requirements by stipulating that the updates for the digital elements agreed to in the sales contract must be provided during the relevant period under the contract. Regarding the objective requirements, the consumer must be provided with the necessary updates to maintain the conformity of the goods with the contract during the period that can be expected based on the nature and purpose of the goods and their digital elements and considering the circumstances and nature of the contract. The consumer must be informed of these updates, per Section 475b (4)(2) BGB. This means that the goods must be free of defects with indispensable digital elements at the time of the risk

78 BeckOKBGB/*Hau/Poseck* (69th edn., 2024), § 434 para. 76; MüKoBGB/*Westermann* (8th edn., 2019), § 434 para. 6.
79 AG Marsberg, judgement of 09.10.2002 – 1 C 143/02, BeckRS 2002, 14584 para. 9; AG Zeven, judgement of. 19 December 2002 – 3 C 242/02, ZGS 2003, 158, 160 et seq., see also: *Mackenrodt*, Technologie statt Vertrag? (2015), p. 257 et seq.
80 *Mackenrodt*, Technologie statt Vertrag? (2015), p. 258.
81 National implementation of Art. 6(d) SGD.

transfer and that the updates necessary to maintain conformity with the contract must be provided for a certain period of time afterwards. Both the provision period and the scope of the update obligation can be agreed upon. For example, it can be agreed that only updates relating to particular functions will be provided. However, it can also be agreed that the digital elements will be improved through upgrades and the scope of services will be expanded. The following applies in principle:

> "The updates agreed in the purchase contract may improve the digital elements of the item, extend its functions, adapt it to technical developments, protect it against new security threats or serve other purposes. The contractual conformity of goods with digital elements must therefore also be examined with regard to the question of whether the digital elements receive updates in accordance with the sales contract. Failure to provide updates agreed in the sales contract constitutes a defect of the good with digital elements. Furthermore, faulty or incomplete updates also constitute a defect, as this means that such updates are not carried out as agreed in the sales contract."[82]

If the period and scope of the update have not been agreed upon, the update period is determined according to an average buyer's expectations.[83] The obligation to update is limited to maintaining the contractual conformity of the item.[84] Unless the parties have contractually agreed otherwise, the seller is therefore not obliged to improve or extend the functions of the good.[85] However, the status quo must be maintained. Therefore, if the bricking by installing an update leads to a restriction of the essential functions of the digital product, the goods with digital elements will no longer be in conformity with the contract. The overall purpose of the update obligation is to ensure that the goods with digital elements can fulfil their functions after they have been delivered to the consumer.[86] So-called "kill updates", which restrict the usability of a smart fridge, do not fulfil this function.[87] A corresponding agreement in the general terms and conditions

82 RegE, BT-Drs. 19/27424, p. 32.

83 RegE, BT-Drs. 19/27434, p. 33; MüKoBGB/*Metzger* (9th edn., 2022), § 327f para. 10; *Staudinger/C Heinze*, BGB (2023), § 327f para. 21.

84 MüKoBGB/*Metzger* (9th edn., 2022), § 327f para. 5.

85 RegE, BT-Drs. 19/27434, p. 33; *Staudinger/C Heinze*, BGB (2023), § 327f para. 11.

86 *Staudinger/C Heinze*, BGB (2023), § 327f para. 9; MüKoBGB/*Metzger* (9th edn., 2022), § 327f para. 1.

87 *Bernzen/Specht-Riemenschneider*, Erman BGB (17th edn., 2023), § 327f para. 7.

that enables such updates is likely to violate the fundamental principles of Section 327f BGB[88] and Section 475b (3)(2) BGB and is therefore invalid under Section 307 (2)(1) BGB. After all, one of the aims of the update obligation is to enable consumers to use their products for longer. The background to this legal provision is not primarily the protection against loss of functionality due to remote access, but rather the preservation of the contractual conformity of the goods digital elements.[89] However, it would be inconsistent with the aims of the updating obligation to this if the manufacturer would be allowed to structure this obligation through general terms and conditions in such a way that the product could fall behind the status it had at the time of delivery. This result is also supported by the fact that the ratio of the updating obligation is not limited to "digital maintenance" and the adaptation to changing external digital circumstances as well as the extension of the useful life: Rather, the updating obligations can also become relevant if the manufacturers or a third party interferes with the digital product through remote access. Recital 30 SGD states that the seller shall be liable for restoring conformity with the contract if an update by the seller or a third party who provides the digital content or digital service under the sales contract causes the non-conformity of a good with digital elements. The European legislator is, therefore, likely to have focused primarily on cases in which the manufacturer installs an inadvertently faulty update or a third party, leading to functional restrictions. However, *targeted* updates that impair functionality should be also seen as "unsuccessful" updates that entitle the consumer to remedies. Something else could only apply if the seller or manufacturer has a legitimate interest in bricking, for example if bricking is a reaction to a delay in payment by the consumer or to another breach of contract. The legislator and case law will have to decide for which purposes bricking may be agreed here and when a clause is invalid within the meaning of Section 307 BGB.

(b) Bricking of Digital Products and Goods with "Dispensable" Digital Products

Sections 327 et seq. BGB provide for a standardised legal guarantee for defects for different types of contracts as provisions for consumer contracts for digital products. In the case of a purchase contract, Sections 327 et

88 National implementation of Art. 7(d) and Art. 8(2) DCD.
89 *Bernzen/Specht-Riemenschneider*, Erman BGB (17th edn., 2023), § 327f para. 1.

seq. BGB apply if the object of purchase is a product with "dispensable" digital products, Section 475a(1) and (2) BGB. Goods with dispensable digital products are goods that contain digital products or are connected to digital products in such a way that the goods can fulfil their basic functions without these digital products, e.g. a car with a navigation system. A differentiation between goods with dispensable digital products or digital elements is not made in other contract types. If a digital product or good containing digital products are rented, Section 578b BGB refers to the warranty rights of Sections 327 et seqq. BGB for these components. In the case of a gift of digital products or goods containing digital products, Section 516a BGB refers to Sections 327 et seq. BGB. The same applies to digital products or goods that contain digital products and that have been created as part of contracts for work and labour to which Sections 327 et seq. BGB apply.

According to Section 327d BGB[90], the entrepreneur is obliged to provide the digital product (e.g. the navigation system) free of defects following Section 327e BGB[91]. Section 327e BGB states that a product is free of defects if it satisfies both subjective and objective requirements. The standards set out in Section 475b BGB apply here, with some additional specifications, such as the functionality of digital products, which is considered part of the subjective and objective requirements. Here too, a negative quality agreement must be expressly and separately agreed, cf. section 327h BGB[92], which is also possible in general terms and conditions.[93] According to Section 327e(2)(3) and 327e(3)(5) BGB, updates must also be provided so that the product fulfils the subjective and objective requirements, Section 327 et seq. BGB. If the purchase contract contains an agreement that allows updates to be made at the expense of the consumer, it is likely to be incompatible with the fundamental principles of Section 327f BGB and therefore invalid under Section 307(2)(1) BGB.

According to Section 327(2) and (3) BGB, the digital product must fulfil the subjective and objective requirements. The quality can result from the relationship of the digital product to the digital environment or to the

90 National implementation of Art. 6 DCD.

91 National implemenation of Art. 7, 8 and 9 DCD.

92 National implementation of Art. 8(5) DCD.

93 *Riehm/Abold*, Rechtsbehelfe von Verbrauchern bei Verträgen über digitale Produkte (2021), Computer und Recht, 530 (534); *Bernzen/Specht-Riemenschneider*, Erman BGB (17th edn., 2023), § 327h para. 13.

environment in general.[94] It is concretised, among other things, by the functionality, i.e. the ability of a digital product to fulfil its functions.[95] If the functionality of the digital product (e.g. the navigation system in a car) is restricted by bricking, the agreed quality is often also affected. In addition, in the case of bricking, a breach of the updating obligations agreed in the contract during the relevant period under the contract can be considered. Bricking by installing an update that is detrimental to the consumer is a faulty update that is not in conformity with the contract. If it is agreed in the sales contract that updates should also be possible to the detriment of the consumer, this agreement is likely to be covered by Section 307(2)(1) BGB.

c) Permanent Provision of Digital Products

If digital products or goods that contain or are connected to digital products are provided permanently, updates must be supplied for the entire duration of the contract.[96] This follows from Section 578b and Section 327e(1)(3) et seq. BGB. Therefore, if the use of a navigation system is owed for a contractually agreed period of time, the standards for assessing bricking are also largely derived from Section 327 et seq. BGB.

d) Result

Bricking will generally lead to a lack of conformity with the contract. Firstly, digital products lack conformity if they are already designed in such a way that functional limitations occur under certain conditions and this cannot be reasonably expected by the consumer unless something else has been effectively agreed upon. Secondly, subsequent bricking also constitutes a lack of conformity, meaning that the seller is obliged to provide an update that restores functionality. However, the parties can also deviate from the updating obligation of the seller by party agreement under the conditions of Section 476(1)(2) BGB which can also be done through general terms and conditions. The decisive factor will therefore be the purposes for which

94 MüKoBGB/*Metzger* (9th edn., 2022), § 327e para. 9; *Staudinger/C Heinze*, BGB (2023), § 327e para. 19.

95 *Bernzen/Specht-Riemenschneider*, Erman BGB (17th edn., 2023), § 327e para. 16; *Staudinger/C Heinze*, BGB (2023), § 327e para. 26.

96 *Staudinger/C Heinze*, BGB (2023), § 327e para. 10.

the entrepreneur may reserve the right to bricking in the general terms and conditions and when a corresponding clause is invalid under Section 307 BGB. In principle, a distinction will must be made as to whether the consumer is in breach of contract or whether the manufacturer is bricking the product for other purposes. Even in the case of a breach of contract, however, it depends on other circumstances, e.g. whether a product is involved that is fundamental to the daily life of the consumer, such as a car. A breach of Section 305c(1) BGB, on the other hand, is unlikely to occur if the manufacturer merely has remote access, as this is a prerequisite for installing an update in the case of connected products.

The legislator should examine whether bricking for specific purposes or planned obsolescence, should be regulated by Section 309 BGB.

3. Right to Analogue and Data Collection-Free Products

Connected products collect data to very different extents. A distinction must be made between data necessary and unnecessary for the products' functionality. The DA gives the user the right to decide on the use of the data within the contract scope under Art. 4(13) DA, insofar as the contractual balance of power allows this. However, the user does not have the right to technically prevent the collection of data that is not necessary for the device's functionality or even to use the device in an analogue manner. The manufacturer determines the technical design. However, control over the data collected would be best achieved if users could decide for themselves whether the data is technically collected at all or whether the device can even be used in analogue mode.

a) Data Generation and Data Collection

A fundamental distinction must first be made between data generation and data collection concepts. This is because both processes can be the starting point for user rights. Data generation means the creation of data through the use of a product, Recital 14 et seq. DA. An analogue product is generally also free of data generation. Data generation-free or analogue products therefore do not generate any data. The term data collection, on the other hand, covers any activity through which the collecting organisation obtains knowledge of the data concerned or establishes technical-factual sovereignty over it.[97] Although a data collection-free product generates data, due to its function, this data is not transferred to the technical-factual access sphere of the product manufacturer or seller but remains in that of the user.

b) Concepts

Firstly, we will present concepts for data collection-free and analogue products. Along with these concepts, we will also suggest possible solutions. Additionally, we will briefly discuss whether existing regulations, namely Art. 25 GDPR, already provide for the right to data collection-free products.

aa) Right to Data Collection-Free and Data Collection-Poor Products

Following Maximilian Becker[98], a right to data collection-free products can initially be conceptualised. A corresponding right, which Becker conceives for personal data, but which could also be transferred to non-personal data, does not exist explicitly yet. For personal data, such a right could be derived from Art. 25(1) GDPR, which, however, only addresses the data holder, not the producer.[99] Art. 25(1) GDPR obliges the data holder to take measures designed to effectively implement the data protection principles laid down in Art. 5(1) GDPR. The principle of data minimisation is mentioned separately, Art. 5(1)(c) GDPR. According to this, personal data shall be adequate, relevant and limited to what is necessary in relation to the purposes for which they are processed. This is to be achieved in particular through data protection-friendly default settings, Art. 25(2) GDPR. Where this is possible, products must therefore be *data collection-free by default*.[100] However, data necessary for the product's functionality must also be collected. Fitness data from a fitness app can be cited as an example if data collection is necessary for communication with a personal coach via the app. In this case, the right to data collection-free products is transformed into a right to data *collection-poor* products.[101]

---

97 *Dammann*, in: Bundesdatenschutzgesetz (8th edn., 2014), § 3 para. 100 et seqq.

98 *Becker*, Ein Recht auf datenerhebungsfreie Produkte (2017), JuristenZeitung, p. 170.

99 *Hansen* in: *Simitis/Hornung/Spiecker*, Datenschutzrecht, Article 25 para. 20.

100 *Hartung* in: *Kühling/Buchner*, DS-GVO/BDSG, Article 25 DS-GVO para. 24.

101 *Becker*, Ein Recht auf datenerhebungsfreie Produkte (2017), JuristenZeitung, p. 170 (176).

A right to data collection-free products *by design* could be achieved with Art. 25 GDPR in relation to personal data if the obligations of Art. 25 GDPR are explicitly extended to manufacturers. A right to data collection-free products would therefore go beyond the existing requirements of Art. 25 GDPR.[102]

For non-personal data, a right to data collection-free products could be established primarily by supplementing the DA. Regulations are required that prohibit the manufacturer or product seller from linking the functionality of the product to the collection of data that is not required for the functionality of the device. In addition, consumers should be informed that they can use the device without data collection or with little data collection and how this can be achieved.

bb) Right to Data-free Products/Right to Analogue Products

However, a legal approach could also already be taken at the data generation stage, either by guaranteeing a right to analogue products or at least data generation-free products. A modular design, for example, could give consumers the option to turn a smart product into a data generation-free product. This is conceivable, for example, by means of a mechanical switch on the device that deactivates all data-relevant functions.[103] Such a switch is also known as a legacy *switch.*[104] A *legacy switch* is not a software command, but a physical interruption of data connections. It should not be possible to bypass it using software.[105] Activating the switch simply makes a smart product no longer smart.[106] For example, a smart thermostat whose smart, connected features are switched off (e.g., via a *legacy switch*) must

102 *Becker*, Ein Recht auf datenerhebungsfreie Produkte (2017), JuristenZeitung, p. 170 (176).

103 *Becker*, Ein Recht auf datenerhebungsfreie Produkte (2017), JuristenZeitung, p. 170 (178); *Ohm/Kim*, Legacy Switches: A Proposal to Protect Privacy, Security, and the Environment from the Internet of Things (2023), Ohio State Law Journal, p. 101 (120 et seq.).

104 *Ohm/Kim*, Legacy Switches: A Proposal to Protect Privacy, Security, and the Environment from the Internet of Things (2023), Ohio State Law Journal, p. 101 (120 et seq.).

105 *Becker*, Ein Recht auf datenerhebungsfreie Produkte (2017), JuristenZeitung, p. 170 (178).

106 *Ohm/Kim*, Legacy Switches: A Proposal to Protect Privacy, Security, and the Environment from the Internet of Things (2023), Ohio State Law Journal, p. 101 (121).

continue functioning as a thermostat. In the analogue state, maximum data protection is guaranteed due to the lack of data collection. However, if smart functions are desired by the user and the *legacy switch* is therefore not used, data protection and data security must be ensured by other means.[107] Therefore, a combination of a *legacy switch* and low-data collection products would be ideal.

c) Interim Result

A combination of *legacy switch* and low-data collection products would therefore be ideal. During the use of smart functions of a product, only the functionally necessary data is generated and collected. If the legacy switch is used, the generation of data can be completely prevented. In this way, consumers are comprehensively protected. On the one hand, they have the choice as to whether data is collected at all. On the other hand, only the minimum amount of necessary data is collected.

4. Remuneration for Non-personal Data

The question of whether consumers should receive, or at least be able to receive, remuneration for providing their data is highly controversial. The arguments against this are that data does not have an objective value, but that this arises from the context in which it is used[108] and – more importantly – that remuneration for the provision of data may create false incentives to pay for data,[109] in favour of the fact that the provision of data (whether for a fee or not) is ultimately also an expression of informational self-determination. Therefore, an analogy to copyright law is being discussed.[110] In addition to the collective remuneration provided for there,

107 *Ohm/Kim*, Legacy Switches: A Proposal to Protect Privacy, Security, and the Environment from the Internet of Things (2023), Ohio State Law Journal, p. 101 (121).

108 *Bisges*, Personendaten, Wertzuordnung und Ökonomie (2017), Multimedia und Recht, p. 301 (305).

109 *Specht*, Dateneigentum und Datenhandel, in: Stiftung Datenschutz, Dateneigentum und Datenhandel (2019), p. 301 (308); *Wandtke*, Ökonomischer Wert von persönlichen Daten (2017), Multimedia und Recht, p. 6 (9 et seq.); *Bisges*, Personendaten, Wertzuordnung und Ökonomie (2017), Multimedia und Recht, p. 301 (305).

110 *Schwartmann/Hentsch*, Parallelen aus dem Urheberrecht für ein neues Datenverwertungsrecht (2016), Privacy in Germany, p. 117 et seq.; *Fezer*, Dateneigentum

individual contractual remuneration models are also possible, as is a data tax or a levy through which the profits of companies that process data and thus generate revenue could flow back to those affected for a specific purpose. Such a data tax was already intensively discussed in 2018, but did not progress beyond a Commission draft.[111] The remuneration models mentioned are presented and discussed below.

a) Individual Remuneration

Individual remuneration for the user could form the consideration for the use of data. Such a contractual solution is also promoted by the DA,[112] which provides for contractual arrangements between the user and the manufacturer as the basis for using non-personal data by the manufacturer, see Art. 4(13) DA and Recital 25 DA. Although there are no requirements for consideration right now, they could certainly be provided for in the future for non-personal data. The user's contribution to data generation is not monocausal; the company's investment in the production of recording and analysing devices and software are also parameters that contribute to creating value from data. In any case, the user's contribution is not insignificant and could therefore justify remuneration of the user.The legislator could therefore make "appropriate consideration" mandatory without, however, positively defining appropriateness. However, there would then be a risk on the part of the company that the remuneration would simply be priced in and passed on to the consumer. Thus, it would seem more sensible to ensure that remuneration is not excluded, at least for non-personal data, to leave the amount to the market and at the same time to provide a simple means of monitoring the use of data. This simple control option should not start with the assertion of legal powers, but should give the consumer himself the opportunity to technically control the use of data. A right to low-data collection products in combination with a legacy switch would make this possible.

(2017), Multimedia und Recht, p. 3 et seq.; *Wandtke*, Ökonomischer Wert von persönlichen Daten (2017), Multimedia und Recht, p. 6 et seq., also argue in favour of a remuneration option.

111 Under the concept of digital tax: Proposal for a Council Directive on a common system of digital tax on revenues from the provision of certain digital services, COM (2018) 148 final.

112 The necessity of a contractual regulation for the use of data is regulated by Art. 4(13) DA in conjunction with Recital 25 DA.

b) Collective Remuneration

Collective remuneration could be realised by setting up a "collecting society for data".[113] A collecting society under the principles of copyright law is authorised to administer the accounts of several rights holders in its own name or in the name of third parties for their collective benefit, cf. Section 2(1) VGG. However, collecting societies are always associated with high administrative and personnel costs. These costs are incurred on the one hand by the collecting society itself, but also by state supervision.[114] Structures and systems would have to be set up from scratch for a collecting society, every use of data would have to be registered and distributions organised. All in all, this effort seems difficult to realise and would also make data usability in the area of non-personal data considerably more difficult in organisational and administrative terms.

c) Data Tax

A draft directive from the European Commission was already being discussed in 2018 under the term "digital tax".[115] The necessity of the digital tax was justified by the fact that current corporate tax regulations were designed for traditional companies,[116] but that the physical presence of a company in a country was not a sufficient connecting factor for tax assessment.[117] In particular, a physical presence in a Member State is not necessary to provide digital services, Recital 2 COM (2018) 148 final.[118] Digital companies also differ structurally from traditional companies.[119] The Commission feared a fragmentation of the internal market and a distortion of competition in the event of Member State solutions.[120] The aim of the draft directive was therefore a tax that enables revenue from the provision

113 *Oehler*, Chancen der selbstbestimmten Datennutzung?! (2016), Wirtschaftsdienst, p. 830 (832).

114 Pursuant to Section 75(1) VGG, the German Patent and Trade Mark Office (DPMA) is responsible for the state supervision of collecting societies under the VGG.

115 The draft digital tax should be considered as part of a package that also includes rules on corporate taxation of a significant digital presence and proposals on double taxation agreements with third countries, see COM (2018) 147.

116 COM (2018) 148 final, p. 2.

117 COM (2018) 148 final, p. 2.

118 COM (2018) 148 final, p. 2.

119 COM (2018) 148 final, p. 2 et seq.

120 COM (2018) 148 final, p. 3.

of certain digital services, is easy to implement and contributes to a level playing field.[121]

aa) Legal Basis and Nature of the Digital Tax

The legal basis for the proposed directive should be Article 113 TFEU.[122] Art. 113 TFEU is limited to indirect taxes; Art. 115 TFEU or Art. 311 TFEU could be considered as the legal basis for direct taxes.[123] Both legal bases require unanimity in the Council.[124] In practical terms, it is therefore a marginal difference as to which legal basis is relevant.

However, whether the proposed digital tax was an indirect tax was disputed,[125] because it was more similar to an income tax, which is a direct tax.[126] In the case of direct taxes, the taxpayer and tax debtor are the same person. In the case of indirect taxes, however, the taxable person and the person liable to pay the tax are different persons.[127] They are levied on consumer goods, for example. This is, for example, value-added tax (VAT) which is also referred to in Art. 113 TFEU. Here, the consumer pays the tax indirectly because the trader adds it to the sales price.

bb) Content and Design of the Digital Tax

Under the draft digital tax, income generated from certain digital services should be taxed; this includes, according to Art. 3(1) COM (2018) 148 final:

---

121 COM (2018) 148 final, p. 4.

122 COM (2018) 148 final, p. 5.

123 *Waldhoff* in: *Calliess/Ruffert*, EUV/AEUV (6th edn., 2022), Art. 113 para. 4.

124 *Brauneck*, Digitalsteuer: Endlich angemessene Steuern für Google, Apple, Facebook und Co. in der EU? (2018), Europäische Zeitschrift für Wirtschaftsrecht, p. 624 (631).

125 In favour: The European Commission, COM (2018) 148 final; Against: *Brauneck*, Digitalsteuer: Endlich angemessene Steuern für Google, Apple, Facebook und Co. in der EU? (2018), Europäische Zeitschrift für Wirtschaftsrecht, p. 624 (628); also critical: *Kokott*, Herausforderungen einer Digitalsteuer (2019), Internationales Steuerrecht, p. 123 (124 et seq.).

126 *Brauneck*, Digitalsteuer: Endlich angemessene Steuern für Google, Apple, Facebook und Co. in der EU? (2018), Europäische Zeitschrift für Wirtschaftsrecht, p. 624 (627 et seq.).

127 *Aichberger* in: *Weber*, Rechtswörterbuch (31th edn., 2023), Direct Taxes.

- the placing on a digital interface of advertising targeted at users of that interface, lit. a;
- the provision of a multi-sided digital interface for users enables them to find and interact with other users and enables the delivery of underlying goods or services directly between users, lit. b;
- the transmission of data collected about users and generated from users' activities on digital interfaces, lit. c.

Digital services should also include communication services such as social media platforms, per Recitals 10 and 12 COM (2018) 148 final. For the transfer of collected user data under Art. 3(1)(c) COM (2018) 148 final, internet analysis tools that make collected user data available for a fee can be mentioned as an example. Digital interfaces are any type of software, including websites or parts thereof and applications, including mobile applications, accessible by users, Art. 2(3) COM (2018) 148 final. The place of taxation, Art. 5(1) COM (2018) 148 final, should depend on the Member State in which the users of the digital service are established during the tax period. The right to levy the digital service tax should arise proportionately in the Member State in which the corresponding income is generated, Art. 6 COM (2018) 148 final.

Although the Commission proposal was only intended to be an interim solution until a global solution was found at the OECD level, no agreement could be reached. Concerns were expressed about possible double taxation. In particular, those countries in which large digital groups have their European headquarters voted against the Commission's proposal.[128] However, Austria, the UK, France, Italy and Spain, among others, adopted national digital taxes. However, the taxation of digital services was suspended in an agreement between these countries and the USA. The suspension currently applies until 30 June 2024, hoping to reach a global solution within the OECD by this date.[129] Germany has not introduced a national digital tax for the time being, also in the hope of a global solution. This is in line with an agreement reached by OECD members on 1 July 2021[130] to initially refrain from any further national "solo efforts" regarding a digital tax and to

128 No digital tax in Europe for the time being, available at https://www.tagesschau.de/wirtschaft/digitalsteuer-107.html, last accessed on 28/03/2024.

129 Austria and other countries extend suspension of digital tax, available at https://www.derstandard.de/story/3000000207740/oesterreich-und-andere-laender-verlaengern-aussetzen-von-digitalsteuer, last accessed on 28/03/2024.

130 Statement on a Two-Pillar Solution to Address the Tax Challenges Arising from the Digitalisation of the Economy, available at https://www.oecd.org/tax/beps/statemen

suspend existing national digital taxes. At national level, a digital tax would, therefore, probably have no chance of success at present or would have to be suspended anyway if it were to be enacted.

V. Result

Three measures in particular should be prioritised from the many legislative options to better protect consumers when using IoT:

First, the Data Act, particularly Art. 4(13) DA, should be supplemented with consumer protection measures. In particular, the functionality of products should not be linked to the authorisation to collect and process data that is not necessary for their function. Second, the various possible forms of bricking should be examined and, depending on consumer detriment and lack of justification, included in the catalogue of Sections 308 and 309 BGB or, at the European level, in the Unfair Terms Directive. Third, a right to data-collection-free and data-collection-friendly products should be provided as part of the Consumer Agenda 2025. This right could also provide a starting point for market solutions to the remuneration that users could receive for providing their non-personal data.

t-on-a-two-pillar-solution-to-address-the-tax-challenges-arising-from-the-digitalisation-of-the-economy-july-2021.pdf, last accessed on 28/03/2024.

Model Contractual Terms for Mandatory Data Sharing: Challenges and Considerations

*Christiane Wendehorst**

Abstract:

The digital economy necessitates effective frameworks for data sharing, including in the context of mandatory data sharing. This paper delves into the development of model contractual terms (MCTs) for data sharing as mandated by the Data Act. It focuses on the role of the Commission Expert Group, explores diverse scenarios of data sharing, and addresses the complexities of statutory obligations while balancing regulatory requirements with contractual freedom. A special focus is put on the challenges that are posed by ambiguities in several core provisions of the Data Act.

I. Introduction

In the rapidly evolving digital economy, data has become a critical asset. Effective sharing of data, especially under mandatory conditions, requires a robust legal framework to ensure that the rights and obligations of all parties are clearly defined and protected. Article 41 of the Data Act[1] addresses this need by mandating the European Commission to develop and recommend non-binding model contractual terms (MCTs) and standard contractual clauses by 12 September 2025. As far as the MCTs are concerned, they are designed to facilitate data access and use, and they must include terms on reasonable compensation and the protection of trade secrets. A second task following from Article 41 of the Data Act – which will not be addressed in this paper – is the preparation of non-binding standard contractual clauses for cloud computing contracts to assist parties in draft-

---

* University of Vienna.

1 Regulation (EU) 2023/2854 of the European Parliament and of the Council of 13 December 2023 on harmonised rules on fair access to and use of data and amending Regulation (EU) 2017/2394 and Directive (EU) 2020/1828 (Data Act) [2023] OJ L 2023/2854.

ing and negotiating contracts with fair, reasonable and non-discriminatory contractual rights and obligations.

This paper explores the various challenges and considerations involved in developing the MCTs for data sharing and use. It examines the statutory framework set by the Data Act, the role of the Commission Expert Group (see infra point III.) in drafting the terms, and the practical implications for stakeholders involved in data sharing.

II. Data sharing scenarios covered by Article 41

The Commission's tasks with regard to MCTs on data access and use are demanding, as the array of potential data sharing scenarios for which we may need contractual terms is vast. From the point of view of the Data Act, this vast array of data sharing scenarios can broadly be categorised into three bigger clusters: data sharing that occurs under Chapter II (and Chapters III and IV) of the Data Act; data sharing that occurs under Chapter III (and Chapter IV) of the Data Act in conjunction with a data sharing obligation following from other law; and data sharing that is covered only by Chapter IV of the Data Act. In addition, there are also further data sharing scenarios, such as data sharing with public sector players under Chapter V. Careful consideration needs to be given to the question which of these scenarios are covered by the mandate in Article 41 of the Data Act and which are not.

1. Data sharing under Chapter II of the Data Act

Firstly, there are the situations where data sharing occurs on the basis of Chapter II of the Data Act, i.e. the scenario is one of a user of a connected product or related service within the meaning of the Data Act and corresponding data holders and third parties within the meaning of the same act.[2] To a certain extent, and at least for some parties and in some aspects, data

2 For a general overview and critical discussion see Dirk Staudenmayer, 'Der Verordnungsvorschlag der Europäischen Kommission zum Datengesetz' [2022] EuZW, 596; Dirk Staudenmayer, 'Privatrechtsregeln für Datenzugangsrechte' [2022] EuZW 1037; Andreas Wiebe, 'Der Data Act – Innovation oder Illusion?' [2023] GRUR 1569; Andreas Wiebe, 'Der Data Act als vertragsrechtlicher Rahmen für Datennutzungsverträge Anwendungsbereich und Vorgaben der Missbrauchskontrolle nach Art. 13 Data Act-E' [2023] CR 777; Moritz Hennemann and Björn Steinrötter, 'Data Act – Fundament des

sharing is 'mandatory' under Chapter II of the Data Act, which is why, in this paper, these data sharing scenarios are referred to as 'mandatory data sharing'. Another possible term would be 'highly regulated data sharing' because the pivotal point for drafting MCTs is not primarily that one of the parties in a legal relationship is under an obligation to share data, but rather that Chapter II of the Data Act includes a range of mandatory legal provisions with which parties falling under these provisions must comply. These provisions may require the sharing of data under certain conditions, but they may equally require that a party refrains from sharing or using data in a particular way, and they may regulate further aspects.

a) Data sharing under Article 3

According to Article 3, connected products and related services should be designed in such a manner that product data and related service data, including the relevant metadata necessary to interpret and use those data, are, by default, directly accessible to the user. Access should be easy, secure, free of charge, and in a comprehensive, structured, commonly used and machine-readable format. This means that, where technically feasible, connected products and related services should allow users to access product data and related services data by themselves, whenever they wish, and without any further interaction with the data holder.[3]

Article 3 of the Data Act does not require in any way that a contract is concluded between the manufacturer or service provider and the user.[4] However, Article 3 does provide for pre-contractual information duties. Before concluding a contract for the purchase, rent or lease of a connected

---

neuen EU-Datenwirtschaftsrechts?' [2022] NJW 1481; Moritz Hennemann and Björn Steinrötter, 'Der Data Act Neue Instrumente, alte Friktionen, strukturelle Weichenstellungen' [2024] NJW 1; Louisa Specht-Riemenschneider, 'Der Entwurf des Data Act' [2022] MMR 809; Louisa Specht-Riemenschneider, 'Data Act – Auf dem (Holz-)Weg zu mehr Dateninnovation?' [2022] ZRP 137; Philippe Heinzke and Björn Herbers and Michael Kraus, 'Datenzugangsansprüche nach dem Data Act' [2024] BB 649; cf. Josef Drexl and others, 'Position Statement of the Max Planck Institute for Innovation and Competition of 25 May 2022 on the Commission's Proposal of 23 February 2022 for a Regulation on harmonised rules on fair access to and use of data (Data Act)' [2022].

3 On the relevance of Article 3 see Hennemann, Steinrötter, 'Data Act' (n. 2) 1483; Hennemann and Steinrötter, 'Der Data Act' (n. 2) 3; Heinzke and Herbers and Kraus (n. 2) 651; Specht-Riemenschneider, 'Entwurf des Data Act' (n. 2) 815; Drexl and others (n. 2) 73.

4 Hennemann and Steinrötter, 'Data Act' (n. 2) 1483; Hennemann and Steinrötter, 'Der Data Act' (n. 2) 2; Heinzke and Herbers and Kraus (n. 2) 651.

product, the seller, renter or lessor – which may or may not be identical with the manufacturer – is under an obligation to provide certain data-related information to the user in a clear and comprehensible manner. Likewise, the provider of a related service is under an obligation to provide certain minimum information before concluding a contract for the provision of a related service.

Such information will normally become part of the notion of conformity according to Article 6 or Article 7(1) of the Sale of Goods Directive[5] or Article 7 or Article 8(1) of the Digital Content and Services Directive[6]. However, even if the information becomes part of the sales, lease, rental or services contract in one way or another under the applicable contract law, the relevant terms concern primarily a description of the features of the connected product or related service and not so much rights and obligations with regard to data access and use as such. This is all the more important to note as the seller, renter, lessor or service provider is not necessarily the data holder.[7] For example, if the information that certain data is generated by the product and can be accessed directly through the control application became part of the sales contract, and that information was false, this may trigger remedies for lack of conformity against the seller, but not necessarily a right for the buyer to access the data as originally stated. It would therefore not be required under Article 41 to draft model 'contractual terms' with regard to the product and service features addressed by Article 3.

However, there are convincing arguments that the restrictions imposed on the user by Article 4 should be applied by analogy also where the user retrieves data under Article 3,[8] which is why some aspects of retrieval under Article 3 should be included in the MCTs for the H2U agreement under Article 4 (on which see below). Also, the MCTs to be drafted under Article

5 Directive (EU) 2019/771 of the European Parliament and of the Council of 20 May 2019 on certain aspects concerning contracts for the sale of goods, amending Regulation (EU) 2017/2394 and Directive 2009/22/EC, and repealing Directive 1999/44/EC (Text with EEA relevance) [2019] OJ L 136/28.

6 Directive (EU) 2019/770 of the European Parliament and of the Council of 20 May 2019 on certain aspects concerning contracts for the supply of digital content and digital services (Text with EEA relevance) [2019] OJ L 136/1.

7 Specht-Riemenschneider, 'Entwurf des Data Act' (n. 2) 813; Hennemann and Steinrötter, 'Der Data Act' (n. 2) 2.

8 Martin Schmidt-Kessel, 'Heraus- und Weitergabe von IoT-Gerätedaten' [2024] MMR 75, 80; Yannic Duller, 'Data Access and Portability' (forthcoming) ch. 7.11 Overlaps undermining the DA's obligations [2024].

41 for the relationship between the data holder and the user may include a placeholder for the information to be provided under Article 3 for cases where the data holder happens to be identical with the seller, renter, lessor or service provider.

b) Bilateral constellations covered by Article 4

Article 4 addresses the bilateral relationship between the user of a connected product or related service and any data holder. In terms of data access and use, Article 4 covers two very distinct aspects.[9]

aa) Holder-to-user (H2U) data sharing

First, Article 4(1) provides for the user's right of access in cases where the user cannot directly access the data from the connected product or related service in accordance with Article 3. In such cases, the user has a right to request the data holder to make product data or related services data that are readily available to the data holder[10] accessible to the user, together with the relevant metadata necessary to interpret and use the data. This access must be provided without undue delay, in the same quality as the data are available to the data holder, easily, securely, free of charge, in a comprehensive, structured, commonly used and machine-readable format and, where technically feasible, continuously and in real-time.

For exercising this right, no contract is required between the data holder and the user,[11] as all that is necessary on the part of the user is a simple request, where feasible through electronic means. However, some of the provisions in Article 4(2) to (12), which refer to this right in one way or another, also refer to contractual agreements between the data holder and the user.

First of all, Article 4(2) clarifies that users and data holders may contractually restrict or prohibit accessing, using or further sharing data, if

9 See also Drexl and others (n. 2) 79.

10 The definition of ‚readily available data' according to Art 2 para 17 reads as 'product data and related service data that a data holder lawfully obtains or can lawfully obtain from the connected product or related service, without disproportionate effort going beyond a simple operation'.

11 Hennemann and Steinrötter, 'Der Data Act' (n. 2) 3.

such processing could undermine security requirements of the connected product, resulting in a serious adverse effect on the health, safety or security of natural persons. Article 4(3)(b) mentions the possibility of an agreement to refer such matters to a dispute settlement body. According to Article 4(6), which addresses trade secret protection, the data holder or, where they are not the same person, the trade secret holder will agree with the user proportionate technical and organisational measures necessary to preserve the confidentiality of the shared data.[12] In the absence of such agreement, the data holder may withhold the sharing of data identified as trade secrets. According to Article 4(9)(b), the user may agree also for this situation to refer the matter to a dispute settlement body.

But also where Article 4(2) to (12) do not explicitly refer to agreements, they contain various prohibitions or obligations for either the data holder or the user, and it could be advisable to include them in a contractual agreement to make sure there are also contractual remedies in the case of breach. In particular the protection of trade secrets is a question explicitly mentioned in the mandate of Article 41, which is why there are strong arguments that the MCTs should cover H2U data sharing under Article 4(1).

bb) H2U data use agreement

The second data sharing scenario addressed in Article 4 is the one dealt with under Article 4(13) and (14).[13] According to Article 4(13), the data holder 'shall only use any readily available data that is non-personal data on the basis of a contract with the user'. Furthermore, Article 4(14) stipulates that data holders 'shall not make available non-personal product data to third parties for commercial or non-commercial purposes other than the fulfilment of their contract with the user'. The provision goes on to stipulate that, even where product data is shared with third parties, data holders

12 On the protection of trade secrets in the context of Chapter II see Andreas Wiebe, 'Access rights at the Intersection with Database Rights and Trade Secret Protection' [2023] GRUR 227.

13 On these provisions see also Hennemann and Steinrötter, 'Data Act' (n. 2) 1483; Hennemann and Steinrötter, 'Der Data Act' (n. 2) 5; Specht-Riemenschneider, 'Entwurf des Data Act' (n. 2) 816; Heinzke, 'Data Act: Auf dem Weg zur europäischen Datenwirtschaft' [2023] BB 201; Duller (n. 8) ch. 7.5.6. Usage limitations of the data holder.

'shall contractually bind third parties not to further share data received from them'.

Whatever the relationship between Article 4(13) and (14) really is, and whichever 'contract' Article 4(14) may be referring to (for details, see below at IV. 2. c)), a contract between the data holder and the user is definitely required whenever the data holder wants to 'use' data. 'Use' arguably means processing the data for the data holder's own purposes beyond ensuring the functionality, security etc. of the connected product or related service and the fulfilment of statutory obligations. As this will very often be the case a contract between data holder and user will have to be concluded in the average case.[14] As fairness of this contract is of the essence for the functioning of the data economy, MCTs for the H2U data use agreement are certainly covered by the mandate in Article 41.

c) Trilateral constellations covered by Article 5

Last but not least, Chapter II of the Data Act also includes a data sharing scenario, which is a trilateral one, involving the data holder, the user and a third party data recipient.[15] According to Article 5(1), the data holder is under an obligation to make readily available product data and related services data, as well as the relevant metadata necessary to interpret and use those data, available to a third party upon request by the user or a party acting on the user's behalf. Data must, again, be made available without undue delay, of the same quality as is available to the data holder, easily, securely, free of charge to the user, in a comprehensive, structured, commonly used and machine-readable format and, where relevant and technically feasible, continuously and in real-time.

---

14 Heinzke and Herbers and Kraus (n. 2) 650; Hennemann and Steinrötter, 'Der Data Act' (n. 2) 7; Wiebe (n. 2) 1571; Duller (n. 8) ch. 7.5.6. Usage limitations of the data holder.

15 On this trilateral scenario see Heinzke and Herbers and Kraus (n. 2) 654; Hennemann and Steinrötter, 'Der Data Act' (n. 2) 3; Specht-Riemenschneider, 'Entwurf des Data Act' (n. 2) 816; Duller (n. 8) ch. 7.6. Right to share data with third parties.

aa) H2R data sharing agreement

Article 5 itself does not mention any contract to be concluded between any of the parties involved. However, similar indirect references to a contract can be found as in Article 4(2) to (12). In particular, Article 5(9) provides that the data holder or, where they are not the same person, the trade secret holder shall agree with the third party all proportionate technical and organisational measures necessary to preserve the confidentiality of the shared data, which is a question explicitly mentioned in the mandate of Article 41. More importantly, Article 5(1) mentions that the data shall be made available by the data holder to the third party in accordance with Articles 8 and 9. Article 8(1) in turn provides that where a data holder is obliged to make data available to a data recipient under Article 5 (or under other law) the data holder has to agree with the data recipient on the arrangements for making the data available.[16] Terms and conditions of this agreement must be fair, reasonable and non-discriminatory[17] as well as transparent, in accordance with Chapter III and Chapter IV of the Data Act. Article 9 deals with the compensation for making the data available, which is likewise a question explicitly mentioned in the mandate of Article 41.

Therefore, the H2R data sharing agreement seems to be at the very centre of the mandate given to the Commission under Article 41. As far as the user's right to request sharing with the third party is concerned, no separate contract is required, but the aspect could and should be integrated in any MCTs for a H2U data sharing scheme (see supra point b) aa)).

bb) U2R agreement

What is less clear is whether there also needs to be a contractual agreement between the user and the third party recipient, and if so whether it could be covered by the mandate in Article 41.

16 On the question whether an agreement on a reasonable renumeration between the data holder and the data recipient is needed before making the data available under Article 5 see Duller (n. 8) ch. 7.6.2.2 Transfer without contract.

17 So called FRAND-principles. See also Hennemann and Steinrötter, 'Der Data Act' (n. 2) 4; Sebastian Louven, 'Vorschriften im Data Act zur Ausgestaltung und Kompensation von Datenbereitstellungspflichten' [2024] MMR 82; Wiebe (n. 2) 1572; Heinzke (n. 7) 207; Duller (n. 8) ch. 7.6. Right to share data with third parties.

Article 5(9) mentions that trade secrets shall be preserved and shall be disclosed to third parties only to the extent that such disclosure is 'strictly necessary to fulfil the purpose agreed between the user and the third party', i.e. Article 5(9) refers at least to a purpose agreed in the U2R relationship. In a similar vein, Article 6(1) provides that the third party recipient shall process the data it receives 'only for the purposes and under the conditions agreed with the user'. It also provides that this party shall 'erase the data when they are no longer necessary for the agreed purpose, unless otherwise agreed with the user in relation to non-personal data'. Article 6 (1)(b) provides that profiling of natural persons is not permitted unless it is necessary to provide 'the service requested by the user'. Finally, Article 6(1)(c) states that the data recipient may not make the data it receives available to another third party, unless the data is made available 'on the basis of a contract with the user' and provided that all necessary measures to preserve the confidentiality of trade secrets are taken.

All these references seem to suggest the existence of an agreement between user and data recipient, but it is only Article 6(1)(b) that explicitly refers to a 'contract', doing so in a specific context. Arguably, the Data Act does not require the conclusion of such a contract, but rests on the assumption that such a contract will normally exist. [18] As the contract would in any case be one about data access and use, at least Chapter IV of the Data Act applies, and the U2R relationship is, in principle, covered by the mandate in Article 41.

2. Data sharing under other law covered by Chapter III of the Data Act

a) Data sharing obligations following from other law

Next come situations where a data holder is obliged to share data with another party under other Union law or Member State law adopted in accordance with Union law, 'other' meaning other than Chapter II of the Data Act. While not falling under Chapter II, these situations are still governed by Chapter III (and Chapter IV) of the Data Act and data sharing has to comply with the provisions of Chapter III.[19] There is a growing body of

18 Axel Metzger and Heike Schweitzer, 'Shaping Markets: A Critical Evaluation of the Draft Data Act' [2023] ZEuP 42, 48.

19 Article 8(1) Data Act.

law giving rise to such data sharing obligations, which may come under different headings, such as 'data access', 'data portability', and others.[20] They have in common that one party is under an obligation to make accessible information that is recorded in a way suitable for automated processing and controlled or controllable by the relevant party to others in a way that allows automated processing of the same information by those others.[21]

b) How to differentiate from information duties

It is not at all straightforward to draw a clear line between data sharing obligations and very traditional information duties or transparency duties, which we have seen in consumer protection law and may other areas of the law for a long time and which may equally require that information be shared in a particular (including machine-readable) way.[22] Such information duties are also included, for example, in Article 3(2) and (3) of the Data Act.

Arguably, the difference between data sharing on the one hand and providing information or ensuring transparency on the other is one of primary aim and focus. Information and transparency duties primarily aim at making other persons (including through any electronic agents these parties may be using) aware of certain facts, and where there is a requirement that information is provided in some kind of machine-readable format suited for automated processing this is to ensure that awareness is in fact created.[23] In other words, the requirement of providing information in a particular recorded format is subordinate to the aim of creating awareness (including for future reference etc.). However, in the case of data sharing obligations it is the other way round: Enabling the recipient to engage in automated processing of the information is at the core of the obligation, i.e.

20 See for example Duller (n. 8) ch. 1 Introduction.

21 See for example Article 6 DMA or sector specific regulation such as (among others) the Payment Service Directive II or the Type Approval Regulation. For a detailed reference see Duller (n. 8) ch. 9 sector-specific data rights.

22 Duller (n. 8) ch. 10 A Taxonomy of European Data Rights.

23 Sometimes, this is referred to as the 'pragmatic' dimension of data, cf. Ulrich Sieber, 'Informationsrecht und Recht der Informationstechnik' – Die Konstituierung eines Rechtsgebietes in Gegenstand, Grundfragen und Zielen' [1989] NJW 2569, 2572; Duller (n. 8) 2.2.4.3 Pragmatic layer.

the information is a resource, asset or commodity[24] that can be compared to raw materials, and whether or not that information will ever create awareness of certain facts is, at best, a secondary concern.

3. Data sharing covered only by Chapter IV of the Data Act

Thirdly, there is the panoply of situations where parties voluntarily agree to share certain data with others. Data sharing may be the main subject matter of a transaction (such as where data is supplied to others against payment)[25] or a side aspect of another transaction (such as where the contract is one about maintenance of production lines and, amongst others, an agreement is made about use of the maintenance data).

One may call this cluster of scenarios 'voluntary data sharing', indicating that the basis or triggering factor is not a statutory obligation of some kind but a contractual arrangement between the parties in the first place. Naturally, this does not exclude that one party was in a weaker bargaining position and that, therefore, the arrangement was somewhat less 'voluntary' for that party than for the other party. This is why Chapter IV of the Data Act also includes provisions that would cover any kind of agreement about data access and use and why, in particular, Article 13 of the Data Act has introduced an unfairness test for contractual clauses on data access and use that applies (also) in B2B transactions.[26] However, from a more formal point of view, this is still private ordering and therefore can be considered to be 'voluntary' data sharing.

It is often not easy, in the context of this third cluster of data sharing scenarios, to differentiate between the access and use of data that is covered by the Data Act and other transactions primarily covered by other pieces

24 ALI/ELI, *Principles for a Data Economy, Data Transactions and Data Rights* (ALI/ELI 2023) Principle 2.

25 Really, the situation is much more complex, and transactions for the supply of data fall into several broader categories, e.g. contracts for the transfer of data, contracts for simple access to data, contracts for exploitation of a data source, contracts for authorization to access or contracts for data pooling. For more detail see ALI/ELI (n. 24) Principle 7.

26 For details see Sebastian Schwamberger, 'Art 13' in Bomhard and others (eds), *EU Data Act* (forthcoming); Sebastian Schwamberger, 'Die Klauselkontrolle in Art. 13 Data Act' [2024] MMR 96; Friedrich Graf v. Westphalen, 'Der neue Data Act – Eine Kaskade AGB-rechtlicher Verbote im unternehmerischen Verkehr' [2024] BB 515; Heinzke (n. 2) 207.

of legislation. Article 2(1) Data Act defines 'data' as 'any digital representation of acts, facts or information and any compilation of such acts, facts or information, including in the form of sound, visual or audio-visual recording'. This definition is in line with the respective definitions in the Data Governance Act[27] and the Digital Markets Act[28]. However, no efforts are made to provide further explanations in the Recitals that would allow to draw a line between data within the meaning of these provisions and other digital phenomena.[29] It seems highly improbable, for example, that Chapter IV of the Data Act covers transactions such as about the supply of software or cryptoassets, or maybe even a contract which a consumer makes with a movie theatre about watching a film, even though the reference to 'sound, visual or audio-visual recording' could be read as suggesting the opposite. Arguably, Chapter IV of the Data Act only covers transactions about the sharing of data where the information aspect occupies centre stage, and not what the ALI-ELI Principles[30] have come to call 'functional data' (including, inter alia, most digital content and digital services within the meaning of the Digital Content and Services Directive[31]), nor what has been called 'representative data' (including any cryptoassets or entries in public records).[32]

4. B2G data sharing under Chapter V of the Data Act

Also Chapter V of the Data Act is about data sharing, but about data sharing of a very different kind, namely making data available to public sector bodies, the Commission, the European Central Bank and Union bodies on the basis of an exceptional need (business-to-government data sharing, B2G). While data sharing under Chapters II to IV occurs on the basis of contracts, this is different with B2G data sharing, which is based on

27 Article 2(1) Regulation (EU) 2022/868 of the European Parliament and of the Council of 30 May 2022 on European data governance and amending Regulation (EU) 2018/1724 (Data Governance Act) OJ L 2022/152, 1.

28 Article 2(24) Regulation (EU) 2022/1925 of the European Parliament and of the Council of 14 September 2022 on contestable and fair markets in the digital sector and amending Directives (EU) 2019/1937 and (EU) 2020/1828 (Digital Markets Act), OJ L 2022/265, 1.

29 Duller (n. 8) ch. 2.1. What is Data?.

30 ALI/ELI (n. 24).

31 ALI/ELI (n. 24) Principle 2.

32 ALI/ELI (n. 24) Principle 2.

the public sector body's request. Although the term 'request' is used also in Article 4(1), it is clear from the context, and in particular from Article 17, that the idea is not to share the data under a contract. The Commission will develop a model template for the request in accordance with Article 17(6), but this model template is not part of the mandate in Article 41. This is why B2G data sharing under Chapter V is also not included in the mandate of the Expert Group. Needless to say, where a public sector body procures data on the market (which it is obliged to try to do before resorting to a request under Chapter V), this is a normal case of voluntary data sharing covered by Chapter IV.

III. The Commission Expert Group

1. Establishment and composition

The European Commission has established an Expert Group to address the tasks outlined in Article 41 of the Data Act.[33] It includes legal experts, industry representatives, and policymakers who bring a wide range of expertise and perspectives to the table. The primary mission of the Expert Group is to develop draft MCTs and SCCs as foreseen by Article 41 that reflect fair, reasonable, and non-discriminatory rights and obligations.[34] This mission is multifaceted, as the Group aims to provide guidance to parties on how to negotiate and draft contracts in various data sharing scenarios and to ensure that the MCTs comply with the Data Act while allowing for some degree of contractual freedom to accommodate different business needs and contexts. A sub-group[35] consisting purely of industry representatives and other stakeholders and acting as a kind of sounding board assists the Group, testing and commenting on the practical utility of the MCTs and SCCs and making sure they respond to the stakeholders'

33 Commission, 'Expert Group on B2B data sharing and cloud computing contracts (E03840)' (23 February 2022) <https://ec.europa.eu/transparency/expert-groups-register/screen/expert-groups/consult?lang=en&groupID=3840> accessed 10 June 2024.

34 Commission, 'Informal Commission expert group on B2B data sharing and cloud computing contracts: Terms of reference' (2022) ch. 3.

35 Commission, 'Expert Group on B2B data sharing and cloud computing contracts / Sub-group – stakeholders (E03840/1)' (01 August 2022) < https://ec.europa.eu/transparency/expert-groups-register/screen/expert-groups/consult?lang=en&fromMainGroup=true&groupID=103092> accessed 10 June 2024.

needs. The Expert Group's work is crucial in navigating the complex legal and practical challenges of data sharing in the digital economy.

2. Tasks of the Expert Group with regard to the MCTs

The task described in Article 41 of the Data Act is a task for the Commission itself, which needs to be fulfilled before 12 September 2025. As the MCTs are to be non-binding, the only possible form is a Commission Recommendation within the meaning of Article 292 TFEU. The Expert Group's tasks with regard to the MCTs on data access and use are closely connected with the Commission's own task.

a) Terms of reference for the Expert Group

According to the terms of reference (ToR),[36] the Expert Group is to assist the Commission by analysing existing B2B data sharing models and practices, identifying problems and commonalities and recommending to the Commission a general horizontal set of balanced MCTs for B2B data sharing that could be applicable for sharing data across sectors. In addition, the task is to analyse data sharing practices in some sectors where there is a need for MCTs and recommend to the Commission MCTs tailored for these sectors. Existing market practice for data sharing should be used as a starting point for the discussion, also taking into account the work of the Support Centre for Data Sharing,[37] as well as the provisions of the Data Act and other Union legislation itself. MCTs for B2B data sharing involving the providers of core platform services designated as gatekeepers shall be outside the scope of the expert group, to the extent they are already covered by the Digital Markets Act[38].

Where the Commission so requests, the experts would also provide guidance to the Commission on other subjects related to fair contractual relations in B2B data sharing as follow-up to the Data Act. Following its

36 Commission, 'Informal Commission expert group on B2B data sharing and cloud computing contracts: Terms of reference' (2022).

37 For more information see https://www.eudatasharing.eu (link not accessible when manuscript submitted).

38 Schwamberger, 'Art. 13' (n. 26) ch. D.II.b Datenzugangsregelungen im europäischen Recht.

work, the expert group may be asked to assist the Commission with expert advice in the possible implementation of its recommendations.

b) Timeline and resources

Originally, the Expert Group's recommendations to the Commission for general and possibly also sectoral MCTs for B2B data sharing were to be finalised at the latest one year after its first meeting, which took place on 22 September 2022. However, it soon became clear that the task of creating the MCTs was huge, in particular as half of the Expert Group members were absorbed with the other task of drafting Standard Contractual Clauses (SCCs) for cloud computing contracts. Also, due to limited personnel capacities, there was little administrative support and no resources for something like a research assistant for Expert Group members. Needless to say, there is also no attribution of drafts to those who volunteer to shoulder major parts of the work, which is why academic members cannot do this in their regular working time and with their university staff (quite apart from the fact that the idea was to make this truly collective work and full drafts by individual members were not necessarily welcomed). Asking a group of busy high-level professionals and academics to produce jointly, for free and on top of their day jobs, what an international law or consultancy firm would possibly produce against a high six-digit amount and what the Support Centre for Data Sharing had not been able to achieve at all, was ambitious. For all these reasons, and also because of different priorities set within the Commission, the timeline was adjusted, and MCTs are not to be expected before autumn 2024.

c) Prioritisation of data access and use scenarios

As has been demonstrated under point II., the array of potential data sharing scenarios for which we may need MCTs is vast. The ToR, according to which the focus of the Expert Group would have been on a general horizontal set of MCTs for B2B data sharing that could be applicable for sharing data across sectors – plus potentially special sets of MCTs for specific sectors – sounded like there was a priority on MCTs for voluntary data sharing, i.e. cases of data sharing only covered by Chapter IV of the Data Act. This impression was confirmed by the idea that industry practices should be the general starting point. Accordingly, the Expert Group started working on MCTs for voluntary data sharing during the first months of its existence.

However, it soon became clear that priorities had to be adjusted, both in view of limited resources and the fact that the final version of Chapters II and III of the Data Protection Act, published in the Official Journal on 22 December, left a high degree of uncertainty as to the meaning of some of its core provisions. MCTs on mandatory data sharing were therefore urgently needed to alleviate some of the problems faced by stakeholders – even if a Commission Recommendation cannot amend an EU Regulation, stakeholders relying on the Commission Recommendation would be on much safer ground than stakeholders trying to figure things out on their own.

Among the possible sets of MCTs for mandatory data sharing, the one on the H2R data sharing agreement stood out in terms of urgency, which is why it was addressed in the first place. In the second place, MCTs for the relationship between data holder and user were tackled, aspiring to combine, in particular, aspects of H2U data sharing (see supra point II. 1. b) aa)) and the H2U data use agreement (see supra point II. 1. b) bb)). Whether any additional sets of MCTs will finally be submitted, and if so, which they could be, is currently not entirely clear.

IV. Challenges in Drafting MCTs for Mandatory Data Sharing under the Data Act

1. General challenges

a) How to balance accuracy, simplicity, and the need for explanation

Data law has become very complicated, and it is the European legislator, not the Expert Group, who has created the complexities. While the European legislator can restrict itself to placing one piece of legislation next to the other, stating that each of them should be 'without prejudice to' the other or choosing a similar formulation,[39] parties who have to comply with each of the pieces of legislation need to integrate all of it in their busi-

39 Björn Steinrötter, 'Verhältnis von Data Act und DS-GVO' [2023] GRUR 217 f.; Wiebe (n. 2) 1577 f.; Martin Schmidt-Kessel, 'Einordnung des Data Act in das Mehrebenensystem des Unionsprivatrechts' [2024] MMR 122, 122; Christian Czychowski, 'Shaping the Data Economy: Ausgestaltung von Datenüberlassungsverträgen aus

ness practices and contract terms. In the light of drastic sanctions which non-compliance with any of the more recent Union legal regimes may, potentially, trigger[40] parties cannot content themselves with complying 'by and large', but have to strive for full compliance across the board.

Requests from the political side, as well as from some stakeholders, many of whom are not very familiar with the intricacies of European data law themselves, have repeatedly urged the Expert Group to produce something short and simple, and criticised some preliminary drafts as being much too long and complicated. However, the MCTs, which come with the 'trust-mark' of the European Commission on them, have to strive for one hundred percent compliance – anything else would mean falling short of expectations which stakeholders rightly have, and they would create liability risks instead of added value. This comes at a cost in terms of length and degree of complexity of any set of MCTs.

What is definitely true is that MSMEs and other parties who cannot afford very sophisticated lawyers, or should not have to afford them in any case, will mostly be the ones to use the MCTs. This means that the MCTs face the challenge of balancing the need for practical, easily digestible guidance with the rigidity of blackletter provisions. Stakeholders require clear and actionable explanations to navigate the complexities of data sharing agreements. The Expert Group must find ways to combine practical advice with legal requirements, ensuring that stakeholders can implement the MCTs effectively. One way of doing this is adding explanations in boxes under many MCTs, putting MCTs into context in a clear and easily comprehensible manner. Another way of doing this is creating multiple types of output, including accompanying guidance documents.

b) How to deal with the diversity of real world cases

Data sharing scenarios are often complex and diverse, involving multiple stakeholders with different roles and responsibilities. For instance, in the automotive industry, the roles of vehicle manufacturers, component manu-

---

Herstellerperspektive Welche Gestaltungspielräume lässt der Data Act?' [2024] CR 80, 82; Hennemann and Steinrötter 'Data Act' (n. 2) 6 f.

40 For the Data Act Art. 40 refers to Art. 83 GDPR. For the General Data Protection Regulation Art. 83 sets the sanctions up to a maximum of 4 % of the yearly turnover; Heinzke, (n. 13) 208; Steinrötter (n. 39) 223; David Bomhard, 'Der Anwendungsbereich des Data Act: Offene Fragen rund um Art. 1 DA' [2024] NJW 71, 74 f.

facturers, fleet operators, lessors, renters and users can overlap, with multiple data holders and multiple users, and parties that are both, creating ambiguity in data sharing agreements.[41] Other sectors, for example the energy market, have very different specificities and requirements.[42] Yet, the provisions of the Data Act are of a horizontal nature and have to be applied in a cross-sectoral manner.

These complexities require the Expert Group to develop MCTs that are general and flexible enough to accommodate different scenarios while providing clear and enforceable terms. One way of doing this is providing options for parties from which they can pick and choose, and/or boxes to be ticked or not, and/or blank spaces for filling in specific content in the individual case.

In some cases, this will be close to impossible. For example, the U2R agreement, if there is a contract at all (on which see supra point II. 1. c) bb)), may be almost any kind of legal relationship. There are at least four standard scenarios: a contract for the development and/or provision of services that require product or related services data;[43] a contract for the 'sale' of product or related services data by the user to third parties against remuneration; the provision by the user of product data or related services data as non-monetary counter-performance[44] for another service; and the

41 Wolfgang Kerber and Jonas Severin Frank, 'Data Governance Regimes in the Digital Economy: The Example of Connected Cars' (2017) Working Paper, 20 <https://ssrn.com/abstract=3064794> accessed 16 July 2024; Josef Drexl, 'Data access and control in the era of connected devices' (BEUC 2018), 160; Andreas Wiebe, 'Protection of industrial data – a new property right for the digital economy?' [2016] GRUR-Int. 877, 878.

42 Thomas Tombal, *Imposing data sharing among private actors* (Wolters Kluwer 2022) 161 ff; Heike Schweitzer and Robert Welker, 'A Legal Framework for Access to Data – A Competition Policy Perspective' in Bundesministerium der Justiz und für Verbraucherschutz and Max-Planck-Institut für Innovation und Wettbewerb (eds.), Data Access, Consumer Interests and Public Welfare (Nomos 2021) 120 ff.

43 This seems to be the paradigm case primarily envisaged by the European legislator, see task 1 of the terms of reference for the Expert Group on B2B data sharing and cloud computing contracts (E03840) (no. 40).

44 See rec. 24, Art. 3 (1) Digital Content Directive; see further Sebastian Lohsse and Reiner Schulze and Dirk Staudenmayer, 'Data as Counter-Performance – Contract Law 2.0? An Introduction' in Sebastian Lohsse and Reiner Schulze and Dirk Staudenmayer (eds), *Data as Counter-Performance – Contract Law 2.0?: Münster Colloquia on EU Law and the Digital Economy V* (Nomos 2020); Sebastian Lohsse and Reiner Schulze and Dirk Staudenmayer, "Smart Products' – A Focal Point for Legal Developments in the Digital Economy' in Sebastian Lohsse and Reiner Schulze and Dirk Staudenmayer (eds.), *Smart Products: Münster Colloquia on EU Law and the*

'donation' of data for what is, at least from the perspective of the user, an altruistic purpose[45]. Each of these four standard scenarios presents unique challenges that must be addressed in the MCTs. For example, in the case of data donations, the MCTs must ensure that the data is used ethically and in accordance with the donor's intentions. In the case of data sales, the MCTs must specify the terms of remuneration and data use, ensuring that the seller's interests are protected. If one wishes to have full sets of MCTs that can be used by parties 'as is', there would thus have to be at least four very different sets. Alternatively, the MCTs could restrict themselves to very few 'crunch points', possibly mostly replicating the restrictions following from Article 6 of the Data Act.

A special challenge is the need to provide MCTs that can possibly work for bespoke high-value transactions between businesses as well as for standardised mass transactions with consumers, and for everything in between, including for transactions concluded by way of machine-to-machine contracting.[46] In particular the H2U agreement will, in practice, usually be 'delivered' together with the connected product, with the user agreeing to the terms when switching it on for the first time or when configuring it (such as by pressing a button 'OK' on a display). This raises difficult contractual issues[47] and data protection issues,[48] but this paper, which concentrates on the MCTs, is not the right place to discuss them.[49] In any case, while the

Digital Economy VI (Nomos 2022); Philipp Hacker 'Daten als Gegenleistung: Rechtsgeschäfte im Spannungsfeld von DS-GVO und allgemeinem Vertragsrecht' [2019] ZfPW 148, 153.

45 Data altruism is now defined in Art. 2 (16) DGA.

46 Christiane Wendehorst, 'Principles for AI in contracting' [2024] EuCML 43; Christiane Wendehorst, '§ 312' in Franz Jürgen Säcker and others (eds.) *MüKoBGB* (CH Beck 2022) para 171 ff.

47 See Martin Schmidt-Kessel, 'Heraus- und Weitergabe von IoT-Gerätedaten' [2024] MMR 75; Hennemann/Steinrötter, 'Data Act' (n. 2); Hennemann and Steinrötter, 'Der Data Act' (n. 2) 6; Specht-Riemenschneider (n. 2) 813.

48 See Specht-Riemenschneider, 'Datennutz und Datenschutz: Zum Verhältnis zwischen Datenwirtschaftsrecht und DSGVO' [2023] ZEuP 638; Specht-Riemenschneider (n. 2) 816; Hennemann and Steinrötter, 'Der Data Act' (n. 2) 5; Steinrötter, 'Verhältnis von Data Act' (n. 39) 216.

49 Among other things, the question arises as to whether the terms of the data use agreement would have to be made available to the user before the user agrees to buy, lease or rent the connected product, otherwise consent to the data use agreement would not be freely given. It might, however, be sufficient for the terms of the agreement to be within the range of what the user could reasonably expect, or for the seller, renter or lessor to provide the user with a right to withdraw from the sale, lease or rental agreement if the user prefers not to accept the data use agreement.

MCTs are being developed as a first step to look like a very traditional contract, with blanks for the names and contact details of the parties and a signature line, it must be borne in mind that their actual use in practice may be very different. It is not easy for the Expert Group to manage this tension.

c) What to do about issues of general contract law

Another question that arises is whether the Expert Group should prepare full sets of MCTs, which parties could, with very few adaptations, use for their transactions 'as is', or whether the MCTs should restrict themselves to the points addressed by the Data Act and leave the rest to the negotiations and applicable law. Needless to say, those parties that would profit most from the MCTs, i.e. MSMEs that cannot afford sophisticated lawyers, would want to have full sets of contract clauses, because what is the benefit if they can use the MCTs for some core data-related points but still have to hire a lawyer for turning them into a full contract. However, the challenge with preparing full sets of MCTs is that they necessarily address issues of general contract law, and general contract law differs from jurisdiction to jurisdiction. So the MCTs could opt for some 'neutral' regime inspired by international or European uniform law (such as the CISG[50]), including soft law (such as the PECL[51] or DCFR[52]). Alternatively, they could restrict themselves to including a choice-of-law clause and addressing some few issues of general contract law that are likely to be solved in the same or almost the same manner all across Europe.

d) What to do about ambiguities in the Data Act?

While the challenges described so far are challenges that the Expert Group has accepted and will somehow be able to manage, the most difficult challenge is posed by the many ambiguities and instances of flawed drafting of the Data Act. Both the haste and the lack of engagement on the part of

50 United Nations Convention on Contracts for the International Sale of Goods (Vienna, 11 April 1980) 1489 UNTS 3 entered into force 1 January 1988.

51 Commission on European Contract Law, *Principles of European Contract Law (PECL)* (1982–2002) (Lando Principles).

52 Study Group on a European Civil Code and Research Group on EC Private Law (Acquis Group), *Principles, Definitions and Model Rules of European Private Law Draft Common Frame of Reference (DCFR)* (sellier european law publishers 2009).

the Member States[53] with which this central piece of legislation has been pushed through is remarkable. Repeatedly, the Expert Group has been confronted with questions of interpretation that it has been unable to resolve.

Voluntary data sharing involves agreements where parties freely negotiate terms. These scenarios allow for greater flexibility and creativity in drafting contracts but also require clear guidelines to ensure fairness and protect sensitive information. In voluntary data sharing, parties have the autonomy to define the terms of their agreement. While it is crucial to ensure that these terms comply with the law, the focus lies on ensuring that they are fair and protect the interests of all parties involved. Mandatory data sharing, on the other hand, is governed by statutory obligations to a much greater extent, and absolute precision of their implementation is paramount.

Only the Court of Justice has the authority to make a decision one way or the other,[54] but it may be many years, possibly a decade or more, before we know. In the meantime, the Expert Group can try to make informed guesses, and ultimately the Commission will have to provide in its recommendation based on Article 41 a somewhat semi-authoritative version that the Commission believes might best reflect the will of the European legislator and be compatible best with practical needs.

2. Ambiguities in the Data Act: Three Illustrations

This paper will give three illustrations for the ambiguities just mentioned: The first is the question whether data access for the user under Article 4(1) can be provided, at the choice of the data holder, on the computing infrastructure of the data holder instead of transferring the data to the infrastructure indicated by the user. The second addresses the question whether the user can waive its 'right' to pass data retrieved under Article 4(1) on to third parties, and the third illustration is the relationship between paragraphs (13) and (14) of Article 4.

53 It is paradigmatic that, for example, Austria did not even bother to give a mandate to negotiate to its delegation.

54 Article 267 AEUV.

a) Is restriction to in situ-access possible?

According to Article 11(1) of the Data Act, a data holder may apply appropriate technical protection measures to prevent unauthorised access to data, including metadata, and to 'ensure compliance with Articles 4, 5, 6, 8 and 9, as well as with the agreed contractual terms for making data available'. As examples of technical protection measures, only 'smart contracts and encryption' are mentioned explicitly. However, it is not entirely clear how smart contracts and encryption could really ensure that, for example, the third party recipient does not use the data for any other purposes than agreed with the user – a purpose, which the data holder is not supposed even to know[55]. Likewise, it is not clear how they could help against the recipient passing the data on to other parties in an unauthorised manner. However, what would be an effective measure, in particular when combined with smart contracts, encryption and other techniques, would be access to the data only on an ICT environment of the data holder – this is what the ALI-ELI Principles call 'simple access' to data.[56] Simple access, which can be combined with the involvement of trusted third parties ('data trust' and/or 'data escrow' services within the terminology of the ALI-ELI Principles[57]), is to be contrasted with 'transfer' of data.[58] The latter would entail putting the user or recipient in full control of the data and enabling the user or recipient to pass the data on, whether or not this is allowed under the contract.

Chapter II remains surprisingly silent as to the exact access modalities. In the English language version, which was the version in which most of the negotiations took place, Articles 3(1) and 4(1) use the term '(make) accessible', whereas Article 5(1) uses the term '(make) available'. The difference is still more obvious in the French language version, where Articles 3(1) and 4(1) use the term '(être/rendre) accessible', whereas Article 5(1) uses the term 'mettre à la disposition'. The German language version, on the other hand, uses the term 'zugänglich' under Article 3(1), and '(stellt) bereit' in both Articles 4(1) and 5(1). Given that, during the negotiations, much more attention was paid to the English version (and possibly the French and further versions), whereas one out of two German speaking countries

55 Art. 5 (4) Data Act. See also Hans Steege, 'Technische Schutzmaßnahmen des Dateninhabers im Data Act' [2024] MMR 91, 94.
56 ALI/ELI (n. 24) Principle 8.
57 ALI/ELI (n. 24) Principle 13, 14.
58 ALI/ELI (n. 24) Principle 7.

did not even participate in the negotiations, it is fair to assume that the English (and French) language versions are much closer to the actual will of the European legislator. This indicates that the meaning in Articles 3(1) and Article 4(1) is the same, whereas the meaning in Article 5(1) is slightly different. Actually, this would also make sense, as data access for the user under Article 3 and Article 4 are to a certain extent interchangeable, with priority given to Article 3, but accepting that the Article 4 mechanism will be preferred by the parties in a range of cases, such as when trade secrets are at stake. Given that the data holder will often not even know the identity of the user (e.g. in a mass transaction), whereas the data holder can make a bespoke contract with a data recipient in the case of an Article 5(1) request, it also makes sense that the Article 5 mechanism allows for different access modalities.

With regard to access under Article 3, Recital 22 states that 'Connected products may be designed to permit the user or a third party to process the data on the connected product, on a computing instance of the manufacturer or within an information and communications technology (ICT) environment chosen by the user or the third party.' If the assumption that the access modalities in Article 3(1) and Article 4(1) are by and large the same (with the obvious difference that, in the first case, the user can retrieve the data without any further interaction with the data holder), this would hold true also for Article 4(1), i.e. the data holder could prefer to give the user access only on a computing instance of the manufacturer. Needless to say, as maintaining such a computing instance, combined with the necessary guarantees and safeguards that the conditions under the Data Act are fulfilled, is expensive, data holders will often choose to simply transfer the data. Conversely, also data access under Article 5 may be more restricted where the data holder and data recipient agree on special technical protection measures to preserve trade secrets.

This interpretation, which was derived from the wording and the context of the provisions, is supported also by considerations on purpose. For if data holders were not allowed to differentiate between data access under Articles 3(1) and 4(1) on the one hand and Article 5(1) on the other it is entirely unclear why users and third party data recipients would choose to go via the Article 5 mechanism. The Article 5 mechanism implies an obligation to pay compensation as well as certain restrictions under Article 6, whereas no compensation is due (at least not for the user) and Article 6 does not apply where data is retrieved under Article 4 and then passed on by the user to the data recipient. The latter does not even require specific infrastructure and skills on the part of the user as the user could request the data to be transferred to a space provided by and accessible to the data recipient. Therefore, if it were not possible that the data holder allows data access under Article 4(1) only on its own computing facilities, hardly anyone would choose the Article 5 mechanism any more, undermining the whole regulatory scheme of Articles 5 to 12. Also, if parties would always take the Article 4 mechanism in lieu of the Article 5 mechanism, manufacturers and service providers must price in from the outset that users will make maximum use of their right under Article 4 and pass on the data to third parties to the maximum extent.

However, while this is the view adopted in this paper, it seems that the majority of authors argues in a different direction, insisting that full data transfer is already owed under Article 4(1).[59] For the work of the Expert Group, this poses a problem, for the type of contractual clauses required under a contract for simple access to data are very different from the clauses required under a contract to transfer data.[60]

b) Can the user waive the right to pass data on?

A related question, which also concerns the relationship between Article 4 and Article 5 and the question of whether Articles 5 to 12 will be undermined in practice by users and data recipients choosing 'retrieve-and-pass-on' via Article 4, is the question of whether the user can contractually waive its right to pass data it has retrieved on to third parties.

The Recitals stress, in several places, that the user has a right to pass data on. For example, Recital 26 states that 'Users should therefore have the right to share non-personal data with data recipients for commercial and non-commercial purposes. Such data sharing could be performed directly by the user, upon the request of the user via a data holder, or through data intermediation services.' However, it is to be noted that this 'right' is only stated in the Recitals, whereas the blackletter of the Data Act itself only suggests the Article 5 mechanism where users wish to share data with a third party. This is also why the general rule in Article 7(2) according to which any contractual term which, to the detriment of the user, excludes

59 Rupprecht Podszun, *Der EU Data Act und der Zugang zu Sekundärmärkten am Beispiel des Handwerks* (Nomos 2023) 70 f.; Steinrötter, 'Data Act und DS-GVO' (n. 48) 222; Wiebe (n. 2) 1571; Duller (n. 8) ch. 7.5.4 In situ access or full control?.

60 ALI/ELI (n. 24) Principle 8.

the application of, derogates from or varies the effect of the user's rights under Chapter II shall not be binding on the user, does not necessarily also include the user's 'right' to pass data on.

Recital 25 mentions the possibility of a waiver. The wording is the following: 'This Regulation does not prevent users, in the case of business-to-business relations, from making data available to third parties or data holders under any lawful contractual term, including by agreeing to limit or restrict further sharing of such data, or from being compensated proportionately, for example in exchange for waiving their right to use or share such data.' Given that the word 'from' is repeated, this passage can only be read as indicating that users can, against proportionate compensation, waive their right to use or share product data or related services data, at least in B2B relations. The view that this is the case only vis-à-vis third parties, but not vis-à-vis the data holder,[61] does not find any support in the wording (a right is normally 'waived' vis-à-vis the person against whom the right is directed), nor does Article 7(2) differentiate in any way between contractual terms agreed with the data holder or with third parties.

The blackletter regulatory text of the Data Act does not mention the user's 'right' to pass data retrieved via Article 4 on to third parties, but only offers the Article 5 mechanism for instances where users wish to share data with third parties. While Article 4 mentions, in a by-the-way manner, data sharing in some places, this is never explicitly phrased as a right. This is why, in this paper, the view is being held that the user's 'right' to pass data on is not a 'right' strictly afforded by the Data Act. The user can therefore waive this right also vis-à-vis the data holder, as long as the Article 5 mechanism remains available to the user. However, in order to pass the unfairness test under Article 13, such a waiver would only be possible against proportionate compensation.

Again, while this is the view of the author, and while many Expert Group members agree that it would be desirable not to let parties undermine the regulatory regime of Articles 5 to 12 of the Data Act, it seems to be a minority position, with the majority of authors reading the Data Act itself differently.[62] For the Expert Group, this poses immense challenges, as such an option for waiver, if allowed under the Data Act, would have to be

61 Oral contribution by EP representative at the Münster Colloquium.

62 Drexl and others (n. 2) 32; Wolfgang Kerber, 'Governance of IoT Data: Why the EU Data Act Will Not Fulfill Its Objectives' (2023) 72 GRUR International 120, 123; Metzger and Schweitzer (n. 18) 56 ff. Heike Schweitzer and Axel Metzger, 'Data Access under the Draft Data Act, Competition Law and the DMA: Opening the Data

included in the MCTs. However, if it is not allowed under the Data Act, the Expert Group would, by including such an option, put its reputation at risk.

c) What is the relationship between Article 4(13) and (14)

The third illustration for challenges posed by ambiguities in the Data Act is the relationship between Article 4(13) and Article 4(14). According to Article 4(13), on the one hand, a data holder shall 'only use any readily available data that is non-personal data on the basis of a contract with the user'. According to Article 4(14), on the other hand, 'data holders shall not make available non-personal product data to third parties for commercial or non-commercial purposes other than the fulfilment of their contract with the user'.

There are several striking differences in terminology between the two provisions: One refers to 'readily available data' (which encompasses both product and related services data, but restricted to those that are available to the data holder without significant effort), the other refers to 'product data' only. One refers to 'the basis of a contract', which is as much as 'as far as agreed in a contract', the other refers to 'for ... the fulfilment of their contract'. One uses the singular of 'a data holder', the other the plural of 'data holders'. It is not clear whether the differences in terminology indicate a difference in substance, and what exactly that difference would be, or whether they are just a result of the fact that paragraph (14) was added at a very late stage in the legislative process and insufficient attention was paid to consistency of language. To add to the complexities, it is also not clear to whom 'their' in paragraph (14) really refers. From a strictly grammatical point of view it should refer to the data holders, but it could theoretically also refer to the third parties, which would be two very different things. Even if it is the contract with the data holder, it could still mean either the H2U data use agreement within the meaning of paragraph (13) or a broader sale, lease or rental contract or service contract. Given that paragraph (14) was inserted at such a late stage, its content seems not to be reflected in the Recitals.

In this paper, the view is taken that paragraph (14) is for cases not already covered by paragraph (13), i.e. where the data holder's right to pass product

Treasures for Competition and Innovation?' [2023] GRUR 337, 347; Duller (n. 8) 7.7 Waving the access right.

and related services data on to third parties within a broader notion of 'use' of the data has not already been agreed in the H2U data use agreement under paragraph (13). This means that, even without any H2U data use agreement, or where passing on of product data to a third party was not considered for some reason when drafting the H2U data use agreement, the data holder may still pass on data to third parties where this is required for the fulfilment of a contract with the user. This would then mean 'fulfilment' in the narrow sense, i.e. where there is a contractual obligation on the part of the data holder that cannot be fulfilled without passing the data on. Paragraph (14) provides mainly clarification in this regard, and the added value may lie primarily in the second sentence, according to which the data holder must contractually bind the third parties not to share the data any further. For this interpretation, any kind of contract between data holder and user that is in any way data-related would be sufficient, i.e. it could as well be a sale, lease or rental contract if the fulfilment of this contract requires the passing on of data to third parties.

What is, admittedly, more difficult to argue is why the wording of paragraph (14) is restricted to 'product data'. However, also this can be explained by the fact that it will usually be necessary to disclose product data to third parties, in particular if providing a related service is required for fulfilment of the contract with regard to the connected product itself, but not so much related services data. According to this reading, sharing of related services data would be allowed only under an H2U data use agreement within the meaning of paragraph (13) but not without such agreement under paragraph (14). There will possibly be some exceptional cases where paragraph (14) needs to be applied by analogy.

For the Expert Group however, once again, this ambiguity, which allows for numerous different interpretations, poses immense difficulties. If the MCTs are to provide any added value to stakeholders, they must be clearer and better intelligible than the Data Act itself, so the Expert Group should not simply restrict itself to restating paragraphs (13) and (14) as they stand, even though this would certainly be the 'safest' option.

V. Conclusion

The mission to draft effective MCTs is fraught with challenges, particularly due to uncertainties in pivotal regulatory interpretations. The Commission's work on a recommendation, to be issued under Article 41 of the

Data Act, is crucial in ensuring fair, reasonable, and non-discriminatory data sharing practices, balancing regulatory requirements with practical guidance for stakeholders. The same holds true for the Expert Group's work, which is of a preparatory and advisory nature.

In addition to the general challenges associated with this formidable task, the Expert Group is also faced with the challenge posed by a number of ambiguities in core provisions of the Data Act. Three illustrations for these ambiguities have been provided: The first is the question whether data access for the user under Article 4(1) can be provided, at the choice of the data holder, on the computing infrastructure of the data holder instead of transferring the data to the infrastructure indicated by the user. The second illustration is the likewise open question whether the user can waive its 'right' to pass data retrieved under Article 4(1) on to third parties, and the third illustration is the relationship between paragraphs (13) and (14) of Article 4, which allows for numerous different interpretations. In this paper, suggestions have been made how to answer these three questions, but it is by no means clear that this is the view that will be taken by the majority of relevant players, let alone the Court of Justice.

In any case, by addressing the diverse scenarios and challenges involved in data sharing, the Expert Group can hopefully create MCTs that facilitate effective and fair data sharing practices. These terms will play a vital role in the digital economy, ensuring that data is shared in a manner that creates better certainty and protects the legitimate interests of all parties involved.

Voluntary Data-Sharing: Bilateral Data-Sharing

Drafting Model Contractual Terms for Voluntary B2B Data Sharing: A Tool to Deal with Unfairness

*Teresa Rodríguez de las Heras Ballell**

I. Data sharing: context, policy goals, and mechanisms

Data have an exceptional transformative potential. Contemporaneous societies and modern economies are heavily dependent upon data. Data-driven solutions, businesses, and decision-makings pervade all sectors of the economy and promise immense benefits for society.[1] As non-rival (and non-excludable or excludable) goods,[2] data can expand and replicate their value and utility for multiple purposes and unlimited uses and reuses without losing quality or dwindling quantity. However, the potential of data as public goods is not fully realised.[3] A well-functioning data market is then instrumental to an optimal allocation of data for the good of society. Promoting the sharing of high-quality, interoperable data fosters innovation, competition, and economic growth. Data sharing encourages innovation and enhances competition in the aftermarket, foments the development of innovative and novel products and services, and even incentives the devising of sustainable practices and business models around or related to the main product market. Then, while the volume of data and the variety of data sources increase, the need to remove any barrier to data sharing is

---

* Professor of Commercial Law, University Carlos III of Madrid, Spain. Member of the Expert Group on B2B Data Sharing and Cloud Computing. The present contribution expresses only the personal opinion of the author and does not necessarily represent neither the opinion of the Expert Group nor the views of the European Commission.

1 OECD (2019), *How's Life in the Digital Age?: Opportunities and Risks of the Digital Transformation for People's Well-being*, OECD Publishing, Paris, https://doi.org/10.1787/9789264311800-en.

2 Data can be public goods (and non-excludable) or club goods (excludable). Duch Brown, N., Martens, B. and Muller-Langer, F., *The economics of ownership, access and trade in digital data*, JRC Digital Economy Working Paper 2017–01, European Commission, 2017, JRC104756.

3 European Strategy for Data: Communication from the Commission to the European Parliament, the Council, the European Economic and Social Committee and the Committee of the Regions, *A European strategy for data*, COM (2020) 66 final.

more pressing and crucial to revert data asymmetries, dismantle data silos, and debilitate (or dilute) data monopolies.

The increasingly popularity and expanding use of connected products have inundated the economy with unprecedent amounts and volumes of data. As the potential value of these data for individuals, businesses, the economy and the society may be outstanding, mobilising such data and properly allocating rights of access and use constitute a decisive policy.[4] Incentives for data sharing should be unlocked and adequate mechanisms for data sharing must be implemented. Data Act[5] crystallizes these policy goals and deploys a data sharing strategy under fair, reasonable, and non-discriminatory terms. To that end, private law[6] rules and, in particular, contract law rules play a central role not only to unleash data sharing but also to attain fairness objectives.

Data Act establishes a harmonised framework to enable the availability, the access, and the use of data in a pervasive economy of connected products and related services. Therefore, rules specifying who is entitled, in which conditions and on which basis to use such product data or related service data, as well as right-allocating mechanisms, have to be laid down. Non-rivalry (and non-excludability, primarily) invites an ambitious, expansive, and multifaceted approach to data sharing. Data Act acknowledges the multiple fronts converging on data sharing and sets out harmonized rules on the making available of product data and related service data to the user[7] of the connected product or related service, the making available of

4 An EU level action on the market has been called since the Building a European Data Economy' Communication in 2017, COM (2017) 9 final.

5 Regulation (EU) 2023/2854 of the European Parliament and of the Council of 13 December 2023 on harmonised rules on fair access to and use of data and amending Regulation (EU) 2017/2394 and Directive (EU) 2020/1828 (Data Act), PE/49/2023/REV/1, *OJ L, 2023/2854, 22.12.2023.*

6 Private law is today experiencing an extraordinary revival revisited from various approaches that challenge a monolithic and simple construction of private law's role in society. Grundmann, Stefan, Micklitz, Hans-Wolfgang & Renner, Moritz (2022), *New Private Law Theory – A very Brief Introduction,* German Law Journal, 23, 801–804. Against such a backdrop, the reinforced role of private law, and in particular, contract law for data governance proves, or at least seems to corroborate this revival.

7 Article 2 (12) Data Act:
'user' means a natural or legal person that owns a connected product or to whom temporary rights to use that connected product have been contractually transferred, or that receives related services
Data Act complements consumer protection legislation and and applies without prejudice to any Union law promoting the interests of consumers.

data by data holders to data recipients, and, in exceptional circumstances and for the performance of a specific task in the public interest, the making available of data by data holders to public sectors bodies.

Mobilising data flows and breaking down data silos to unleash data potential and to create a fluid data market are the drivers of data sharing contracts.[8] An optimal allocation of data requires considering and repairing possible market failures. Data sharing contracts, while driven by party autonomy, must face the fairness challenge. Transactions costs, asymmetries, or gatekeeping strategies render fairness a common and key problem in the entire data ecosystem. Hence, Data Act addresses the fairness problem and provides for various solutions and tools. *Inter alia*, on the hand, rules on unfair contractual terms in (B2B) data sharing contracts between enterprises (Article 13 Data Act). On the other hand, non-binding model contractual terms on data access and use for B2B data sharing contracts to be developed and recommended by the Commission (Article 41 Data Act).[9]

The aim of this contribution is to explore the role of the Model Contractual Terms for data sharing contracts, discuss the key issues to be addressed and solved, and assess its potential to serve as a tool to deal with unfairness in data sharing practice.

II. Data sharing: data, parties, and relationships

The MCT stem from the Data Act. Hence, the MCT pivot on its legal definitions[10] and are expected to operate within its scope of applications.

---

8 Contrary to the conventional disclosure paradox, information (data) is not always nonexcludable. In this context, contracts can play a fundamental role in building trust relationships and facing information asymmetries. Burstein, Michael J., *Exchanging Information Without Intellectual Property* (December 2012), Texas Law Review, Vol. 91, 227, Available at SSRN: https://ssrn.com/abstract=2038772.

9 The Expert Group on B2B data sharing and cloud computing contracts (E03840) – https://ec.europa.eu/transparency/expert-groups-register/screen/expert-groups/consult?lang=en&groupID=3840 – has the mission of assisting the Commission in its work on developing model contractual clauses for B2B data sharing and standard contractual clauses for cloud computing contracts. The author is member of the Expert Group. All views and opinions in this contribution are personal and do neither bind nor represent the European Commission or the Expert Group.

10 According to the Data Act (Art. 2):
'connected 'product' means an item, that obtains, generates or collects, data concerning its use or environment, and that is able to communicate product data via an electronic communications service, a physical, connection or on-device access and

Thus, the MCT are to be developed for contracts covering product data and/related service data.[11] As the Data Act explicitly recognises, it covers both personal data and non-personal data (Art. 1(2) Data Act). Should the data to be shared qualify as personal data, parties must ensure that there is a valid legal basis under the GDPR[12] for the data holder making the data available to the data recipient, and the data sharing contract will specify the modes of provision. If data are non-personal the contract itself provides the legal basis as well as the mode of data sharing.

The broad notion of personal data under the GDPR risks to absorb almost entirely the expanding data sphere generated by connected product and related services.[13] Despite the real or remote possibility of associating product-generated data with the user, and consequently with a data subject, certainly, numerous data are primarily related to environment, operation or performance. Frankly remote from the data subject in a certain way. More precisely, a part of product data and related service data appear to respond better to the logic of co-generated data. Product data are generated by the use of the product. Related service data represent user actions or events related to the connected product, recorded intentionally by the user or generated as a by-product of the user's action during the provision of a related service by the provider. Consequently, data are generated because the product has been designed to that end, while, it is the use, but also the mere idle consumption or the interconnection with other ecosystems. Coping with the data protection requirements in this challenging scenario

whose primary function is not the storing, processing or transmission of data on behalf of third parties, other than the user.
'Related service' means a digital service other than an electronic communications service, including software, which is connected with the product at the time of the purchase in such a way that its absence would prevent the product from performing one or more of its functions, or which is subsequently connected to the product by the manufacturer or a third party to add to, update or adapt the functions of the product.

11 Zins, Chaim, *Conceptual Approaches for Defining Data, Information, and Knowledge*, Journal of the American Society for Information Science and Technology, 22 January 2007, 58 (4): 479–493.

12 Regulation (EU) 2016/679 of the European Parliament and of the Council of 27 April 2016 on the protection of natural persons with regard to the processing of personal data and on the free movement of such data, and repealing Directive 95/46/EC (General Data Protection Regulation) (Text with EEA relevance). *OJ L 119, 4.5.2016, 1–88.*

13 Purtova, Nadezhda, *The law of everything. Broad concept of personal data and future of EU data protection law*, Law, Innovation and Technology. 10 (1), 2018, 40–81.

is becoming increasingly tedious and burdensome.[14] Therefore, it is not unreasonable to think further and maybe reconsider or, at least, revisit the, undoubtedly commendable, assumptions of the personal data protection. It is inevitable to wonder whether the notion of personal data is compatible with a densely interconnected economy and a profound transformation[15] of our original connection of digital life.[16] The blurring of the distinction between reality and virtuality; the blurring of the distinctions between human, machine and nature; the reversal from information scarcity to information abundance; and the shift from the primacy of entities to the primacy of interactions invite a further consideration, even radical, of the distinction, never conclusive nor unambiguous, between personal data and non-personal data.

A contract-driven approach to data economy with the main aim to unleash the full potential of data for the benefit of society lies in this fossilised duality personal/non-personal. Without suggesting by all means a deterioration of the level of protection for personal data, it is enticing the idea of rethinking the contours of the notion of personal data in a world of connected machines.

The MCT have to deal with this quandary and carefully internalize the proper data protection regimes for those data that qualifies as personal data. The magnitude of personal data presence tends naturally to enlarge where the user is a natural person.

Whereas the use of the connected product and the related service can be supported by various contracts (sale, rent, lease), the MCT are focused on the subsequent data sharing triggered by such use. The contracts can be concluded concurrently or successively though.

The personal scope of the MCT advises the formulation of different set of rules. First, MCT designed for contracts pursuant to Article 4(6) the Data Act between a data holder and a user of a connected product or

---

14 Schwartz, Paul M. and Solove, Daniel J., *The PII Problem: Privacy and a New Concept of Personally Identifiable Information* (December 5, 2011), New York University Law Review, Vol. 86, 1814, 2011, UC Berkeley Public Law Research Paper No. 1909366, GWU Legal Studies Research Paper No. 584, GWU Law School Public Law Research Paper No. 584, Available at SSRN: https://ssrn.com/abstract=1909366.

15 Floridi, Luciano, *The Online Manifesto. Being Human in a Hyperconnected Era*, Springer, 2015, 1. The Online Manifesto was launched on 8 February 2013 and presented at an inaugural event in Brussels held by DG Connect, the European Commission Directorate General for Communications Networks, Content & Technology.

16 Simon, Judith & Ess, Charles, *The ONLIFE Initiative—a Concept Reengineering Exercise*, Philosophy & Technology, 2017, 28. 10.1007/s13347-015-0189-8.

related service where the data holder wishes to use any non-personal data generated by the use of the product or related service. With appropriate modifications, this first scenario covers those agreements where a data holder wishes to use any co-generated data with the contribution of the user, including by being a data subject within the meaning of the GDPR. Second, MCT designed for contracts between a data holder and a third party data recipient where, in business-to-business relations, a data holder is obliged to make data available to a third party data recipient upon request by a user under Article 5 of the Data Act, in accordance with the provisions of Chapter III of the Data Act. Third, MCT designed for contracts between a user of a connected product or related service and a third party data recipient where the user requests a data holder to make data available to the third party data recipient pursuant to Article 5 of the Data Act; or the user has requested the data holder to access data in accordance with Article 4 of the Data Act and makes the data available to the third party data recipient. Finally, MCT designed for contracts between a data holder and a data recipient willing to share data (or make data available to a data recipient) voluntarily and independent of any request by a user or similar party.

III. Model Contractual Terms

As per Article 41 Data Act, the Commission shall develop and recommend non-binding model contractual terms on data access and use. Such model contractual terms (MCT) should contain, in particular, terms on reasonable compensation and protection of trade secrets. It shall be completed by 12 September 2025. The legal provision does also refer to the development of non-binding standard contractual clauses (SCC) for cloud computing contracts. Thus, the combined but differentiated treatment in the same provisions of both markets reflects the understanding and the assumption that there are fairness problems in both B2B data sharing and cloud computing and market failures that present commonalities, while, however, these problems surface and materialize in different ways in each of the two markets. Therefore, considering the commonalities as well as the differences, the Commission is entrusted with the tasks of developing MCT for B2B data sharing and SCC for cloud computing contracts.

With the mission[17] of assisting the Commission in the work of developing the MCT and the SCC,[18] the Expert Group on B2B Data Sharing and Cloud Computing Contracts is created.[19]

1. Unveiling the unfairness problem in the B2B data sharing market

The primary question to address is why there is an unfairness risk in the B2B data sharing market. A study[20] complementing and contributing to the impact assessment of the (proposal for a) Data Act[21] sets the background and provides basic premises and key assumptions.

17 Expert Group on B2B Data Sharing and Cloud Computing Contracts, Terms of Reference:
"3. Tasks
The expert group shall assist the Commission by:
analysing existing B2B data sharing models and practices, identifying problems and commonalities and recommending to the Commission a general horizontal set of balanced model contract terms for B2B data sharing that could be applicable for sharing data across sectors, including for data generated by machines and the use of products and related services;
analysing data sharing practices in some sectors where there is a need for model contract terms and recommending to the Commission model contract terms tailored for these sectors;
analysing existing practices for cloud contract terms and recommending to the Commission a general set of standard contractual clauses for cloud contracts.
issuing recommendations/suggestions to the Commission on other subjects related to fair contractual relations in B2B data sharing as follow-up to the Data Act and Cloud Marketplace, following a proposal by the Commission services."

18 As previously developed for the transfer of personal data: Commission Implementing Decision (EU) 2021/914 of 4 June 2021 on standard contractual clauses for the transfer of personal data to third countries pursuant to Regulation (EU) 2016/679 of the European Parliament and of the Council (Text with EEA relevance), C/2021/3972, *OJ L 199, 7.6.2021, 31–61.*

19 Register of Commission Expert Groups, Expert Group on B2B data sharing and cloud computing contracts (E03840): https://ec.europa.eu/transparency/expert-groups-register/screen/expert-groups/consult?lang=en&groupId=3840&fromMeetings=true&meetingId=48306.

20 European Commission, Directorate-General for Justice and Consumers, Graux, H., Somers, G., Van Camp, S. et al., *Study on model contract terms and fairness control in data sharing and in cloud contracts and on data access rights – Final report*, Publications Office of the European Union, 2022, https://data.europa.eu/doi/10.2838/174720.

21 Impact Assessment report and support studies accompanying the Proposal for a Data Act available at

Contract law is the main driver for data sharing but leads to unfairness and underutilisation should market failures prevent parties from sharing data in free, competitive, transparent, and fair conditions. Market failures range from lack of competition and data monopoly situations, to gatekeeping-enabling value chains, or non-disputable data ecosystems or markets. As in other markets or sectors, data market can be distorted by market players holding a dominant position and imposing imbalanced conditions in the sharing, provided that there is any incentive for the dominant holder to deal and share, rather than retaining the data and holding the position. Should innovation and competition in the principal market or in connected markets depend upon data access, a substandard level of data sharing ruins the potential of data as non-rival and non-excludable economic goods.

Thus, the first type of market failure is related to these asymmetric position of market players within a scenario of high levels of data concentration.[22] Data can reinforce tipping, raise barriers to entry barriers and increase the economic power of large data holders that can benefit from strong network effects and economies of scope and scale in data. To identify and adequately categorize this failure is key to ideate and devise an effective and fit-for-purpose intervention. Whether competition-law type measures[23] are sufficient and efficient, or ex-ante regulatory measures should be, solely or in combination, provided for.[24] While the spotlight on the dominance may direct the attention towards measures attacking or mitigating market power, the data unavailability or scarcity problem may be instead rather aggravated by unbalanced or unfair terms.

---

https://digital-strategy.ec.europa.eu/en/library/impact-assessment-report-and-support-studies-accompanying-proposal-data-act.

22 Crémer, Jacques, Montjoye, Yves-Alexandre, Schweitzer, Heike, *Competition Policy for the Digital Era:* Final Report, Luxembourg 2019, Publications Office of the European Union, 2019.

23 Graef, Inge, *Market definition and market power in data: The case of online platforms*, World Competition Law and Economics Review, 38(4), 2015, 473–506; Martens, B, *An economic policy perspective on online platforms*, JRC Technical Report 2016/05, 2016; Stucke, M. and M. Grunes, *Debunking the myth over big data and antitrust*, Antitrust Chronicle, 2015, 5; Tucker D. R. and H. B. Wellford, *Big mistakes regarding big data,* Antitrust Source, American Bar Association, 2014.

24 Assuming that, and to the extent that, the level of data sharing in the market is proved to be a problem and provided that (free) contractual arrangements between the market players do not suffice. Kerber, Wolfgang, *Rights on Data: The EU Communication 'Building a European Data Economy' From an Economic Perspective*, 2017, https://papers.ssrn.com/sol3/papers.cfm?abstract_id=3033002.

A second type of market failure is not necessarily provoked by more or less traditional market dominance situations but rather be triggered by gatekeeping scenarios. Strategic positions in the value chain may raise barriers in the data flow and erect such data holders in gatekeepers creating bottlenecks and imposing unfair conditions to downstream participants. Interestingly, in these cases, the data holder deploying strategical gatekeeping strategies does not necessarily occupy a dominant position and, however, it can foreclose the development of connected markets, corelated activities, or ancillary services. This adverse effect in narrowing down or locking side or related markets is particularly damaging for competition and innovation. The non-rivalrous use potential of data is seriously compromised and missed.

These market failures can cross-cut the data ecosystem or surface with particular intensity and seriousness in specific niches or sectors. The market fails to effectively mobilise data value and avoids an optimal allocation of data. Although contracts are the primary mechanisms for enabling data sharing, party autonomy is leading to underperformance and suboptimal data sharing.

Lack of competition, non-disputable markets, and gatekeeping strategies explain, at least, one side of the identified problem: suboptimal level of B2B data sharing. Whereas they also lay the problematic foundations for the second side of the identified problem: the unfairness risk. The resultant imbalance of negotiating power and the existence of weak incentives for data sharing of those dominant or gatekeeping data holders precipitate conditions conducive to possible unfair clauses in data sharing contract.

A proper understanding of the sources of and the basis for the unfairness risk is crucial for the formulation of effective solutions. Therefore, it well worth wondering whether non-binding MCT for B2B data sharing serve the policy objectives and how deal with the unfairness problem in B2B relationship. The question cannot be adequately answered without acknowledging and incorporating into the analytical framework a third vector that crosses data market. Little, undeveloped, and non-elaborate market practice for data sharing. This factual state of play brings about two dealings-hindering factors: high transaction costs and high uncertainty. A pernicious combination of low experience, little market practice, high uncertainty, and significant transactions costs to manage hinders economic interaction and can even paralyse contracting. Albeit not exclusively, these factors do specially impact SMEs less prepared to handle uncertainty, inexperience and transaction costs in a competitive manner.

The value of the MCT initiative and its effectiveness in achieving the policy goals increase significantly where the problems of transactions costs, limited praxis, and uncertainty are included into the equation. The development of MCT for businesses, of any size, to rely on and utilize in their data sharing contracts is certainly a highly-effective fit-for-purpose solution. The beneficial effects to raise a data market and enable and accelerate data transactions are evident and substantial. MCT prove to be a practical, influential, and market-creating tool to achieve the policy goals.

In conjunction with other policy interventions, such as the fairness control over contractual terms related to data access and use between enterprises, the MCT play a contributory role in unleashing the full potential of data in the Union.

2. MCT as a tool to deal with unfairness

The joint analysis of the impact assessment report, the support studies of the proposal, and the final text of the Data Act allow to sketch the multiple-function role of MCT in the policy intervention. The succinct statements of Recital 111 of the Data Act and the concentrated and brief wording of its Article 41 condense, nonetheless, the four drivers guiding the policy role of MCT.

a) MCT and presumed fairness objectives

First, promoting data sharing by recommending MCT, albeit non-binding and voluntary, can instil fairness objectives in the market. The presumption is that the MCT are drafted to achieve certain fairness objectives. Thus, once the parties have identified a common or compatible economic purpose and mutual benefit in sharing data, by utilizing the MCT, parties would naturally pursue and attain the "embedded" fairness objectives. As per Article 41 Data Act, MCT would provide parties with terms to conclude contracts with "fair, reasonable and non-discriminatory contractual rights and obligations". In that regard, contractual terms would be modelled to achieve such fairness objectives, so parties could simply align with them.

The binding or non-binding character of the MCT and the possibility of the parties to depart from the set of MCT as a "fair contract model" shall determine the effectiveness of MCT in imbuing market practice with such fairness goals.

b) MCT for reducing transactions costs

Second, by jointing resorting to MCT in their dealings, parties would significantly reduce transaction costs in negotiating, drafting, valuating, and performing. This is probably the most visible benefit of MCT as a policy intervention in a market afflicted by limited contractual practice, little experience in data sharing, lack of expertise in the matter, and even certain imbalances in the negotiating power. The longed-for reduction of transaction costs might, however, be attained at the cost of "over-standardising" contracting praxis, "corseting" party autonomy, or even relegating the very economic interests that parties do seek in their business negotiations. Mindful of such undesired effects in the market, a MCT-based policy strategy needs to carefully consider on which conditions the model terms should operate.

While opting for their possible binding character more intensely interferes into parties' autonomy, promoting flexibility and voluntariness with non-binding MCT inevitably raise doubts about the actual effect of the cost-reduction objective insofar as negotiation and drafting costs may abruptly reappear, and even exacerbated, if parties have to discuss the application of the MCT, agree on their use in the contract, and subsequently select the applicable terms and renegotiate the remaining ones where, if possible, an agreement to use the MCT has not been reached. The possibility that parties can either not apply the MCT or substantially alter their terms in the final agreement question puts, to a certain extent, in jeopardy the ultimate aim of ensuring by MCT fairness objectives, as parties could elude them either by renegotiating the model terms individually or by readjusting the fairness equilibrium of the entire contract. Besides, should MCT be non-binding and voluntary the risks of imbalance in the negotiating power of the parties are not totally eliminated. Certainly, it cannot be ignored that the existence of MCT alleviate asymmetries and can empower the disadvantageous party with a yardstick to measure the reasonableness of the counterparty's proposal and with a benchmark to start and conduct negotiations. Hence, while MCT represent a more effective tool to reduce transaction costs rather than to achieve fairness objectives in data sharing contracts, the actual use of MCT in the market may, nonetheless, lead to satisfying *de facto* outcomes related to both policy goals.

c) MCT as a practical tool

Third, MCT provide a *practical tool* to help enterprises, in particular, SMEs to conclude data sharing contracts. Recital 111 highlights this role of MCT as a practical tool. With this descriptive term, the role of MCT seems to distance from pure policy goals and fairness objectives and perform more practical functions. MCT are presented to as to serve as educational, helpful tools that assist enterprises, specially of small size, in their contracting practice. This role is not *per se* rooted into fairness objectives, unless improving SMEs' data contracts knowledge and fortifying their data contracting skills are deemed indeed rebalancing mechanisms. In fact, the value of MCT as a practical tool for SMEs, in particular, directly connect with the lack of expertise and the limited data-sharing practice as drivers of the identified market failures and triggers of the policy intervention.

The educational value and the role as a practical tool can be particularly enhanced with suited drafting and formatting strategies. In certain terms, and where it is required or relevant, the MCT can provide options for the parties to choose in their drafting of the agreement. Options are to serve as real substantive or material alternatives, purely alternative drafting versions, or mechanisms to adapt the MCT to different sectors or transactional contexts.

For instance, in delimiting the scope of the agreement the parties can refer to detailed Annexes (option 1) or describe or list the data covered by the contract in one of the contractual terms. That is essentially a drafting option without substantial impact on the agreement.

Or, the MCT can contain as an option a clause stipulating the compensation for additional support or a penalty clause (or liquidated damages). Here, these options help the parties to exercise their party's autonomy within the perimeters of the MCT and still benefit from the benchmarking value of pre-drafted terms that, if parties agree on the matter, can be incorporated into the contract. By providing these clauses as optional, the MCT sign that stipulations governing such issues are not essential and the parties can find their own equilibrium of interests. Particularly advisable is the use of options in those clauses, normally general clauses, where there is not preferred option in terms of fairness but they must simply reflect the free agreement of the parties. A simple example of the term on the duration of the agreement and the starting date can illustrate those cases. The parties can agree that the Agreement *[OPTION 1:]* comes into effect at the date of the signature, by both Parties, or that *[OPTION 2:]* it comes into effect on *[insert date]* and is concluded for *[OPTION 2a:]* an indeterminate period or *[OPTION 2b:]* a period of *[insert period]*, until termination. In considering which of these options to choose, the Parties should be guided primarily by the user's request. If the request is for a one-time supply of data, the first option is appropriate. If the request is for a continuous supply of data, the Parties will need to choose the second option and agree on either the first or second sub-option, depending on whether or not the User has specified a particular time period.

Finally, with the use of options the MCT get a modular shape. Flexibility and adaptability to needs, sectors or circumstances. A good example might be where the MCT contain options for data recipients qualifying as SMEs.

Drafting and material options as well as (additional) optional terms imbue MCT with an adequate adaptability feature and, in a certain way, reinforce its potential value as a toolkit for the parties.

Besides, considering the identified lack of experience in data sharing in the market and little practice among the enterprises more exposed to unfairness risks, in principle those of more modest size, accompanying explanations, commentaries, and/or illustrations would enlighten its educational purpose. Thus, the MCT would turn into a contractual guidance where parties can find not only model contractual terms, but also a guide to understand the extent, assess the consequences, and construct the MCT for ensuring an informed contractual decision. While the MCT literally materialize the mandate of the Commission pursuant to Article 41 Data Act, a guidance format may go beyond and exceed expectations. In particular, it should be critically assess whether the wording of the commentaries may risk to become recommendations.

d) MCT as a "fair model contract" or as a "model for a fair contract"

Yet, Recital 111 of Data Acts provides another perspective on the potential role of MCT that intimately relate with the fairness aspirations. When used widely and integrally, the recital states, MCT influence contractual praxis and drive contractual relations towards fairer data access, use, and sharing practices. It is an interesting construction of the role of MCT that assumes a medium/long term impact on the market, a silent and progressive effect on commercial practice, and a natural and pervasive permeation of the fairness objective embedded in the MCT in the contracts more and more frequently concluded under or inspired by the MCT. This perspective takes a distance from the market functioning and the parties' behaviour and proposes a low level of intervention. It relies on a continuing accommodation of the market and the contracting practices to MCT that would naturally become a benchmark.

The idea that MCT encapsulate a "fair contract model" is particularly intriguing. Article 13 Data Act provides for a definition of unfair contractual term based on gross deviation from good commercial practice in data access and use.[25] Subsequently, in the following paragraphs, Article 13 Data Act specify contractual terms that, considering its object or effect, shall be, in particular, unfair, and terms that shall be presumed unfair for the purposes of the fairness control defined in paragraph 3. As MCT may distil best practices in the market they could become a yardstick to measure fairness. Should MCT be conceived and accepted as good commercial practice, they would play an extremely valuable role in giving shape and content to the standard of good commercial practice. Nonetheless, that would not immunize the contract concluded by the parties using the MCT from judicial scrutiny and possible total or partial voidance. Therefore, as expounded below, the interplay of the MCT with the applicable legislation, both at national level and EU one, and with the exercise of party's autonomy.

3. Key strategical decisions in the drafting of MCT

The development of MCT needs to be preceded by the adoption of key decisions to articulate the interplay with party autonomy, on the one hand, and with applicable legislation, on the other. The policy option for standardizing contract making opens profound and fundamental debates on the meaning and the extent of private law as a regulatory tool.[26] Besides, the Data Act does not replace contract law rules. On the contrary, rules on formation, validity and effects of contracts, as well as on the consequences of termination, remain unaffected.

Yet, agreements based on, or incorporating the MCT cannot be isolated from the legal rules on contracts included, where applicable, the consumer legislation in relation to unfair terms in consumer contracts, consumer

25 Article 13(3) Data Act:
"A contractual term is unfair if it is of such a nature that its use grossly deviates from good commercial practice in data access and use, contrary to good faith and fair dealing".

26 Micklitz, Hans-Wolfgang, *The Visible Hand of European Regulatory Private Law*, The Transformation of European Private Law from Autonomy to Functionalism in Competition and Regulation, EUI LAW, 2008/14 – https://hdl.handle.net/1814/8707.

rights, and unfair commercial practices. But more singularly, Data Act, by providing for a rule on unfair terms in B2B data contract, adds the layer of fairness control which stacks on general contract law rules. Naturally, the MCT do not cure invalidating causes nor exempt the agreements from complying with the applicable legislation. Therefore, it is to be wondered how the MCT can effectively deal with the unfairness problem in data sharing.

To that end, several strategical decisions in the drafting of MCT and for determining their expected use in the market are instrumental to assess the effectiveness' prospect in the achievement of policy goals.

MCT for B2B data sharing contracts have a non-binding character. The non-binding character of the MCT reconciles standardization with party's autonomy, but it stirs the debate on which incentives parties have to align their contractual agreements with the MCT. In particular, in a market with power imbalance, it is inevitable to wonder whether the dominant party would have any incentive to renounce their power to impose unilaterally beneficial terms and how the less advantageous party can place the necessary incentives on the counterparty to jointly agree on the use of the MCT. In such a scenario, where a term is unilaterally imposed, the fairness control provided for by Article 13 Data Act comes to fore. In that regard, the MCT provide a model that prevent parties (the party who can and would be willing to) from falling under Article 13 Data Act.

The non-binding character of the MCT ensures the respect for party's autonomy to allocate risks, distribute costs, and fulfil their economic interests through their agreement. Should MCT succeed in reflecting good practices and providing a reasonably balanced agreement, the aim to reduce transactions costs is largely realised. Nonetheless, the satisfaction of fairness objectives invites further consideration. In the exercise of their party's autonomy, parties can amend any of the balanced model terms or replaced them by less equilibrated rights or obligations. Unless the MCT remain integrally used and fully incorporated into the final agreement between the enterprises, the risk of imbalance persists. As a matter of fact, the fair balance attained by the MCT, as a consistent body of contractual terms, may end up diluting if the economic equilibrium of the entire agreement is reverted. By altering certain terms of the final agreement, or by adding other terms on rights and obligations, on the performance conditions or on liability, for instance, the fairness embodied in the MCT may be reverted. The MCT provide a "fair contract model", but solely to the extent that it remains balanced, it may be alleged.

Nonetheless, such attempts to disequilibrate the balance of the agreement, that the non-binding character of the MCT cannot impede, would be often subsequently stopped by Article 13 where the unilaterally imposed term that is likely to create an imbalance and boycott the fairness objective pursued by the MCT, as a whole, falls under its scope. Thus, in the departing from the MCT, the parties (more precisely, the party who forces the deviation and aims to unilaterally impose an alternative term), the MCT as a policy intervention loses immediate effectiveness, but the fairness-control policy solution plays its role. This two-step process seems to achieve an adequate balance in achieving fairness objectives.

Another delicate balance has to be struck between the MCT and the applicable legislation. How much the MCT should go beyond the legal provisions in order to signify an actual added value. Should MCT go beyond the applicable law in detailing and specifying rights and obligations and in complementing the data-related provisions with other ancillary terms, the non-binding character questions again their acceptance rate. Whereas if the MCT are simply reproducing the legal provisions, their function remains confined to a practical tool with more limited added value.

From the same perspective, it is to be discussed whether the MCT should provide an entire "model contract" or a set of model contractual terms, exclusively related to the data-related obligations and rights, that need to be integrated in the very agreement that parties would enter into. There are considerations to ponder in both directions. The option for an entire and standalone model contract excels in the pursuit of providing parties, especially SMEs, with a practical tool in the drafting and concluding contracts for data sharing, and, if adopted by the parties, reduce transaction costs in, at least, the first stages of contract formation. By constituting a coherent, complete model contract, it can even better encapsulate the fairness objectives, as it is. Nonetheless, it cannot be disregarded that parties can dissemble or deconstruct the model contract in their negotiations, or one strong party can ignore or customize the MCT in its own benefit. So, the achievement of fairness objectives is moving away.

Yet, the option to offer an entire model contract has to face the question of how to unify all types of contractual models or standardize contractual responses to various sectoral needs and practices. Therefore, a balance is to be struck between ensuring the utility of the MCT and accommodating flexibility, party' autonomy, and sectoral and transaction-specific needs with the inclusion of drafting options.

In drafting MCT to constitute an entire model contract, there is other issues to address and solve. Whether the MCT should be only addressing data-related aspects and provide the core of the contract as far as data sharing is concerned without diving into those clauses pertaining to general contract. Should the MCT include terms on duration, consequences of termination, remedies for non-performance, and general clauses such as choice of law, interpretation or dispute settlement. There are two main points to take into account. First, to which extent in such general (or ancillary) provisions there are any specificities arising from the type of contract (data sharing modalities) or the object of the contract (data). If so, proposing MCT in that matter would certainly assist parties in their deals. Second, whether national law would differ in issues covered by such terms such as remedies. In such a case, the model term would be replaced by the national law provision or adjusted to national laws.

The interplay with general contract law is a complex and intriguing area to explore. Not only the legal nature of data is amply debated, but also the typology of contracts that can articulate an agreement for data sharing is diverse and, to a certain extent, disputed. Ambiguities or uncertainties on the type of contracts to be concluded – sale-based, license-based, service-based approaches – cannot neither ignore nor simply eluded by using the MCT. Certainly, the use of MCT, especially if they provide a complete and standalone model contract, alleviate the pressure on the parties to acknowledge the contract type, but, in reality, it is merely postponed to a later state. Data contracts need to be legally categorized. Even if the MCT seem to evade the characterisation problem and avoid any legal recognition, at least explicitly, it will be relevant for gap-filling, for interpretation purposes, and, definitively, for subsequently referring to (subsidiary) applicable legislation if the agreement, as it will inevitably happen, is incomplete.

4. MCT and the typology of data contracts: selected issues

Data transactions range from contracts for the processing of data to agreements for the provision of data.[27] The above-described characteristics of

27 ALI-ELI Principles for a Data Economy – Data transactions and data rights at https://www.ali.org/media/filer_public/ff/7c/ff7c5006-058e-4254-885d-b5d5725fd8be/date-economy-td2.pdf and https://europeanlawinstitute.eu/fileadmin/user_upload/p_el

data together with the diversity of modes of provision render the legal characterization of the data contract particularly challenging.[28]

On the one hand, some data transactions are clearly contracts for services with regard to data – such as contracts for the processing of data or contracts for data escrow.

On the other hand, in those data transactions that are contracts for the supply or provision of data, there are several modes of provision: transfer of data, simple access to data, sharing or pooling of data.[29] Although, it has been proved to be insufficient and to a certain extent rather imperfect for a legal characterisation, a distinction between a sale-based approach and a license-based approach to describe contracts for the supply of data depending on the mode of provision is commonly used. A 'sales' approach would suggest that the data recipient is entitled to determine the purposes

i/Projects/Data_Economy/Principles_for_a_Data_Economy_Final_Council_Draft.pdf.

28 For illustration purposes, it could be used the Convention on International Sale of Goods (CISG) as a test scenario. For the purposes of Article 3 CISG, it must be identified the primary obligation of the party who furnishes the goods (if data are goods) or the preponderant part of his obligations. CISG-AC Opinion no 4, Contracts for the Sale of Goods to Be Manufactured or Produced and Mixed Contracts (Article 3 CISG), 24 October 2004.Rapporteur: Professor Pilar Perales Viscasillas, Universidad Carlos III de Madrid.

29 The ongoing project on data contracts that UNCITRAL (United Nations Commission for International Trade Law) is carrying out is proposing neutral terminology (using for accessing, sharing, porting, transferring or providing data) to avoid prejudicing the type of contract, but it is providing for various modes of provision that direct towards traditional typified contracts (essentially sale-based approach, license-based approach, access-based mode). The latest available version of the default rules is published as the document A/CN.9/WG.IV/WP.183 Default rules for data provision contracts
Article 1. Definitions
"For the purpose of these rules:
(a) "Data" is a representation of information in electronic form;
(b) "Using" data includes performing one or more operations on data, and extends to accessing, sharing, porting, transferring or providing data"
Article 5. Mode of provision
"(1) The data is provided by:
(a) Delivering the data to an information system designated by the data recipient;
(b) Making the data available to the data recipient or to a person designated by data recipient in an information system under the control of the data provider.
(2) The data provider and data recipient shall cooperate with each other where such cooperation could reasonably be expected with respect to the mode of provision of the data under the contract, including technical, organizational and security measures".

and means of processing the data provided by the other party who would have waived any residual right in data. Conversely, a 'license' approach would suggest that the data recipient is entitled to process the data only for the purposes, by the means or in relation to the operations provided for in the contract. Unlike in a sales approach, the data recipient is only entitled to specified uses of the data as defined by the 'license'.

As for the obligation of the data provider (data holder), in those data transactions designed as data access contracts, there is not a 'delivery' of data but the implementation of measures to authorize and enable access to data by the data recipient.

Should a contract for the provision of data be articulated as a 'sale of data', the obligation to deliver requires to agree on effective actions to transfer the 'control' over the supplied data. Whereas the role of control as a functional equivalence to 'transfer of possession' can work for representative data, in a contract for the supply of data as records of information (as in the data sharing contexts is assumed), the transfer of control may not be on an exclusivity basis and it is rather entailing permitting the data recipient to determine purposes and subsequent uses.

In the drafting of the MCT, modes agreed to provide the data with the aim of realising the sharing of data need to be decided. Parties should, in the agreement itself or in a separate Appendix, include all the details of how access is to be provided. The modes of access and use of data are not neutral in terms of legal characterisation. So, the choice for and the deployment of the access and use modalities are not a banal and irrelevant decision. On the contrary, that entails assuming as well as defining a type/s of contract underlying the data sharing practice.

Parties can decide how data shall be provided. Various modes are possible. First, data can be provided as a full transfer – i.e. a copy of the data is transferred to a medium within the data recipient's control. Second, data can be provided by way of transmission triggered by the data holder (push) – such as online transmission, upload into the data recipient's cloud space or delivery of a tangible medium on which the data is stored. Third, data can be made available by way of retrieval triggered by the data recipient (pull) – such as upon being provided with an API, access credentials to the data holder's cloud space or similar tools that enable the data recipient to access and extract the data. Yet, there is no objection or prohibition in the Data Act to implement a model based on in situ access to the Data. Thus, the data must be accessed and processed on a medium within the data holder's or a trusted third party's control, such as by the data recipient logging into a dedicated space on the data holder's or trusted third party's servers. But there are other technical possibilities that can create different data sharing structures, including access on the requesting user's device, but more importantly that crystallizes diverse contractual obligations.

In addition to the basic question of the mode of provision the parties must consider and decide on a variety of further issues, such as the frequency (whether access is provided in real-time or not), the expected performance conditions (which delays or update intervals are acceptable), and a number of organizational, technical, and legal considerations (access credentials, technical specifications, authorised users, format, etc). But, even the most exhaustive, detailed, and purportedly complete agreement (or MCT) cannot anticipate, contemplate, and resolve all possible problems to be raised in the performance of the contract. A default legal framework applicable to the (type of) contract is needed.

As explained above, parties should be aware of the practical and also legal consequences of each mode of data provision. The specification of all performance conditions, albeit in a full and comprehensive manner, does not allow to elude the question of the type of obligations the parties are to comply with. Performance conditions (frequency, format, place, specifications) are not capriciously agreed by the parties in a vacuum. They do and should emanate from the very nature of the contract/obligations. Timely and proper compliance of the obligations related to the provision of data needs to be contextualized in the mode of provision selected by the parties. Neither the notion of conformity nor the available remedies are impermeable to the type of contract that the particular mode of data provision reflects.

In general terms, it may be questioned whether the conformity standards[30] provided for, for instance, sale contracts work well for data transactions. Quantity, quality, fitness for purpose and reference to samples and models may apply to data. However, there are some considerations that should be taken into account in applying such standards to data conformity. Quality of data includes a variety of factors or attributes such as traceability or lawfulness (lawful collection and/or processing). Real-time and continuous supply of data may be critical as well to define the conformity of

30 CISG-AC Opinion No. 19, Standards and Conformity of the Goods under Article 35 CISG, Rapporteur: Professor Djakhongir Saidov, King's College London, United Kingdom, Adopted by the CISG Advisory Council following its 25th meeting, in Aalborg Denmark, on 25 November 2018.

data with the contracts (fitness for purpose). Ordinary use of data requires that data are supplied together with the metadata, domain tables, semantics and other specifications required for normal data use. The assessment of the fitness for purpose cannot be confirmed until the data is effectively used for the expected purpose (AI training, personalized ad campaign, predictions, market study). Among many other intriguing questions, the obligation to examine[31] the goods may be impracticable in data transactions or entail a 'use' of the supplied data.

The characteristics of data, as described above, may need to revisit the remedies in case of default and ensure that they are suitable to data provision transactions. It may be interesting to rethink some aspects[32] such as, *inter alia*: how to repair non-conforming data; what the delivery/supply of substitute data entails as far as the supplied non-conforming data are concerned; or how to restitute supplied data in case of avoidance of the contract.

Yet, applying the passing-of-risk provisions to contract for the supply of goods raise some challenging questions: whether the loss of data is a real risk if copies of data are available to be redelivered; how to accommodate the passing of risk provisions to 'data transfer' models as well as to 'data access' models; how data to be supplied are 'clearly identified to the contracts' for the purposes of risk passing; what is the meaning of damaged data (corrupted, inaccurate, hacked, malware, insufficient); how to establish the 'place' to take over the data other that the place of business.

The selected examples above aim to unveil the complexity of data contracts and the fundamental need to address these substantive issues. The pervasion of data economy by contract law must be realized with all consequences and to the full extent. Contract law logic should not be ignored or perverted in order to serve data contracts. Adaptations, and innovation in contract law to embrace data economy are certainly welcomed and commendable. But the soundness and sustainability of a data sharing market strongly depends upon the coherence and solidity of the underlying contract-law infrastructure.

31 CISG-AC Opinion No. 1, Electronic Communications under CISG, 15 August 2003, Rapporteur: Professor Christina Ramberg, Gothenburg, Sweden.

32 CISG-AC Opinion No. 21, Delivery of Substitute Goods and Repair under the CISG, Rapporteurs: Professor (em.) Dr. Ingeborg Schwenzer, LL.M., University of Basel, Switzerland, and Dr. Ilka H. Beimel, Germany. Adopted unanimously by the CISG Advisory Council following its 27th meeting in Puerto Vallarta, Mexico, on 3 and 4 February 2020.

A Fair Share? – Data Contracts and Unfair Terms Control

Moritz Hennemann

I. Introduction: The 'Contractualisation' of EU Data Law

Data Law is heavily driven by Contract Law instruments.[1] The new framework for data exchanges, data access, and data use established by the Data Act (DA) and the Data Governance Act (DGA) relies in various ways on contractual settings and contractual interventions to the benefit of (potentially) weaker parties.[2] Contracts have formed in the past[3] and will form in future the coordinating infrastructure of the data economy.[4]

The *contract bias* of the Data Act is underlined – besides Open Data-scenarios – by the fact that the relevant actors are typically linked by and

1 Moritz Hennemann/Björn Steinrötter, Der Data Act – Neue Instrumente, alte Friktionen, strukturelle Weichenstellungen, Neue Juristische Wochenschrift (NJW) 2024, 1 (6 et seq.); Sebastian Omlor, Unfair Contractual Terms under the Data Act, ERPL 2024, 173 (175); Dirk Staudenmayer, Der Verordnungsvorschlag der Europäischen Kommission zum Datengesetz – Auf dem Weg zum Privatrecht der Datenwirtschaft, Zeitschrift für Europäisches Wirtschaftsrecht (EuZW) 2022, 596 (596 et seq.). Cf. the negotiations on data provision contracts on the international level at UNCITRAL, Report of the Working Group IV (Electronic Commerce) on the work of its sixty-fifth session (New York, 10–14 April 2023), A/CN.9/1132, pp. 3 et seq.; UNCITRAL, Report of the Working Group IV (Electronic Commerce) on the work of its sixty-sixth session (Vienna, 16–20 October 2023), A/CN.9/1162, pp. 10 et seq.; UNCITRAL, Working Group IV (Electronic Commerce) Sixty-sixth session, Vienna, 16–20 October 2023, Default rules for data provision contracts (first revision), A/CN.9/WG.IV/WP.183, p. 12.

2 Rec. 5 reads: "Private law rules are key in the overall framework for data sharing. Therefore, [the Data Act] adapts rules of contract law and prevents the exploitation of contractual imbalances that hinder fair access to and use of data."

3 Cf. for the general contract law framework for data contracts Moritz Hennemann, Datenlizenzverträge, Recht Digital (RDi) 2021, 61; for empirical evidence, also on the existing challenges, see Martin Fries/Marc Scheufen, Vertragsgestaltung beim Data Sharing – Empirie und Best Practice, RDi 2023, 419.

4 Moritz Hennemann/Björn Steinrötter, Der Data Act – Neue Instrumente, alte Friktionen, strukturelle Weichenstellungen, NJW 2024, 1 (6 et seq.); Friedrich Graf von Westphalen, Das Datengesetz und seine umfassende AGB-Kontrolle für KMUs, EuZW 2023, 1121 (1122). See also Axel Metzger/Heike Schweitzer, Shaping Markets: A Criticial Evaluation of the Draft Data Act, Zeitschrift für Europäisches Privatrecht (ZEuP) 2023, 42 (62 et seq.).

steer their relationship by contractual means.[5] Users (Art. 2 no. 12 DA) buy, rent and lease IoT-products. Users conclude, if non-personal data is at stake, data use agreements according to Art. 4 para. 13 DA. Users may seek data exchanges and may initiate data access to the benefit of the third-party data recipient (Art. 2 no. 14 DA) via Art. 5 DA. The respective relationships[6] are effectuated by data contracts. To complicate the picture, it is important to bear in mind that the aforementioned contracts might be arranged via further parties, especially data intermediation services (Art. 2 no. 11, Art. 10 et seq. DGA) offer respective platform services. Recipients of data may also be data altruism organisation – and the process of a 'data donation' might also be framed contractually.[7] Finally, parties might agree on data access and data use on a voluntary basis and independently of the Art. 4 and 5 DA scenarios.

Rights and duties within respective contracts are potentially heavily intertwined (cf. e.g., in the case of Art. 5 para. 9 DA). In parts, contracts might be legally or *de facto* linked and / or dependent on each other. The Data Act presumes and creates contractual networks[8] that are not easy to handle – also as they do not typically fit neatly into traditional contract law doctrine.

II. Seeking Fairness: The Unfair Terms Control by Art. 13 Data Act

Fairness within these diverging contractual relationships is a central policy goal of the EU. Rec. 2 DA underlines that "[b]arriers to data sharing prevent an optimal allocation of data for the benefit of society. Those barriers include (...) the abuse of contractual imbalances with regard to data access

5 In detail Dirk Staudenmayer, Der Verordnungsvorschlag der Europäischen Kommission zum Datengesetz – Auf dem Weg zum Privatrecht der Datenwirtschaft, EuZW 2022, 596 (596 et seq.); Axel Metzger/Heike Schweitzer, Shaping Markets: A Criticial Evaluation of the Draft Data Act, ZEuP 2023, 42 (62 et seq.).

6 Between the user and the third party as well as the third party and the data holder (Art. 2 no. 13 DA).

7 Moritz Hennemann, in: Louisa Specht-Riemenschneider/Moritz Hennemann, Data Governance Act – Handkommentar, 2023, Art. 21 mn. 6 et seq. as well as Art. 25 mn. 4 et seq. and 34 et seq.

8 See Martin Schmidt-Kessel/David Bomhard, EU-Datengesetz ante portas, MMR 2024, 69 (70) and Andreas Wiebe, Der Data Act – Innovation oder Illusion?, GRUR 2023, 1569 (1570);Moritz Hennemann/Björn Steinrötter, Der Data Act – Neue Instrumente, alte Friktionen, strukturelle Weichenstellungen, NJW 2024, 1 (7); Andreas Wiebe, Der Data Act als vertragsrechtlicher Rahmen für Datennutzungsverträge – Anwendungsbereich und Vorgaben der Missbrauchskontrolle nach Art. 13 Data Act-E, CR 2023, 777 (782).

and use." The EU legislator tackles these imbalances with a new unfair terms control for data contracts.[9] The mandatory[10] Art. 13 DA provides the respective provisions for b2b-scenarios – irrespective of the fact whether non-personal or personal data is at stake. Unilaterally imposed terms must stand an (un)fairness test against "good commercial practice (...) contrary to good faith and fair dealing", but not against trade practices.[11] To this end, Art. 13 DA is drafted as a sharp sword. Unfair terms are qualified as

9 See in general on Data Act and unfair terms control Lukas Beinke/Ingvar Daute, Der Fairnesstest des Data Act – Verdrängung der nationalen Klauselkontrolle?, RDi 2024, 69; Friedrich Graf von Westphalen, Das Datengesetz und seine umfassende AGB-Kontrolle für KMUs, EuZW 2023, 1121; Friedrich Graf von Westphalen, Der neue Data Act – Eine Kaskade AGB-rechtlicher Verbote im unternehmerischen Verkehr, BB 2024, 515; Sebastian Omlor, Unfair Contractual Terms under the Data Act, ERPL 2024, 173; Sebastian Schwamberger, Die Klauselkontrolle in Art. 13 Data Act – Erste Analyse zu Anwendungsbereich, Missbräuchlichkeit und Durchsetzung, MMR 2024, 96; Dirk Staudenmayer, Der Verordnungsvorschlag der Europäischen Kommission zum Datengesetz – Auf dem Weg zum Privatrecht der Datenwirtschaft, EuZW 2022, 596; Andreas Wiebe, Der Data Act als vertragsrechtlicher Rahmen für Datennutzungsverträge – Anwendungsbereich und Vorgaben der Missbrauchskontrolle nach Art. 13 Data Act-E, CR 2023, 777; as well as Matthias Leistner/Lucie Antoine, IPR and the use of open data and data sharing initiatives by public and private actors, 2022, pp. 105 et seq.; ELI [John Thomas et al.], Public Consultation on the Data Act, pp. 25 et seq., https://www.europeanlawinstitute.eu/fileadmin/user_upload/p_eli/Projects/Data_Economy/ELI_Response_Public_Consultation_on_a_Data_Act.pdf. More generally, Florian Möslein, Digitized Terms: The Regulation of Standard Contract Terms in the Digital Age, European Review of Contract Law (Eur. Rev. Contract Law) 2023, 300.

10 Cf. Art. 13 para. 9 DA as well as Sebastian Omlor, Unfair Contractual Terms under the Data Act, ERPL 2024, 173 (178); Dirk Staudenmayer, Der Verordnungsvorschlag der Europäischen Kommission zum Datengesetz – Auf dem Weg zum Privatrecht der Datenwirtschaft, EuZW 2022, 596 (602). Furthermore, Art. 8 para. 2 DA – non-waivable to the detriment of the user according to Art. 12 para. 2 DA – also stipulates: "A contractual term concerning access to and the use of data, or liability and remedies for the breach or termination of data-related obligations, shall not be binding if it constitutes an unfair contractual term within the meaning of Article 13 (...)." Cf. also Andreas Wiebe, Der Data Act als vertragsrechtlicher Rahmen für Datennutzungsverträge – Anwendungsbereich und Vorgaben der Missbrauchskontrolle nach Art. 13 Data Act-E, CR 2023, 777 (784 et seq.).

11 Sebastian Schwamberger, Die Klauselkontrolle in Art. 13 Data Act – Erste Analyse zu Anwendungsbereich, Missbräuchlichkeit und Durchsetzung, Multimedia und Recht (MMR) 2024, 96 (96); Sebastian Schwamberger, in: David Bomhard/Martin Schmidt-Kessel (eds.), EU Data Act, 2024, Art. 13 [p. 11, 17] (forthcoming). The need to include trade practices is underlined by ELI [John Thomas et al.], Public Consultation on the Data Act, p. 26, https://www.europeanlawinstitute.eu/fileadmin/user_upload/p_eli/Projects/Data_Economy/ELI_Response_Public_Consultation_on_a_Data_Act.pdf.

non-binding (Art. 13 para. 1 DA)[12], are therefore directly void (*ex tunc*) and not only voidable by declaration.[13] Art. 13 DA thereby also underlines the fact that the Data Act is not only gaining ground by *public enforcement*, but has included a *private enforcement* layer.[14] Rec. 58 DA highlights the rationale of the Data Act's approach[15]:

> "Where one party is in a stronger bargaining position, there is a risk that that party could leverage such a position to the detriment of the other contracting party when negotiating access to data with the result that access to data is commercially less viable and sometimes economically prohibitive. Such contractual imbalances harm all enterprises without a meaningful ability to negotiate the conditions for access to data, and which may have no choice but to accept take-it-or-leave-it contractual terms."

In difference to b2c-settings, an information deficit of one party or a market failure with respect to transparent terms is not the central concern of the Data Act for b2b-settings.[16] Rather, the economic power of one party –

---

12 Cf. furthermore Art. 13 para. 7 DA according to which terms severable from the unfair terms shall remain binding; in detail – also with regard to a potential gap-filling – Sebastian Omlor, Unfair Contractual Terms under the Data Act, ERPL 2024, 173 (189 et seq.).

13 See Dirk Staudenmayer, Der Verordnungsvorschlag der Europäischen Kommission zum Datengesetz – Auf dem Weg zum Privatrecht der Datenwirtschaft, EuZW 2022, 596 (601); Andreas Wiebe, Der Data Act als vertragsrechtlicher Rahmen für Datennutzungsverträge – Anwendungsbereich und Vorgaben der Missbrauchskontrolle nach Art. 13 Data Act-E, CR 2023, 777 (783). Differently, Sebastian Schwamberger, in: David Bomhard/Martin Schmidt-Kessel (eds.), EU Data Act, 2024, Art. 13 [p. 64] (forthcoming) arguing in favour of voidability. Cf. also Sebastian Omlor, Unfair Contractual Terms under the Data Act, ERPL 2024, 173 (189).

14 For a detailed discussion see Sebastian Schwamberger, Die Klauselkontrolle in Art. 13 Data Act – Erste Analyse zu Anwendungsbereich, Missbräuchlichkeit und Durchsetzung, MMR 2024, 96 (99 et seq.); Sebastian Schwamberger, in: David Bomhard/Martin Schmidt-Kessel (eds.), EU Data Act, 2024, Art. 13 [pp. 61 et seq.] (forthcoming); Andreas Wiebe, Der Data Act als vertragsrechtlicher Rahmen für Datennutzungsverträge – Anwendungsbereich und Vorgaben der Missbrauchskontrolle nach Art. 13 Data Act-E, CR 2023, 777 (784).

15 Cf. also Andreas Wiebe, Der Data Act als vertragsrechtlicher Rahmen für Datennutzungsverträge – Anwendungsbereich und Vorgaben der Missbrauchskontrolle nach Art. 13 Data Act-E, CR 2023, 777 (779).

16 Cf. Sebastian Schwamberger, in: David Bomhard/Martin Schmidt-Kessel (eds.), EU Data Act, 2024, Art. 13 [p. 10] (forthcoming). The information duty of Art. 3 para. 2 Data Act covers this dimension.

leaving the other party no real options to negotiate – shall be countered.[17] Despite the open wording of rec. 58, the Data Act does not seek to regulate prices or adequate counter-performances for a specific data set, for data access and / or data use. Rec. 59 underlines "the principle of contractual freedom as an essential concept in business-to-business relationships" respectively.

Art. 13 para. 8 DA makes clear that the unfair terms control does not cover terms defining the main subject matter of the contract, the adequacy of the price for the data supplied in exchange.[18] Especially with regard to immaterial goods, it is not always easy to make a distinction between terms covering the main subject matter and other terms.[19]

In line with existing approaches of unfair terms control, only the further 'conditions' for data access and use are at stake. The unfair terms control thereby tries to contribute to 'fair' relationships between the actors on the markets, but without eliminating negotiations at arm's length, competitive pressure, or even a market-based approach. The Data Act explicitly and rightly acknowledges that 'fair' in this context is not to be equalled with "fully balanced". Rec. 61 stipulates:

> "The vast majority of contractual terms that are commercially more favourable to one party than to the other (…) are a normal expression of the principle of contractual freedom and continue to apply."

Indirectly, the Data Act shall also create trust in data contracting by offering a protective layer for all market participants faced with take-it-or-leave-it terms. Thereby, the unfair terms control shall boost not only data sharing practices in general, but also the actual use of the new access instruments provided by the Data Act in particular. "[A]n optimal allocation of data for the benefit of society" (rec. 2) is envisioned.[20] To effectuate a respective

17 Sebastian Schwamberger, in: David Bomhard/Martin Schmidt-Kessel (eds.), EU Data Act, 2024, Art. 13 [pp. 10, 40] (forthcoming).

18 See also Sebastian Schwamberger, in: David Bomhard/Martin Schmidt-Kessel (eds.), EU Data Act, 2024, Art. 13 [p. 61] (forthcoming); Dirk Staudenmayer, Der Verordnungsvorschlag der Europäischen Kommission zum Datengesetz – Auf dem Weg zum Privatrecht der Datenwirtschaft, EuZW 2022, 596 (601). One has, however, also to bear in mind Art. 8 and 9 DA, cf. Dirk Staudenmayer ibid.

19 See Moritz Hennemann, Datenlizenzverträge, RDi 2021, 61 (65) with further references.

20 Cf. also Sebastian Schwamberger, in: David Bomhard/Martin Schmidt-Kessel (eds.), EU Data Act, 2024, Art. 13 [p. 10] (forthcoming).

'fair' contracting, the model contract terms developed on the basis of Art. 41 DA will be of further and focal assistance (cf. also rec. 62).[21]

III. The Entry Gates: Structure and Scope of Art. 13 Data Act

1. b2b-Settings

The unfair terms control of Art. 13 DA does only apply in b2b-settings ("by an enterprise on another enterprise"[22]).[23] The EU legislator thereby enlarges the unfair terms control to a field that is at least traditionally seen as alien to a standard term control. This is not to say that standard term control has not already some anchors also in EU law[24] (and is also established in some of the member states[25]). With regard to b2c-settings, the EU legislator assumes that consumers are adequately protected by the Unfair Terms Directive 93/13/EEC[26] and the respective national laws. Rec. 28 reads:

> "In contracts between a data holder and a consumer as user of a connected product or related service generating data, Union consumer law, in particular [directive] 93/13/EEC (...) applies to ensure that a consumer is not subject to unfair contractual terms."

21 See also Sebastian Schwamberger, in: David Bomhard/Martin Schmidt-Kessel (eds.), EU Data Act, 2024, Art. 13 [pp. 37 et seq.] (forthcoming); Friedrich Graf von Westphalen, Der neue Data Act – Eine Kaskade AGB-rechtlicher Verbote im unternehmerischen Verkehr, BB 2024, 515 (516); Andreas Wiebe, Der Data Act als vertragsrechtlicher Rahmen für Datennutzungsverträge – Anwendungsbereich und Vorgaben der Missbrauchskontrolle nach Art. 13 Data Act-E, CR 2023, 777 (785 et seq.).

22 See for the definition(s) of enterprises in this respect Sebastian Schwamberger, in: David Bomhard/Martin Schmidt-Kessel (eds.), EU Data Act, 2024, Art. 13 [p. 16] (forthcoming).

23 Favouring a focus on b2b-contracts UNCITRAL, Report of the Working Group IV (Electronic Commerce) on the work of its sixty-fifth session (New York, 10–14 April 2023), A/CN.9/1132, p. 5. Rather critical e.g., Matthias Leistner/Lucie Antoine, IPR and the use of open data and data sharing initiatives by public and private actors, 2022, pp. 105 et seq.

24 Cf. Dirk Staudenmayer, Der Verordnungsvorschlag der Europäischen Kommission zum Datengesetz – Auf dem Weg zum Privatrecht der Datenwirtschaft, EuZW 2022, 596 (597 et seq.) as well as Sebastian Schwamberger, in: David Bomhard/Martin Schmidt-Kessel (eds.), EU Data Act, 2024, Art. 13 [p. 11] (forthcoming) in this regard.

25 Cf. Andreas Wiebe, Der Data Act als vertragsrechtlicher Rahmen für Datennutzungsverträge – Anwendungsbereich und Vorgaben der Missbrauchskontrolle nach Art. 13 Data Act-E, CR 2023, 777 (779) with further references.

26 Cf. also Art. 1 para. 9 DA.

The implication of an existing net of protection is not in any way convincing.[27] Where it is true that the general criteria of national unfair terms control (such as the general clause of § 307 para. 1 and 2 German Civil Code) might be broad enough to deal with data contracts in b2c-settings.[28] It must be borne in mind that the Directive 93/13/EEC as well as national law (at least so far) do typically not include data-specific provisions, parameters or classifications via 'black' or 'grey' lists.[29] At least until substantial case law has been handed down by courts, the reference to national unfair terms control therefore goes along with substantial legal uncertainties and a huge interpretational corridor. This legislative 'gap' is partially mitigated by the fact that, in future, Art. 13 DA might serve as an indicator of fairness (standards) also in b2c-settings.[30] The different goals pursued and thresholds set by Art. 13 DA compared to consumer contracts must, however, be borne in mind when interpreting respective national standards.

2. Contractual Scenarios Covered

In substance, Art. 13 DA does not exactly define the data contracts it is targeted at.[31] Para. 1 only refers to "contractual term[s] concerning access to and the use of data or liability and remedies for the breach or the

27 Cf. for demands to amend the Data Act respectively Louisa Specht-Riemenschneider in this volume.

28 See also Moritz Hennemann, Datenlizenzverträge, RDi 2021, 61 in this regard.

29 Cf. Lukas Beinke/Ingvar Daute, Der Fairnesstest des Data Act – Verdrängung der nationalen Klauselkontrolle?, RDi 2024, 69 (70).

30 Cf. in this regard Lukas Beinke/Ingvar Daute, Der Fairnesstest des Data Act – Verdrängung der nationalen Klauselkontrolle?, RDi 2024, 69 (71); Sebastian Omlor, Unfair Contractual Terms under the Data Act, ERPL 2024, 173 (177) (correctly pointing to the fact that this does – *inter alia* – not include the standard of Art. 13 para. 6 DA); Andreas Wiebe, Der Data Act als vertragsrechtlicher Rahmen für Datennutzungsverträge – Anwendungsbereich und Vorgaben der Missbrauchskontrolle nach Art. 13 Data Act-E, CR 2023, 777 (786).

31 In detail on data access and data use in this context Sebastian Schwamberger, in: David Bomhard/Martin Schmidt-Kessel (eds.), EU Data Act, 2024, Art. 13 [pp. 17 et seq.] (forthcoming). For the discussion on the applicability of Art. 13 DA in the context of Art. 25 DA see Carlo Piltz/Johannes Zwerschke, Cloud Switching nach dem Data Act aus der Beratungsperspektive – Zentrale Herausforderungen für die vertragliche Ausgestaltung hindernisfreier Wechsel zwischen Datenverarbeitungsdiensten, Computer und Recht (CR) 2024, 153 (156) and Gregor Lienemann, in: Moritz Hennemann et al. (eds.), Data Act, 2024 (forthcoming).

termination of data related obligations".[32] The scope is therefore potentially vast.[33]

First and foremost, Art. 13 DA covers the – often intertwined and potentially interdependent – contractual relationships in the data access-context of Art. 4 DA (including the data use agreement according to Art. 4 para. 13 DA[34]) and in the data portability-context of Art. 5 DA (user-data holder, data-holder-third party, user-third party).[35] With regard to the latter, however, also Art. 8, 9, and 11 DA need to be factored in.[36] Second, Art. 1 para. 3 lit. c DA adds that Art. 13 DA "applies to any private sector data accessed and used on the basis of contract between enterprises". Public actors are therefore not covered by Art. 13 DA.[37] Third, it is, however, not explicitly specified whether Art. 13 DA only applies to contracts where data

32 According to Art. 50 DA, Art. 13 DA applies to contracts concluded after 12.09.2025. It shall apply from 12.09.2027 to contracts concluded on or before 12.09.2025 if the contract is of indefinite duration and is due to expire at least 10 years from 11.01.2024.

33 Cf. similar discussions on the international level UNCITRAL, Report of the Working Group IV (Electronic Commerce) on the work of its sixty-fifth session (New York, 10–14 April 2023), A/CN.9/1132, pp. 4 et seq.: "It was observed that the working definitions of ["data" and "data provision contract"] were broad and that, as a result, the types of contracts covered by the default rules would be vast, potentially encompassing contracts for the supply of digital content and digital services, contracts for the transfer of digital assets, and contracts involving some information sharing. (...) Support was expressed for the view that, rather than finetune the definitions in abstract, the Working Group should proceed by reference to the types of transactions taking place in practice, as well as the types of obligations to which those transactions gave rise. In that regard, it was observed that the parties were interested in data for the information that it represented, which was typified by transactions in "big data". Broad support was expressed for excluding from scope "functional data" such as software, "representative data" such as digital assets, and other types of data such as the result of trust services. (...) It was also observed that data was transacted in ways other than the simple transfer of data between two parties. In that regard, it was pointed out that the ALI/ELI Principles distinguished several different types of data provision contracts, for which different obligations were identified, and addressed the involvement of third-party intermediaries. Some support was expressed for including data pooling contracts and contracts with data intermediaries within the scope of work."

34 In detail Sebastian Schwamberger, in: David Bomhard/Martin Schmidt-Kessel (eds.), EU Data Act, 2024, Art. 13 [p. 22] (forthcoming).

35 Sebastian Schwamberger, in: David Bomhard/Martin Schmidt-Kessel (eds.), EU Data Act, 2024, Art. 13 [pp. 31 et seq.] (forthcoming).

36 Sebastian Schwamberger, in: David Bomhard/Martin Schmidt-Kessel (eds.), EU Data Act, 2024, Art. 13 [pp. 23 et seq.] (forthcoming).

37 Sebastian Schwamberger, in: David Bomhard/Martin Schmidt-Kessel (eds.), EU Data Act, 2024, Art. 13 [p. 16] (forthcoming).

access or data use is the main subject matter of the contract – opening the interpretational possibility that Art. 13 DA establishes a control regime for data access and data use terms in any type of contract (e. g. a sale of land property where some additional data about the building is provided to the buyer). Rec. 60 seems to support such a broad understanding:

> "[T]he rules (...) should apply only to those elements of a contract that are related to making data available, that is contractual terms concerning access to and use of the data as well as liability or remedies for breach and termination of data related obligations. Other parts of the same contract, unrelated to making data available, should not be subject to the unfairness test (...)."

Two factors speak to the opposite.[38] First, the Data Act is apparently targeted at data and data exchanges – as underlined by Art. 1 para. 1 DA. Second and even more significant, Art. 13 para. 8 DA implicitly underlines that only contractual settings of some data exchange are within the scope of Art. 13 DA when it refers "to the adequacy of the price, as against the data supplied in exchange". Consequently, only those contracts fall into the scope of Art. 13 DA where a data exchange – may it be the main subject or an ancillary performance – constitutes a stand-alone, often negotiated or priced separately, element of the subject (e. g. in the context of the sale of an IoT-product, which may, of course, also be a smart building / immovable property).[39]

Finally, Art. 13 DA does not only cover data contracts in the context of Art. 4 and 5 DA scenarios, but applies also to other data contracts (e. g. a data sharing agreement between the user and another party).[40]

---

38 Cf. also the proposal of Art. 2 para. 3 of the default rules for data provision contracts by UNCITRAL, Working Group IV (Electronic Commerce) Sixty-sixth session, Vienna, 16–20 October 2023, Default rules for data provision contracts (first revision), A/CN.9/WG.IV/WP.183, p. 4: "These rules do not apply to contracts in which the preponderant part of the obligations of the data provider consists in the supply of services with respect to the data;"; the paragraph is critically examined, cf. UNCITRAL, Report of the Working Group IV (Electronic Commerce) on the work of its sixty-sixth session (Vienna, 16–20 October 2023), A/CN.9/1162, p. 12.

39 Sebastian Schwamberger, in: David Bomhard/Martin Schmidt-Kessel (eds.), EU Data Act, 2024, Art. 13 [p. 20] (forthcoming).

40 Axel Metzger/Heike Schweitzer, Shaping Markets: A Criticial Evaluation of the Draft Data Act, ZEuP 2023, 42 (63); Lukas Beinke/Ingvar Daute, Der Fairnesstest des Data Act – Verdrängung der nationalen Klauselkontrolle?, RDi 2024, 69 (70); Sebastian Omlor, Unfair Contractual Terms under the Data Act, ERPL 2024, 173 (179); Andreas Wiebe, Der Data Act als vertragsrechtlicher Rahmen für Datennutzungsverträge –

3. Unilaterally Imposed

Art. 13 DA only applies to contractual terms that are *unilaterally imposed*.[41] According to Art. 13 para. 6 sent. 1 DA a term is "unilaterally imposed (...) if it has been supplied by one contracting party and the other contracting party has not been able to influence its content despite an attempt to negotiate it."[42] Art. 13 DA is focussed on take-it-or-leave-it-scenarios.[43] Rec. 59 adds that "[a] term (...) simply provided by one party and accepted by the other" or "a term (...) negotiated and subsequently agreed in an amended form" are not unilaterally imposed.[44] Whereas the latter scenario is rather straightforward, the first one has risen several doubts.[45] What constitutes an 'acceptance'?[46] What constitutes an 'attempt to negotiate'?[47] It is clear from the context that an 'attempt' refers to an actual action of the other party. A standard term stating that any clause is not unilaterally imposed is no way out.[48] But a mere acceptance of the contract by the other party

Anwendungsbereich und Vorgaben der Missbrauchskontrolle nach Art. 13 Data Act-E, CR 2023, 777 (779).

41 Sebastian Schwamberger, Die Klauselkontrolle in Art. 13 Data Act – Erste Analyse zu Anwendungsbereich, Missbräuchlichkeit und Durchsetzung, MMR 2024, 96 (97 et seq.).

42 Art. 13 para. 6 sent. 2 and 3 DA further stipulates that „[t]he contracting party that supplied the contractual term bears the burden of proving that that term has not been unilaterally imposed" and that "[t]he contracting party that supplied the contested contractual term may not argue that the term is an unfair contractual term."; in detail Sebastian Omlor, Unfair Contractual Terms under the Data Act, ERPL 2024, 173 (181).

43 Sebastian Omlor, Unfair Contractual Terms under the Data Act, ERPL 2024, 173 (180).

44 Cf. also – with reference to the case law of the German Federal Court of Justice – Friedrich Graf von Westphalen, Das Datengesetz und seine umfassende AGB-Kontrolle für KMUs, EuZW 2023, 1121 (1123 et seq.).

45 Cf. e.g. Moritz Hennemann/Björn Steinrötter, Der Data Act – Neue Instrumente, alte Friktionen, strukturelle Weichenstellungen, NJW 2024, 1 (4).

46 Cf. Friedrich Graf von Westphalen, Der neue Data Act – Eine Kaskade AGB-rechtlicher Verbote im unternehmerischen Verkehr, BB 2024, 515 (517) as well as Andreas Wiebe, Der Data Act als vertragsrechtlicher Rahmen für Datennutzungsverträge – Anwendungsbereich und Vorgaben der Missbrauchskontrolle nach Art. 13 Data Act-E, CR 2023, 777 (780) in this regard.

47 In detail Sebastian Schwamberger, in: David Bomhard/Martin Schmidt-Kessel (eds.), EU Data Act, 2024, Art. 13 [pp. 52 et seq.] (forthcoming).

48 Dirk Staudenmayer, Der Verordnungsvorschlag der Europäischen Kommission zum Datengesetz – Auf dem Weg zum Privatrecht der Datenwirtschaft, EuZW 2022, 596 (600).

without objection (eg by just pushing a respective online-button) is not sufficient to come into the scope.[49] However, will the other party simply start mock negotiations to come into the scope?[50] Is it not often the case that a (weaker) party might not see a realistic chance to change the terms and just sign?[51] Potentially yes. Framed positively, however, Art. 13 DA sets an incentive for parties with a lower bargaining power to engage with the contractual terms, to evaluate the commercial relevance of the conditions, and seek to determine the data implications at stake.[52]

IV. Unfairness: The Parameters of Art. 13 para. 3 to 5 Data Act

The unfairness of a term is the central factor of Art. 13 DA.[53] Terms, however, "[reflecting] mandatory provisions of Union law, or provisions of Union law which would apply if the contractual terms did not regulate the matter, shall not be considered to be unfair" according to Art. 13 para. 2 DA.[54] On the opposite, terms reflecting national law are covered[55], but an unfairness seems to be rather unlikely in most of the cases.

According to the general clause of Art. 13 para. 3 DA a term is unfair "if it is of such a nature that its use grossly deviates from good commercial practice in data access and use, contrary to good faith and fair dealing."[56]

49 Sebastian Omlor, Unfair Contractual Terms under the Data Act, ERPL 2024, 173 (180).

50 Cf. Sebastian Omlor, Unfair Contractual Terms under the Data Act, ERPL 2024, 173 (180 et seq.); Sebastian Schwamberger, in: David Bomhard/Martin Schmidt-Kessel (eds.), EU Data Act, 2024, Art. 13 [p. 54] (forthcoming); Andreas Wiebe, Der Data Act als vertragsrechtlicher Rahmen für Datennutzungsverträge – Anwendungsbereich und Vorgaben der Missbrauchskontrolle nach Art. 13 Data Act-E, CR 2023, 777 (780).

51 Cf. also Sebastian Omlor, Unfair Contractual Terms under the Data Act, ERPL 2024, 173 (181).

52 Cf. also Friedrich Graf von Westphalen, Der neue Data Act – Eine Kaskade AGB-rechtlicher Verbote im unternehmerischen Verkehr, BB 2024, 515 (517) underlining that the burden of an 'initiative' is on the other party.

53 In detail Sebastian Schwamberger, Die Klauselkontrolle in Art. 13 Data Act – Erste Analyse zu Anwendungsbereich, Missbräuchlichkeit und Durchsetzung, MMR 2024, 96 (98 et seq.).

54 In detail Sebastian Omlor, Unfair Contractual Terms under the Data Act, ERPL 2024, 173 (183).

55 Sebastian Schwamberger, in: David Bomhard/Martin Schmidt-Kessel (eds.), EU Data Act, 2024, Art. 13 [p. 29] (forthcoming).

56 Deviating from other frameworks, Art. 13 DA does not consider non-transparent terms to be non-binding, see Sebastian Omlor, Unfair Contractual Terms under the

The material threshold of Art. 13 DA is therefore rather narrow. Art. 13 DA has rightly be classified as "ultima ration approach"[57]. Rec. 61 points to "excessive contractual terms where a stronger bargaining position has been abused" and underlines that "grossly deviating from good commercial practice would include, *inter alia*, objectively impairing the ability of the party upon whom the term has been unilaterally imposed to protect its legitimate commercial interest in the data in question." To define 'good commercial practice', however, is far from easy. Existing data access rights in sector-specific regimes might give a first indication.[58] The challenge remains that not only a general 'good commercial practice' does not seem to exist so far, but in many cases not even a commercial practice at all (as mandatory access rights have not been the standard so far).[59] If such a practice exists (or will be boosted by the Data Act), it shall not be overlooked that the respective practice might not necessarily be 'good', especially if only a minor number of actors shapes this practice.[60]

Data Act, ERPL 2024, 173 (185); Sebastian Schwamberger, Die Klauselkontrolle in Art. 13 Data Act – Erste Analyse zu Anwendungsbereich, Missbräuchlichkeit und Durchsetzung, MMR 2024, 96 (96). The Data Act unfair terms control regime does not explicitly mention transparency, cf. also Sebastian Schwamberger, in: David Bomhard/Martin Schmidt-Kessel (eds.), EU Data Act, 2024, Art. 13 [pp. 11, 60] (forthcoming); Andreas Wiebe, Der Data Act als vertragsrechtlicher Rahmen für Datennutzungsverträge – Anwendungsbereich und Vorgaben der Missbrauchskontrolle nach Art. 13 Data Act-E, CR 2023, 777 (783). However, rec. 25 – in the context of Art. 3 para. 2 DA – seems to indicate that transparency is factored in to some extent.

57 Sebastian Omlor, Unfair Contractual Terms under the Data Act, ERPL 2024, 173 (185, 188).

58 Sebastian Schwamberger, in: David Bomhard/Martin Schmidt-Kessel (eds.), EU Data Act, 2024, Art. 13 [p. 33] (forthcoming).

59 Andreas Wiebe, Der Data Act als vertragsrechtlicher Rahmen für Datennutzungsverträge – Anwendungsbereich und Vorgaben der Missbrauchskontrolle nach Art. 13 Data Act-E, CR 2023, 777 (782).

60 Dirk Staudenmayer, Der Verordnungsvorschlag der Europäischen Kommission zum Datengesetz – Auf dem Weg zum Privatrecht der Datenwirtschaft, EuZW 2022, 596 (599); Sebastian Schwamberger, in: David Bomhard/Martin Schmidt-Kessel (eds.), EU Data Act, 2024, Art. 13 [p. 30] (forthcoming); Andreas Wiebe, Der Data Act als vertragsrechtlicher Rahmen für Datennutzungsverträge – Anwendungsbereich und Vorgaben der Missbrauchskontrolle nach Art. 13 Data Act-E, CR 2023, 777 (782).

1. Potential Fairness Dimensions in Data Contracts

Fairness is a multi-faceted factor. What constitutes a *fair* term in the context of data access and data use? 'Data contracts' refers to different settings as they are of relevance for various forms of individual, common, and collective data access and use.[61] Typically, data contracts include elements of data definition, use, and transfer conditions as well as liability aspects[62], but are not based on an established type of contract. So far, the legislator has not defined central obligations, legitimate interests, intertwined fairness aspects, or a standard blueprint balancing interests at stake (*Leitbild*).[63] As data will not always involve trade secrets and is not generally protected by IP rights, parameters of Trade Secret Law and IP Law can only be applied with great caution.[64] Although the ALI-ELI Principles for the Data Economy[65] and the UNCITRAL work with respect to data provisions con-

61 Cf. on different types ALI-ELI Principles For A Data Economy – Data Transactions and Data Rights (2021), https://www.principlesforadataeconomy.org/fileadmin/user_upload/p_principlesforadataeconomy/Files/Principles_for_a_Data_Economy_ELI_Final_Council_Draft.pdf. Cf. also UNCITRAL, Report of the Working Group IV (Electronic Commerce) on the work of its sixty-fifth session (New York, 10–14 April 2023), A/CN.9/1132, pp. 3 et seq. as well as UNCITRAL, Report of the Working Group IV (Electronic Commerce) on the work of its sixty-sixth session (Vienna, 16–20 October 2023), A/CN.9/1162, pp. 10 et seq.

62 Cf. Martin Fries/Marc Scheufen, Vertragsgestaltung beim Data Sharing – Empirie und Best Practice, RDi 2023, 419 (422 et seq.).

63 Moritz Hennemann, Datenlizenzverträge, RDi 2021, 61 (65). See also Sebastian Schwamberger, in: David Bomhard/Martin Schmidt-Kessel (eds.), EU Data Act, 2024, Art. 13 [p. 34] (forthcoming); Lukas Beinke/Ingvar Daute, Der Fairnesstest des Data Act – Verdrängung der nationalen Klauselkontrolle?, RDi 2024, 69 (70). Cf. also Andreas Wiebe, Der Data Act als vertragsrechtlicher Rahmen für Datennutzungsverträge – Anwendungsbereich und Vorgaben der Missbrauchskontrolle nach Art. 13 Data Act-E, CR 2023, 777 (779, 781).

64 See Andreas Wiebe, Der Data Act als vertragsrechtlicher Rahmen für Datennutzungsverträge – Anwendungsbereich und Vorgaben der Missbrauchskontrolle nach Art. 13 Data Act-E, CR 2023, 777 (782).

65 ALI-ELI Principles For A Data Economy – Data Transactions and Data Rights (2021), https://www.principlesforadataeconomy.org/fileadmin/user_upload/p_principlesforadataeconomy/Files/Principles_for_a_Data_Economy_ELI_Final_Council_Draft.pdf.

tracts[66] provide first and substantial assistance in this regard, these soft law instruments remain – naturally – non-binding indications.[67]

What could be potential fairness dimensions of data access and data use against these diverse backgrounds?[68] From the outset, *fairness* might be linked to the subject matter of the contract, the actual data set or data categories at stake. *Fairness* could be understood as referring to *data quality* and / or *data conformity*.[69] In the ongoing UNICITRAL negotiations "origin (authenticity), completeness, accuracy[,] (...) timeliness[,] (...) traceability[,] (...) fitness for purpose (...), data format and structure, and the availability of updates"[70] as well as quantity[71] are mentioned.[72] One has,

66 UNCITRAL, Report of the Working Group IV (Electronic Commerce) on the work of its sixty-fifth session (New York, 10–14 April 2023), A/CN.9/1132, pp. 3 et seq.; UNCITRAL, Working Group IV (Electronic Commerce), Sixty-fifth session, New York, 10–14 April 2023, Default rules for data provision contracts, A/CN.9/WG.IV/WP.180; UNCITRAL, Report of the Working Group IV (Electronic Commerce) on the work of its sixty-sixth session (Vienna, 16–20 October 2023), A/CN.9/1162, pp. 10 et seq.; UNCITRAL, Working Group IV (Electronic Commerce) Sixty-sixth session, Vienna, 16–20 October 2023, Default rules for data provision contracts (first revision), A/CN.9/WG.IV/WP.183.

67 Sebastian Schwamberger, Die Klauselkontrolle in Art. 13 Data Act – Erste Analyse zu Anwendungsbereich, Missbräuchlichkeit und Durchsetzung, MMR 2024, 96 (99); Sebastian Schwamberger, in: David Bomhard/Martin Schmidt-Kessel (eds.), EU Data Act, 2024, Art. 13 [pp. 29, 35 et seq.] (forthcoming); Andreas Wiebe, Der Data Act als vertragsrechtlicher Rahmen für Datennutzungsverträge – Anwendungsbereich und Vorgaben der Missbrauchskontrolle nach Art. 13 Data Act-E, CR 2023, 777 (785).

68 The EU Commission at an early stage once pointed to transparency, shared value creation, respect for each other's commercial interests, undistorted competition, and minimised data lock-in, see EU Commission, Guidance on sharing private sector data in the European data economy – "Towards a common European data space", SWD (2018) 125 final, p. 3.

69 Cf. also on data quality on the international level UNCITRAL, Report of the Working Group IV (Electronic Commerce) on the work of its sixty-fifth session (New York, 10–14 April 2023), A/CN.9/1132, p. 7.

70 UNCITRAL, Report of the Working Group IV (Electronic Commerce) on the work of its sixty-fifth session (New York, 10–14 April 2023), A/CN.9/1132, p. 7.

71 UNCITRAL, Report of the Working Group IV (Electronic Commerce) on the work of its sixty-sixth session (Vienna, 16–20 October 2023), A/CN.9/1162, p. 14.

72 Cf. also the proposal of Art. 7 of the default rules for data provision contracts by UNCITRAL, Working Group IV (Electronic Commerce) Sixty-sixth session, Vienna, 16–20 October 2023, Default rules for data provision contracts (first revision), A/CN.9/WG.IV/WP.183, pp. 9 et seq.

however, to bear in mind that Art. 13 para. 8 DA explicitly excludes the main subject matter of the contract from the control regime.[73]

Fairness therefore seems to refer to other conditions of access and use. The UNCITRAL Working Group IV refers *inter alia* to "(i) limitations on the purpose for which the data recipient used the data, (ii) the "residual" rights retained by the data provider to use the data, (iii) the timing for the provision of data, and (iv) the duration of the data provision contract." Manifold further and diverse aspects come into play in this regard: the modes of access and transfer, exclusivity arrangements[74], the location for data storage[75], the duration of the contract, needs to cooperate during the contract period, access to data or a copy after termination[76], the role and rights of third parties, allowed after-use, onward-transfer[77] and sub-contracting[78] as well as confidentiality obligations[79].

Especially, the factual and legitimate *usability* of data defines not only modes of analysis, but also further monetarisation chances attached. Against this background, a point of reference for the usability is highly needed. What is the standard blueprint for defining unfairness in this context (next to the parameters of Art. 4 et seq. DA)? Independently of the Data Act, it has been argued that contracts shall mirror the inherent innovative potential of data and shall therefore – as a standard rule – enable a data use by both parties.[80] The UNCITRAL Working Group IV generally mirrors this framing and dedicates (rightly) a separate article on the "[u]se of provided data". The current version of Art. 8 of the default rules for data provision contracts reads *inter alia*[81]:

73 Cf. also Matthias Leistner/Lucie Antoine, IPR and the use of open data and data sharing initiatives by public and private actors, 2022, pp. 106, 108.
74 Cf. Moritz Hennemann, Datenlizenzverträge, RDi 2021, 61 (67).
75 Cf. Moritz Hennemann, Datenlizenzverträge, RDi 2021, 61 (67). Cf. for the difficulty to define the actual location UNCITRAL, Report of the Working Group IV (Electronic Commerce) on the work of its sixty-fifth session (New York, 10–14 April 2023), A/CN.9/1132, p. 9.
76 Cf. Moritz Hennemann, Datenlizenzverträge, RDi 2021, 61 (66).
77 Cf. Moritz Hennemann, Datenlizenzverträge, RDi 2021, 61 (66).
78 Cf. Moritz Hennemann, Datenlizenzverträge, RDi 2021, 61 (67).
79 Cf. Moritz Hennemann, Datenlizenzverträge, RDi 2021, 61 (66).
80 See e.g. Moritz Hennemann, Datenlizenzverträge, RDi 2021, 61 (65 et seq.).
81 UNCITRAL, Working Group IV (Electronic Commerce) Sixty-sixth session, Vienna, 16–20 October 2023, Default rules for data provision contracts (first revision), A/CN.9/WG.IV/WP.183, pp. 11 et seq.

"(1) As between the parties to the contract:

(a) The data recipient is entitled to use the data for any lawful purpose and by any lawful means, [subject to any agreed limitations];
(b) The data provider is entitled to continue using the data, including by providing it to third parties."

The approach of Working Group IV sets important parameters for the data contracts in scope ("contractual framework").[82] Art. 8 underlines with para. 1 subpara. a) that the general usability of the data by the data recipient is perceived as the standard. This also seems to be a legitimate starting point for data access and data use contracts covered by Art. 13 DA. The same holds true – outside Art. 4 and Art. 5 DA scenarios – for the provider's continuing 'right' to use the data in question – also differentiating data provision contracts clearly from a 'sale'-like framing.[83] Within Art. 4 and Art. 5 DA scenarios and with respect to non-personal data, however, Art. 4 para. 13 and 14 DA lay the ground for an opposite approach.

A further and highly relevant dimension of fairness might also refer to the analysis gained, the value added to a specific data set, and other forms of common *participation* in the underlying value (these dimensions might, however, also be part of the main subject matter of the contract). Independently of the Data Act, it was proposed to 'attribute' insights gained – as standard rule – to the one actually pursuing the analysis of the data.[84] This actor has typically made an investment into the instruments to analyse, has created the corresponding 'value', and shall be able to monetise respective gains. In order to assess a potential unfair participation in this regard, it is, however, necessary to analyse the underlying contract. If the contract is targeted at a common value generation (e. g. in a data pooling scenario),

82 Cf. UNCITRAL, Working Group IV (Electronic Commerce) Sixty-sixth session, Vienna, 16–20 October 2023, Default rules for data provision contracts (first revision), A/CN.9/WG.IV/WP.183, p. 12: "Article 8 establishes a basic framework for the rights and obligations of the parties with respect to the use of the data provided under the contract. It is premised on the peculiar qualities of data that distinguish data provision contracts from contracts for the sale of goods. (...) Conversely, data is generally not recognized as an object of property rights (...) and is therefore not amenable to ownership nor to the rights that the law attributes to ownership. Given the absence of a comprehensive property-like regime for data rights, (...), data provision contracts remain the primary source of law regulating the use of data. (...) [A]rticle 8 [therefore] avoids the concepts of "sale" or "licence" (...)."

83 Cf. the footnote before.

84 See e.g. Moritz Hennemann, Datenlizenzverträge, RDi 2021, 61 (65).

the respective – contractually agreed on – cooperation between the parties must be mirrored.[85] In a similar way, the UNCITRAL Working Group IV refers to *derived data* in Art. 9 respectively. As the standard rule that the data recipient is generally free to derived data (subpara. a), the data provider may only use derived data on the basis of an (explicit) contractual agreement with the data recipient (subpara. b).[86]

Fairness might even refer to the attribution of legal risks attached – especially if personal data or trade secrets are of relevance.[87] Art. 8 of the UNCITRAL default rules underlines this dimension – and also covers third party rights:[88]

> "(3) (...):
>
> (a) The data provider shall ensure that the data recipient is in a position lawfully to use the data [for the purpose or by the means specified in the contract]; (...)
> (c) The data recipient shall ensure that the data is not used in a manner that infringes the rights of the data provider or of a third party with respect to the use of the data; (...)"

Finally, *fairness* could be evaluated with respect to the network of contractual relations that typically go along with the Art. 4 and Art. 5 settings.[89] *Leistner* and *Antoine* have correctly – during the negotiations on the Data

85 Moritz Hennemann, Datenlizenzverträge, RDi 2021, 61 (66).

86 UNCITRAL, Working Group IV (Electronic Commerce) Sixty-sixth session, Vienna, 16–20 October 2023, Default rules for data provision contracts (first revision), A/CN.9/WG.IV/WP.183, p. 15; cf. also ibid. on the difficulties to define derived data adequately. See also UNCITRAL, Report of the Working Group IV (Electronic Commerce) on the work of its sixty-sixth session (Vienna, 16–20 October 2023), A/CN.9/1162, p. 15: "It was suggested that paragraph (b) should be amended to clarify that, as a default rule, the data provider was not entitled to use derived data. The Working Group agreed with that suggestion."

87 Cf. also on the lawfulness of data UNCITRAL, Report of the Working Group IV (Electronic Commerce) on the work of its sixty-fifth session (New York, 10–14 April 2023), A/CN.9/1132, p. 7.

88 UNCITRAL, Working Group IV (Electronic Commerce) Sixty-sixth session, Vienna, 16–20 October 2023, Default rules for data provision contracts (first revision), A/CN.9/WG.IV/WP.183, p. 12. Cf. also UNCITRAL, Report of the Working Group IV (Electronic Commerce) on the work of its sixty-sixth session (Vienna, 16–20 October 2023), A/CN.9/1162, pp. 14 et seq.

89 See already sub I. above.

Act – pointed to the fact that the fairness control of Art. 13 does not mirror agreements going beyond traditional bilateral relationships[90]:

> "Further, from our viewpoint, the question whether and to which extent and, if at all, in which particular way the fairness test pursuant to Article 13 should apply with respect to multi-party data sharing networks/pools or – more general – to multilateral agreements at the moment remains unanswered by the Data Act. Certainly, if the unfairness test was applied to multilateral agreements and contract negotiations, the definition of a 'unilaterally imposed' term would have to be adjusted or complemented accordingly. In fact, the concept of 'unilaterally imposed'-terms seems hardly workable in larger multi-party network contracts. (...) [R]econsidering the role of sharing networks and multipolar settings within the framework proposed by the Data Act seems necessary (...) since diverse provisions are not suitable for cooperative models and multipolar settings."[91]

Unfortunately, this reconsideration has not taken place. Multipolar dimensions are not directly mirrored. It remains an open question to what extent the various contracts are legally 'connected'.[92] The Data Act nevertheless shows the inherent need – already discussed in other settings[93] – to engage with contractual networks as well as the rights and obligations attached. As the Data Act assumes manifold contractual connections between the different actors, the Act leaves first and foremost room for a context- and contract- 'sensible' interpretation of contractual obligations, including for

90 Contract law is generally and typically drafted and designed along bilateral ('relative') agreements despite systemic connections and systemic interdependencies, see in detail Moritz Hennemann, Interaktion und Partizipation – Dimensionen systemischer Binding im Vertragsrecht, 2020.

91 Matthias Leistner/Lucie Antoine, IPR and the use of open data and data sharing initiatives by public and private actors, 2022, p. 107.

92 Cf. Martin Schmidt-Kessel/David Bomhard, EU-Datengesetz ante portas, MMR 2024, 69 (70) and Andreas Wiebe, Der Data Act – Innovation oder Illusion?, GRUR 2023, 1569 (1570) as well as Moritz Hennemann/Björn Steinrötter, Der Data Act – Neue Instrumente, alte Friktionen, strukturelle Weichenstellungen, NJW 2024, 1 (7); Andreas Wiebe, Der Data Act als vertragsrechtlicher Rahmen für Datennutzungsverträge – Anwendungsbereich und Vorgaben der Missbrauchskontrolle nach Art. 13 Data Act-E, CR 2023, 777 (782).

93 Cf. with further references to the discussion Moritz Hennemann, Interaktion und Partizipation – Dimensionen systemischer Binding im Vertragsrecht, 2020.

defining fairness in the context of Art. 13 DA.[94] Furthermore, the Data Act even explicitly goes in different settings beyond the contractual (relative) relationships at stake.[95] The Data Act also highlights settings in which contractual agreement is of relevance for defining another. Art. 5 para. 9 DA stipulates for example that "[t]rade secrets shall be preserved and shall be disclosed to third parties only to the extent that such disclosure is strictly necessary to fulfil the purpose agreed between the user and the third party." – thereby underlining the relevance of the purpose agreed between the user and the third party for the relationship between the data holder and the third party.

2. 'Black' and 'Grey' List of Art. 13 Para. 4 and 5 Data Act

The 'black' and 'grey' lists by Art. 13 para. 4 and 5 Data Act do only partly mirror the aforementioned fairness dimensions. The two paragraphs shall provide legal certainty (rec. 62) on which clauses are (para. 4) or are presumed to be (para. 5) unfair.[96] In the latter case, the party imposing the term might rebut the presumption (rec. 62). The 'black' and 'grey' lists by Art. 13 DA mirrors approaches well-known from other frameworks (e. g. §§ 308 and 309 German Civil Code[97]) and have been modelled after Art. 84 and 85 of the proposed Common European Sales Law (CESL).[98]

---

94 Cf. *inter alia* Andreas Wiebe, Der Data Act als vertragsrechtlicher Rahmen für Datennutzungsverträge – Anwendungsbereich und Vorgaben der Missbrauchskontrolle nach Art. 13 Data Act-E, CR 2023, 777 (782).

95 Martin Schmidt-Kessel/David Bomhard, EU-Datengesetz ante portas, MMR 2024, 69 (70).

96 In detail Sebastian Schwamberger, in: David Bomhard/Martin Schmidt-Kessel (eds.), EU Data Act, 2024, Art. 13 [pp. 41 et seq.] (forthcoming). On the advantages and disadvantages of the combination of a general clause with a 'black' and a 'grey' list see Dirk Staudenmayer, Der Verordnungsvorschlag der Europäischen Kommission zum Datengesetz – Auf dem Weg zum Privatrecht der Datenwirtschaft, EuZW 2022, 596 (598).

97 See in detail for a comparison between the Data Act and the German unfair terms control according to §§ 307 et seq. Friedrich Graf von Westphalen, Der neue Data Act – Eine Kaskade AGB-rechtlicher Verbote im unternehmerischen Verkehr, BB 2024, 515 (516 et seq.).

98 Dirk Staudenmayer, Der Verordnungsvorschlag der Europäischen Kommission zum Datengesetz – Auf dem Weg zum Privatrecht der Datenwirtschaft, EuZW 2022, 596 (598 et seq.); Lukas Beinke/Ingvar Daute, Der Fairnesstest des Data Act – Verdrängung der nationalen Klauselkontrolle?, RDi 2024, 69 (70); Andreas Wiebe, Der Data Act als vertragsrechtlicher Rahmen für Datennutzungsverträge – Anwendungsbereich

If not covered by either para. 4 or 5, the general unfair test of para. 3 might still apply, but rec. 62 underlines that "the terms listed as unfair contractual terms (...) should serve as a yardstick to interpret the general unfairness provision." Additionally, one has to bear in mind that in an Art. 4 DA or an Art. 5 DA scenario the further yardsticks (e. g. Art. 4 para. 6 to 8 DA and Art. 5 para. 9 and 11 DA) must be considered.[99] Respective guardrails are non-waivable to the detriment of the user, Art. 7 para. 2 DA.

Para. 4 refers to the exclusion or limitation of liability for intentional acts or gross negligence (lit. a), to the exclusion of remedies in the case of non-performance or liability in the case of a breach of obligations (lit. b), and to the exclusive right to determine data conformity (lit. c). Only para. 4 lit. c is data-specific.[100] The other aspects rather refer to general fairness dimensions. Para. 5 also refers to general fairness dimensions to some extent. Covered are a limitation of remedies and a limitation and an extension of liability (lit. a), a prevention of termination (lit. d), and a termination at an unreasonably short notice (lit. f). On the opposite, para. 5 lit. b, c, e, and g are data-specific.[101] Covered are settings of detrimental access to and use of data (lit. b), the prevention of a use of data, of a limitation of use, and of an exploitation of value (lit. c), a prevention of obtaining a data copy (lit. e), and a substantial change of price or substantive condition re nature, format, quality or quantity (lit. g) – the latter aspect being qualified in cases of contracts of an indeterminate duration by para. 5 subpara. 1. Having the potential fairness dimensions in mind, one can generally attribute the different data-specific clauses to three general dimensions of unfairness: (1) *data*, (2) *access and use*, and (3) *ancillary* aspects.

---

und Vorgaben der Missbrauchskontrolle nach Art. 13 Data Act-E, CR 2023, 777 (781). In general, see Sebastian Schwamberger, in: David Bomhard/Martin Schmidt-Kessel (eds.), EU Data Act, 2024, Art. 13 [p. 11, 30] (forthcoming).

99 See Sebastian Schwamberger, in: David Bomhard/Martin Schmidt-Kessel (eds.), EU Data Act, 2024, Art. 13 [p. 47] (forthcoming).

100 Cf. also Matthias Leistner/Lucie Antoine, IPR and the use of open data and data sharing initiatives by public and private actors, 2022, pp. 105 et seq.; Andreas Wiebe, Der Data Act als vertragsrechtlicher Rahmen für Datennutzungsverträge – Anwendungsbereich und Vorgaben der Missbrauchskontrolle nach Art. 13 Data Act-E, CR 2023, 777 (780).

101 Cf. also Matthias Leistner/Lucie Antoine, IPR and the use of open data and data sharing initiatives by public and private actors, 2022, p. 108; Sebastian Omlor, Unfair Contractual Terms under the Data Act, ERPL 2024, 173 (187); Andreas Wiebe, Der Data Act als vertragsrechtlicher Rahmen für Datennutzungsverträge – Anwendungsbereich und Vorgaben der Missbrauchskontrolle nach Art. 13 Data Act-E, CR 2023, 777 (781).

The reference to the exclusive right to determine data conformity (para. 4 lit. c) as well as to a substantial change of price or a substantive condition re nature, format, quality or quantity (para. 5 lit. g) is linked to the *data* dimension (1). Covered are aspects of *data quality*. Whilst both scenarios seem to be related to the definition of the main subject matter of the contract, a precise differentiation is needed. Para. 4 lit. c presumes that the data conformity has been defined by the parties of the contract and only covers scenarios in which one party may determine unilaterally the data conformity against this very standard agreed.[102] Para. 5 lit. g is engaged with scenarios of unilateral amendments to the data conditions agreed on. A detrimental access to and use of data (para. 5 lit. b) as well as a prevention of a use of data, of a limitation of use, and of an exploitation of value (para. 5 lit. c) cover the *access and use* dimension (2). An *ancillary* aspect (3) is covered by para. 5 lit. e when referring to a prevention of obtaining a data copy. Para. 5 lit. b, c and e are linked to the fairness dimensions of a parallel or an after-use of data and thereby to monetarisation chances. Especially, para. 5 lit. c covers important fairness dimensions with respect to the analysis to be gained and the value added to the specific data set.[103] Para. 5 lit. b might also assist in reflecting other legitimate interests in the context of the contract.

V. Art. 13 Data Act and Private International Law

The interplay between Art. 13 DA and Private International Law (PIL) is not fully clear. From a PIL perspective, Art. 13 DA always applies if one of the EU member states' Contract Law applies. If the respective data contract is, however, governed by a non-EU Contract Law, Art. 13 DA does not apply.[104] Art. 13 DA is not to be considered as an overriding mandatory norm according to Art. 9 Rom I-Regulation.[105] Rather, the applicable Contract

102 Cf. also Matthias Leistner/Lucie Antoine, IPR and the use of open data and data sharing initiatives by public and private actors, 2022, p. 106 in this regard.

103 Andreas Wiebe, Der Data Act als vertragsrechtlicher Rahmen für Datennutzungsverträge – Anwendungsbereich und Vorgaben der Missbrauchskontrolle nach Art. 13 Data Act-E, CR 2023, 777 (783).

104 Andreas Wiebe, Der Data Act als vertragsrechtlicher Rahmen für Datennutzungsverträge – Anwendungsbereich und Vorgaben der Missbrauchskontrolle nach Art. 13 Data Act-E, CR 2023, 777 (784).

105 Moritz Hennemann/Björn Steinrötter, Der Data Act – Neue Instrumente, alte Friktionen, strukturelle Weichenstellungen, NJW 2024, 1 (8); Dirk Staudenmayer,

Law is to be determined according to the Rom I-Regulation – offering parties in b2b-settings the general possibility to choose the applicable law (Art. 3 Rom I-Regulation).[106]

VI. Art. 13 Data Act and National Unfair Terms Control

The interplay between Art. 13 DA and existing frameworks of unfair terms control is also not clear.[107] The relationship to national rules is regarded to be a pressing issue. Does Art. 13 DA for example apply next to the German unfair terms control by §§ 307, 310 BGB if the contract is generally governed by German Contract Law? Rec. 9 stipulates that "[u]nless otherwise provided for (...), [the Act] does not affect national contract law, including rules on the formation, validity or effect of contracts, or the consequences of the termination of a contract." Rec. 9 thereby indicates that the Act might actually *affect* national contract law ("unless...").[108] As Art. 13 DA provides a fully fletched approach to unfair terms control, there is no room for an additional standard term control with respect to the terms on data access and use in b2b-settings.[109] Accordingly, clauses which are not controlled

Der Verordnungsvorschlag der Europäischen Kommission zum Datengesetz – Auf dem Weg zum Privatrecht der Datenwirtschaft, EuZW 2022, 596 (602); Sebastian Schwamberger, Die Klauselkontrolle in Art. 13 Data Act – Erste Analyse zu Anwendungsbereich, Missbräuchlichkeit und Durchsetzung, MMR 2024, 96 (96); Sebastian Schwamberger, in: David Bomhard/Martin Schmidt-Kessel (eds.), EU Data Act, 2024, Art. 13 [pp. 15, 61] (forthcoming); Andreas Wiebe, Der Data Act als vertragsrechtlicher Rahmen für Datennutzungsverträge – Anwendungsbereich und Vorgaben der Missbrauchskontrolle nach Art. 13 Data Act-E, CR 2023, 777 (784).

106 Moritz Hennemann/Björn Steinrötter, Der Data Act – Neue Instrumente, alte Friktionen, strukturelle Weichenstellungen, NJW 2024, 1 (8); Andreas Wiebe, Der Data Act als vertragsrechtlicher Rahmen für Datennutzungsverträge – Anwendungsbereich und Vorgaben der Missbrauchskontrolle nach Art. 13 Data Act-E, CR 2023, 777 (784).

107 In detail Lukas Beinke/Ingvar Daute, Der Fairnesstest des Data Act – Verdrängung der nationalen Klauselkontrolle?, RDi 2024, 69 (71); Andreas Wiebe, Der Data Act als vertragsrechtlicher Rahmen für Datennutzungsverträge – Anwendungsbereich und Vorgaben der Missbrauchskontrolle nach Art. 13 Data Act-E, CR 2023, 777 (780).

108 Cf. Sebastian Omlor, Unfair Contractual Terms under the Data Act, ERPL 2024, 173 (177).

109 Sebastian Omlor, Unfair Contractual Terms under the Data Act, ERPL 2024, 173 (177). In detail Sebastian Schwamberger, in: David Bomhard/Martin Schmidt-Kessel (eds.), EU Data Act, 2024, Art. 13 [p. 68] (forthcoming). Different approach

because the standard of being "unilaterally imposed" (Art. 13 para. 6 DA) is not fulfilled, are also not subject to a national control.[110] The same holds true for a transparency control of terms which is explicitly not included in the Data Act[111].[112] Contractual terms outside data access and use in b2b-settings, however, might be subject to the existing national instruments (especially b2c-scenarios).[113]

VII. The Way Forward

Art. 13 DA is of great relevance and will probably also influence future EU and / or national b2c-rules.[114] It establishes a new layer of protection for commercial data exchanges, data access scenarios, and data use settings. It is more than obvious that this layer might not be needed if parties negotiate at arm's length. However, Art. 13 DA does not apply if the terms at stake are actually negotiated between them – terms are not unilaterally imposed

---

by Lukas Beinke/Ingvar Daute, Der Fairnesstest des Data Act – Verdrängung der nationalen Klauselkontrolle?, RDi 2024, 69 (72 et seq.).

110 Sebastian Omlor, Unfair Contractual Terms under the Data Act, ERPL 2024, 173 (178).

111 Cf. Sebastian Omlor, Unfair Contractual Terms under the Data Act, ERPL 2024, 173 (185); Dirk Staudenmayer, Der Verordnungsvorschlag der Europäischen Kommission zum Datengesetz – Auf dem Weg zum Privatrecht der Datenwirtschaft, EuZW 2022, 596 (602); Sebastian Schwamberger, in: David Bomhard/Martin Schmidt-Kessel (eds.), EU Data Act, 2024, Art. 13 [pp. 11, 60] (forthcoming); Andreas Wiebe, Der Data Act als vertragsrechtlicher Rahmen für Datennutzungsverträge – Anwendungsbereich und Vorgaben der Missbrauchskontrolle nach Art. 13 Data Act-E, CR 2023, 777 (783).

112 Rightly spotted by Sebastian Schwamberger, in: David Bomhard/Martin Schmidt-Kessel (eds.), EU Data Act, 2024, Art. 13 [p. 68] (forthcoming). An aspect of transparency is covered by Art. 3 para. 2 DA.

113 Sebastian Omlor, Unfair Contractual Terms under the Data Act, ERPL 2024, 173 (176 et seq.). Sebastian Schwamberger, in: David Bomhard/Martin Schmidt-Kessel (eds.), EU Data Act, 2024, Art. 13 [p. 68] (forthcoming); Andreas Wiebe, Der Data Act als vertragsrechtlicher Rahmen für Datennutzungsverträge – Anwendungsbereich und Vorgaben der Missbrauchskontrolle nach Art. 13 Data Act-E, CR 2023, 777 (780).

114 With regard to the latter cf. also Moritz Hennemann, Datenrealpolitik – Datenökosysteme, Datenrecht, Datendiplomatie, University of Passau IRDG Research Paper Series 22–18, https://papers.ssrn.com/sol3/papers.cfm?abstract_id=4267390; Andreas Wiebe, Der Data Act als vertragsrechtlicher Rahmen für Datennutzungsverträge – Anwendungsbereich und Vorgaben der Missbrauchskontrolle nach Art. 13 Data Act-E, CR 2023, 777 (786).

in this setting. If terms are just accepted without any further evaluation by the other party, the unfair term control does also not apply. In some b2b-setting in which the unfair terms control does apply, the control might be regarded as overly protective[115] – being the consequence of the broad approach taken by the legislator when linking Art. 13 to all b2b-settings. In many scenarios, taking the respective analysis of the EU Commission[116] for granted, however, commercial parties confronted with standard terms will actually be in need of a basic security net. By 'denying' the weaker party the option just to 'accept' the terms and conditions, the Data Act sets an incentive to engage with the contractual terms, to evaluate the commercial relevance of the conditions, and seek to determine the data implications at stake.

Having its rather large scope of application in mind, Art. 13 DA therefore bears the enormous potential to counter excessive bargaining power and settings of exploitation as well as to reduce contractual imbalances more thoughtfully. Applied (hopefully) in a considerate manner, it offers sharp modes of interventions to the benefit of data sharing and data monetarisation. To effectuate a respective 'fair' contracting, balanced model contract terms are much needed. If those developed (e. g. on the basis of Art. 41 DA) are considered to be practical feasible by the actors at stake, they will act as a significant catalysator for contracting as such and the data economy as a whole.

115 Cf. also Axel Metzger/Heike Schweitzer, Shaping Markets: A Criticial Evaluation of the Draft Data Act, ZEuP 2023, 42 (63): "By contrast, for major machine users, e.g. airlines, one can expect that the collected machine data is of sufficient commercial relevance. Businesses should be in a position to consider the relevant clauses on data access carefully or take the risk of unfavourable conditions. A review of standard terms is not appropriate in this case."

116 EU Commission, A European strategy for data, COM (2020) 66 final, p. 8; EU Commission, Impact Assessment Report – Data Act, SWD (2022) 34 final, p. 11. Cf. also Sebastian Schwamberger, in: David Bomhard/Martin Schmidt-Kessel (eds.), EU Data Act, 2024, Art. 13 [p. 7] (forthcoming).

Smart contracts for data transactions and the Data Act

Georg Borges*

I. Importance and challenges of data transactions

1. Opportunities and special features of data transactions

New technologies harbour enormous potential for progress and prosperity. This applies to artificial intelligence,[1] particularly machine learning, as well as the generation of new knowledge from the processing of large amounts of data (so-called big data)[2]. Additionally, the interconnection and automation of industrial processes, known as Industry 4.0, contributes significantly to this potential.[3]

These technologies are fundamentally based on the processing of large volumes of data,[4] which can only be efficiently utilised through multiple uses of this data. Notably, "data sharing", i.e., the multiple use of the same data sets, requires the transfer of such data and an agreement as the legal basis for the data transfer.[5] The same challenge arises for other fundamental trends in business and administration, namely the so-called Industry 4.0, i.e., the automation and interconnection of industrial production, or the

---

* Professor of Law; Director, Institute of Legal Informatics, Saarland University; Distinguished Visiting Professor, University of Johannesburg. The author acknowledges Dr. Afolabi Adekemi's valuable assistance with this article.

1 *Jyoti/Schubmehl*, The Business Opportunity of AI, 2023, p. 1 ff., available at: https://static1.squarespace.com/static/5ffd6f883ff3ea0604bd4aea/t/65bb4dadd450c37f5834f0c0/1706170677395/IDC+AI+Report.pdf (last accessed 19.7.2024); *Nagel*, Welfare through digitalisation, available at: https://www.bundesbank.de/en/press/contributions/welfare-through-digitalisation-digital-transformation-is-crucial-for-higher-labour-productivity-912984 (last accessed 17.7.2024).

2 *Arlinghaus/Kus/Kajüter/Teuteberg*, HMD 58 (2021), 565, 566; *Borges*, in: Borges/Keil (eds.), Rechtshandbuch Big Data, 2024, § 1 para. 1 ff.

3 See, *Duan/Xu*, Data Analytics in Industry 4.0: A Survey, p. 3 ff., available at: https://link.springer.com/article/10.1007/s10796-021-10190-0 (last accessed 15.5.2024).

4 *Borges*, in: Borges/Keil, Rechtshandbuch Big Data (fn. 2), § 1 para. 19.

5 See *Borges*, in: Borges/Keil, Rechtshandbuch Big Data (fn. 2), § 5 para. 1 ff.

digitalisation of public administration.[6] Here, too, data transfer and the legal basis for such transfer are essential.

As with transactions involving traditional goods and services, data transactions consist of two basic components: the data transfer on the one hand, and the legal basis for the data transfer on the other hand. Data can be transferred in various ways, particularly by making it available for retrieval, i.e., enabling access to data via an electronic communications service, physical connection or on-device access.[7] The legal basis for such transfers typically entails a contractual agreement but may also consist of an administrative act or a legal obligation, such as under the Data Act.[8] In this respect, it is noteworthy that the Data Act encompasses multiple legal bases. For example, it regulates the legal obligation to transfer data in Articles 4 and 5, while also mandating the parties involved to conclude an agreement for the transfer of the data under Article 8 of the Data Act.[9] The Data Act uses the term "Data Sharing" to designate the transfer of data, while the underlying agreement is called "Data Sharing Agreement".

2. Challenges of data sharing

To date, despite its importance for the digital economy, data sharing has taken place far less than expected.[10] This is arguably largely due to the

---

6 Cf. on tax law *Kirchhof,* DStR 2023, 355 ff.

7 Article 2 (15), Regulation (EU) 2023/2854 of the European Parliament and of the Council of 13 December 2023 on harmonised rules on fair access to and use of data and amending Regulation (EU) 2017/2394 and Directive (EU) 2020/1828 (Data Act), OJ L, 2023/2854, 22.12.2023.

8 Regulation (EU) 2023/2854 of the European Parliament and of the Council of 13 December 2023 on harmonised rules on fair access to and use of data and amending Regulation (EU) 2017/2394 and Directive (EU) 2020/1828 (Data Act), OJ L, 2023/2854, 22.12.2023.

9 For more details, see *Berberich,* in: Borges/Keil, Rechtshandbuch Big Data (fn. 2), § 3 para. 103 ff.

10 *Borges,* in: Borges/Keil, Rechtshandbuch Big Data (fn. 2), § 5 para. 30; *Hennemann/von Ditfurth,* NJW 2022, 1905, 1906; *Schäfer,* Datenkooperation durch Datenpooling, 2023, p. 54; according to a study commissioned by the European Commission, only 39 % of the companies surveyed exchange their data, of which 52 % report obstacles, see *Arnaut/Pont/Scaria/Bergmann/Leconte,* Study on data sharing between companies in Europe, 2018, p. 74 ff., available at: https://op.europa.eu/en/publication-detail/-/publication/8b8776ff-4834-11e8-be1d-01aa75ed71a1/language-en (last accessed 19.7.2024).

special characteristics of data as an economic asset. Notably, compared to most goods, data can be used in parallel by multiple people for different purposes without any complexity.[11] Therefore, unlike the use of goods, the use of data is not rivalrous, i.e., it does not exclude the (simultaneous) use of data by several people.[12]

Also, the use of data is not legally reserved for a specific legal entity, as exclusive rights of data usage do not exist in principle.[13] Instead, the exclusive right to use data is protected solely by the exclusive right of disposal. Once third parties access data, this exclusivity is lost. Moreover, the third party generally receives the same actual right of disposal and, unless there are exceptional rights to the contrary, also gains full legal use of the data.[14] For this reason alone, the general reluctance to share data[15] is justifiable.

Another noteworthy challenge related to data sharing is the inability of the data owner to accurately assess the economic impact of the data transfer because they do not fully comprehend the value of their data.[16] In making this assessment, data owners must consider that receiving a copy of the data puts the data recipient in the same position previously held solely by the data owner.[17] Consequently, without accurate knowledge of the data's actual value, the data owner will have difficulties determining a fair consideration (compensation) for sharing the data.[18]

Similar difficulties exist on the part of the data recipient, i.e., the party receiving the data or the possibility of its use. Data recipients can determine

11 European Law Institute, Characteristics of Data, available at: https://www.principlesforadataeconomy.org/the-project/ (last accessed 15.5.2024); *Zech*, CR 2015, 137, 139.

12 *Borges,* in: Borges/Keil, Rechtshandbuch Big Data (fn. 2), § 5 para. 4; *Paal/Hennemann,* Big Data as an Asset, 2018, p. 18 f., available at: https://www.abida.de/sites/default/files/Gutachten_ABIDA_Big_Data_as_an_Asset.pdf (last accessed 19.7.2024); *Schäfer,* Datenkooperation durch Datenpooling (fn. 10), p. 54; *von Ditfurth,* Datenmärkte, Datenintermediäre und der Data Governance Act, 2024, p. 38.

13 *Berberich,* in: Borges/Keil, Rechtshandbuch Big Data (fn. 2), § 3 para. 3; *Schur,* in: Leupold/Wiebe/Glossner (eds.), IT-Recht, 4th ed. 2021, Part 6.9. para. 24; *Weidert/Bug,* in: Borges/Keil, Rechtshandbuch Big Data (fn. 2), § 16 para. 25.

14 *Borges,* in: Borges/Keil, Rechtshandbuch Big Data (fn. 2), § 5 para. 20; for more details on potentially conflicting rights, see *Berberich,* in: Borges/Keil, Rechtshandbuch Big Data (fn. 2), § 3 para. 29 ff.

15 *Arnaut/Pont/Scaria/Bergmann/Leconte,* Study on data sharing between companies in Europe (fn. 10), p. 44; *Borges,* in: Borges/Keil, Rechtshandbuch Big Data (fn. 2), § 5 para. 30; *Richter/Slowinski* IIC 2019, 4, 7.

16 *Borges,* in: Borges/Keil, Rechtshandbuch Big Data (fn. 2), § 5 para. 50 f.

17 *von Ditfurth* (fn. 12), p. 45.

18 *Borges,* in: Borges/Keil, Rechtshandbuch Big Data (fn. 2), § 5 para. 50 f.

the value of the data (utilisation) to the extent that they know the intended use and the benefits it brings. However, they often lack knowledge of the data quality[19] and, therefore, find it difficult to assess the suitability of the data for their intended use. Consequently, this lack of knowledge diminishes the value of the data from the recipient's view.

Also, just as the data owner, the data recipient is typically unable to determine the value of the data for further use. However, this understanding is vital since the data recipient, upon receiving a copy of the data, assumes a position similar to that of the data owner. These challenges often result in agreements on data sharing that are fraught with high uncertainties, accompanied by corresponding risks and transaction costs.[20]

Furthermore, it is noteworthy that individual data sets often have low value without economic relevance until it is aggregated with a larger database.[21] When aggregated into a comprehensive database, it becomes economically relevant.[22] Merging data into a sufficiently comprehensive database is, however, a major challenge for applications that are based on database utilisation. This challenge persists, especially when dealing with frequently updated data that remains relevant only for a short period of time. For example, this is the case with weather data or financial data, which have a significantly higher value as current information than when used as historical data. This aggregation and continuous updates often lead to a large number of data transmission processes and, thus, data transactions.

This means that, not least due to the lower value of smaller data sets, the effectiveness of data transactions is a decisive factor in the comprehensive use of data needed to unleash the full potential of big data and AI.

---

19 Cf. on the term and characteristics of data quality, *Borges,* in: Borges/Keil, Rechtshandbuch Big Data (fn. 2), § 7 para. 121 ff.; *Druey,* Information als Gegenstand des Rechts, 1995, p. 243 ff.; *Sarre/Pruß,* in: Auer-Reinsdorff/Conrad (eds.), Handbuch IT- und Datenschutzrecht, 3rd ed. 2019, § 2 para. 51 ff.

20 *von Ditfurth* (fn. 12), p. 44 f.

21 *Alaimo/Kallinikos/Aaltonen,* in: Nambisan/Lyytinen/Yoo (eds.), Handbook of Digital Innovation, 2020, p. 162, 174.

22 *Borges,* in: Borges/Keil, Rechtshandbuch Big Data (fn. 2), § 1 para. 2; § 5 para. 2.

3. The European legislature's approach to promoting data sharing

The various challenges facing the efficient use of data can only be overcome through a combination of different technical, organisational and, not least, legal measures. The European legislature is evidently striving to establish the legal framework for the efficient use of data through the development of the European data law.[23] In doing so, the legislature is relying on various instruments and regulatory concepts.

a) Obligations to share data

To promote data sharing, the legislature relies on legal obligations for data sharing, which have recently become increasingly intrusive. For instance, the rules of the Public Sector Information (PSI) Directive of 2003[24] already regulated certain aspects of access to public sector data.[25] In the new version, i.e., the "Open Data Directive" of 2019[26], the regulation is extended to ensure better access to data.[27] However, neither directive contained any obligation for the public sector to make data available.[28] This regulation was further expanded in the Data Governance Act ("DGA") 2021[29]. While the PSI Directive or the Open Data Directive does not apply to data that are subject to intellectual property rights of third parties or which constitute trade secrets of third parties (cf. Art. 1 para. 2 PSI Directive), such data now falls under the scope of accessible data pursuant to Article 3 para. 1 of the

23 For an overview, see *Borges*, in Borges/Keil, Rechtshandbuch Big Data (fn. 2), § 1 para. 30 ff.; in detail *Apel/Huber*, JuS 2024, 410; *Hoernig/Ilharco*, Policy Paper 26 – European Data Strategy: Regulatory & Policy Aspects, 2023, p. 3 ff., available at: https://www.ipp-jcs.org/wp-content/uploads/2023/08/IPP-Paper-EU-Data-Strategy-v6-3.pdf (last accessed 19.7.2024).

24 Directive 2003/98/EC of the European Parliament and of the Council of 17 November 2003 on the re-use of public sector information, OJ EU L 345, 31.12.2003, 90.

25 See for example, *Hartl/Ludin*, MMR 2021, 534 f.; *Fuchs*, ZGI 2022, 151, 152 f.

26 Directive (EU) 2019/1024 of the European Parliament and of the Council of 20 June 2019 on open data and the re-use of public sector information (recast), OJ EU L 172, 26.6.2019, 56.

27 See, Art. 1 (1) Directive (EU) 2019/1024, *ibid.*

28 Cf. recital 26 Directive (EU) 2019/1024, *ibid.*

29 Regulation (EU) 2022/868 of the European Parliament and of the Council of 30 May 2022 on European data governance and amending Regulation (EU) 2018/1724 (Data Governance Act), OJ L 152, 3.6.2022, 1.

DGA. Therefore, the European legislature pursues the goal of making the public sector's "data treasure" available to the public as far as possible.[30]

Furthermore, in the private sector, the access rights provided in Articles 4 and 5 of the Data Act are likely to be of decisive importance.[31] It is generally assumed that commercially utilised machines will often be connected.[32] This means that data from these commercial machines, in principle, will be available for future use by both the machine operator and third parties. This availability will be facilitated through data transactions between the involved parties in accordance with Article 8 of the Data Act.

Even more intrusive are the rules of the recently approved[33] European Health Data Space,[34] which centralises the administration and utilisation of all patient data of European citizens under state regulation for various purposes.

b) Incentives for data sharing

Significantly, the legislature also incentivises voluntary data exchange. For example, the DGA's rules on data altruism,[35] are intended to create a basis for trust in intermediaries that manage the use of data from data donors,[36] so-called data altruistic organisations.[37] Overall, the DGA rules on data intermediaries, which are intended to strengthen trust in data sharing, are certainly of crucial importance.[38]

Furthermore, the balance of interests between holders of rights to data and the interests of third parties in the use of data may be considered a

30 Cf. recital 6 of the DGA, *ibid.*

31 *Staudenmayer,* NJW 2024, 1377, 1380 f.; *Ziegler/Nagl,* ZfDR 2023, 57, 68 f.

32 *Schäfer,* Datenkooperation durch Datenpooling (fn. 10), p. 64; *Ziegler/Nagl,* ZfDR 2023, 57, 65.

33 See, European Commission, European Health Data Space, available at: https://health.ec.europa.eu/ehealth-digital-health-and-care/european-health-data-space_en (last accessed 9.7.2024).

34 European Commission, Proposal for a Regulation of the European Parliament and of the Council on the European Health Data Space, COM (2022) 197 final.

35 See further, *Borges,* in: Borges/Keil, Rechtshandbuch Big Data (fn. 2), § 5 para. 245 ff.

36 *Borges,* in: Borges/Keil, Rechtshandbuch Big Data (fn. 2), § 5 para. 248.

37 This term, which is not defined in the DGA, refers to data intermediaries that are active in the area of data altruism (see Art. 18 DGA). They have the option to be listed in a public register and, once registered, to use the designation "data altruism organisation recognised in the Union" (cf. Art. 17 para. 2 DGA).

38 Cf. recitals 5, 32 DGA; *Hennemann/von Ditfurth,* NJW 2022, 1905, 1907.

decisive factor in data sharing. Here, the European legislature has made important fundamental decisions, for example, by refraining from introducing "data ownership" and restricting the excessive protection of personal data in new regulations.[39] This approach is notably evident in the rules governing the European Health Data Space, which certainly mark a paradigm shift in data protection law.

c) Infrastructure for efficient data transactions

With regard to the infrastructure for data transactions, the European legislature relies primarily on private-sector data transmission and private infrastructure and limits itself to regulating the legal framework, for example, for intermediaries. The concept of the health data space, which relies on state services and state administration of data allocation, has so far been an exception.

Regarding the elements of efficient data transactions, the activity of the European legislature has so far been very restrained. Indeed, the Data Governance Act establishes basic requirements for intermediaries, with legal obligations ensuring legal certainty in this regard. There is no doubt that the obligation to provide data, for example, under the Data Act or the planned regulation on the health data space, will also lead to the efficiency of data transactions insofar as the question of whether to provide data does not have to be negotiated. Also, the "model contractual terms" (Art. 41 Data Act) and the Data Act's "clause control" according to Article 13 Data Act help in this respect if they lead to generally recognised standards for data sharing.[40]

In terms of data transactions or their automation, the importance of which should not be underestimated, European data law has been relatively sparse to date. However, in this regard, Article 36 of the Data Act plays a pioneering role with its provisions on smart contracts. It is therefore of particular interest whether the legal issues relating to automated data transactions (II. below) are sufficiently resolved by the existing legal framework for data transactions (III. below).

---

39 *Borges,* in: Borges/Keil, Rechtshandbuch Big Data (fn. 2), § 1 para. 39; *Etzkorn,* RDi 2024, 116, 118 f.; *Schmidt-Kessel,* MMR 2024, 75, 78; on the discussion at the draft stage *Bomhard/Merkle,* RDi 2022, 168, 175.

40 For more details, see *Borges,* in: Borges/Keil, Rechtshandbuch Big Data (fn. 2), § 5 para. 265 ff.

II. Automation of data transactions

The actual transmission of data, as described earlier, typically occurs based on a contractual agreement serving as the legal basis. The automation of data transactions therefore represents a case group of the automation of contractual relationships.

1. Automation of contractual relationships

Although the automation of contractual relationships is not a new topic, digitalisation and the use of artificial intelligence have certainly reached a new dimension in terms of their practical significance, scope, and dogmatic foundations.

Contractual relationships can be divided into three phases: contract initiation, contract conclusion and contract execution. All three phases are accessible to automation. The term automation is used here in a narrow sense and refers to the aim of carrying out the respective action in the context of initiating, concluding or executing a contract automatically, i.e., without human intervention.

The one-sided automation of contracts in all three phases has long been known in the form of vending machines[41] and is used today not least in the provision of services or the sale of products via websites.

Bipartite automation, in which both parties do not act manually, i.e., by human action, but by software (agents) or machines (automats, robots), is still quite rare and is mainly found in the so-called B2B area, less so in the B2C area, i.e., in a contract between entrepreneur and consumer. However, even in business relationships between companies, complete two-way automation of contracts in all three phases is still rare and is currently being trialled primarily in projects.

An interesting example of such projects is the German Industry 4.0 Legal Testbed project,[42] in which the complete two-way automation of contractual relationships in networked industry is being designed and implemented as a prototype.[43] Specifically, in this project, the automation of contract

41 *Simmchen*, MMR 2017, 162, 164 ("(d)er erste Prototyp der Smart Contracts" ["the first prototype of smart contracts"]).

42 Cf. https://legaltestbed.org/en/start/ (last accessed 15.5.2024).

43 Cf. "General project information", available at: https://legaltestbed.org/en/in-detail/ (last accessed 15.5.2024).

initiation through an automated trustworthiness check and the automation of contract negotiations was designed and also implemented through the use of contract agents and an infrastructure for the automated exchange of trust-relevant information and the automated assessment of trustworthiness.[44] The automated conclusion of contracts by so-called contract conclusion agents enables the conclusion of the contract, the electronic signing of the contract by both parties, the documentation of the contract, and the storage of the contract in a blockchain-based smart contract. The automation of contract execution through smart contracts, which has been instantiated for industrial services (transport) and the purchase of goods (provision of goods for production on order)[45], includes contract management, such as the calculation of payment claims, the triggering of payments and the documentation of the service description. The smart contracts are stored and executed on a blockchain. The actual services, such as transport or the production and delivery of goods, naturally take place outside the blockchain. By combining the modular elements, a complete, two-way automation of this contractual relationship can be achieved.

2. Smart contracts

Automated contract execution takes place by means of smart contracts.

a) The concept of smart contracts

The term smart contract is highly controversial[46] and has been used with different meanings since it was coined by *Nick Szabo*. In his short publications, *Szabo* speaks rather vaguely of a "set of promises" and refers to vending machines as an example.[47] The term's vagueness is already

44 Cf. "Properties and features of Legal Testbed", available at: https://legaltestbed.org/en/in-detail/ (last accessed 15.5.2024).

45 See https://legaltestbed.org/en/usecases/ (last accessed 15.5.2024).

46 *Riccardo de Caria*, in: DiMatteo et al. (eds.), The Cambridge Handbook of Smart Contracts, Blockchain Technology and Digital Platform, Cambridge 2019, p. 19, 21 ff.; *Catchlove*, Smart Contracts: A New Era Of Contract Use, 2017, p. 6, available at: https://papers.ssrn.com/sol3/papers.cfm?abstract_id=3090226 (last accessed 15.5.2024).

47 Cf. *Szabo*, Smart Contracts: Building Blocks for Digital Markets, 1996, available at: https://www.fon.hum.uva.nl/rob/Courses/InformationInSpeech/CDROM/Literatu

apparent here, as the vending machine is not a bundle of conditions but a machine that performs various actions based on predefined conditions, whereas *Szabo's* definition describes more of an intellectual concept. Today, the term is typically used to describe a computer program that triggers a contractually relevant action on the basis of predefined conditions.[48]

As such a contractually relevant action, the focus is on the automated provision of consideration, usually payment, for a service rendered. However, the concept and meaning of smart contracts are by no means limited to this. In Germany, for example, there has recently been a discussion of agreements in which the provision of the main service is automatically interrupted in the case of recurring obligations.[49]

If the smart contract were defined as a computer program that triggers an action based on predefined conditions, the definition would be inadequate, as it is the nature of a computer program to perform certain actions based on predefined input values. The term smart contract only gains its contours through the reference to the contract.

Szabo's definition already referred to a "set of promises". This refers to contractual performance promises. According to today's legal understanding of a contract, a single contractual promise is sufficient, so the "set" mentioned by *Szabo* could just be one promise. The description "in computable form" mentioned by *Szabo* indisputably refers to a computer program, with the specification that the program should trigger or cause the execution of the performance promise. Thus, a smart contract can be defined as a computer program designed for the automated performance of certain contractually defined actions, in particular for the complete or partial fulfilment of contractual performance promises.

---

re/LOTwinterschool2006/szabo.best.vwh.net/smart_contracts_2.html (last accessed 8.5.2024); *Szabo*, Formalizing and Securing Relationships on Public Networks, 1997, available at: https://firstmonday.org/ojs/index.php/fm/article/view/548/469 (last accessed 8.5.2024).

48 See for example, *Buchholtz*, JuS 2017, 955, 956; *Fries*, NJW 2016, 2860, 2861; *Jakl*, MMR 2019, 711, 712; *Kaulartz/Heckmann*, CR 2016, 618; *Kipker/Birreck/Niewöhner/Schnorr*, MMR 2020, 509; *Oster*, ZfPW 2023, 387, 389; *Ostoja-Starzewski*, InTerR 2021, 213, 215.

49 See, for example, BGH judgement of 26.10.2022 - XII ZR 89/21 (Under review was the legality of an agreement that permitted the remote deactivation of a car battery's charging ability after the extraordinary termination of the rental agreement); see also, *Jaensch*, DAR 2023, 131 ff.; *Paulus/Matzke*, CR 2017, 769, 772 ff.; *Wilhelm*, WM 2020, 1807, 1812 ff.

Over the past decade, the concept of smart contracts and, in some cases, the term itself, was associated with the concept of blockchain. This connection is particularly evident when the smart contract is defined as a blockchain-based technology.[50] The particular benefit of blockchain is that it enables tamper-proof initiation and documentation, including the provision of (electronic) services if necessary. However, this advantage is offset by considerable disadvantages, notably the high cost of operating a blockchain and other severe limitations, such as very little flexibility in the design of the actions to be performed. One of the main areas of application of blockchains for the execution of services is therefore the transfer of intangible goods, in particular, financial transactions, where the advantages (fast, secure execution of the service) outweigh the high level of cost involved.

Today, there is a consensus that blockchains and smart contracts are fundamentally different concepts that can, but do not have to be, combined.[51]

b) Smart contract versus contract

As explained above, a smart contract is a computer program that allows the complete or partial fulfilment of contractual performance promises. A smart contract is therefore not a contract.[52] This statement is trivial since a contract is a legal transaction between several parties, but a computer program is a text. The only relevant question is therefore whether a smart contract is a contractual text in the sense of a model for a contract to be concluded.

The relationship between the smart contract and the contract must therefore be clarified. This relationship is described in very different ways, and different concepts can also be identified in the matter. This is made more difficult by the fact that the relationship has various aspects that are not uniformly differentiated or described in discussions.

---

50 See, e.g., *Blocher*, AnwBl 2016, 612, 618, available at: https://anwaltsblatt.anwaltverein.de/files/anwaltsblatt.de/Rubriken/news/2016/AnwBl%202016,%20612_Blocher.pdf (last accessed 19.7.2024); *Zheng*, et al., FGCS 2020, 475 ff.; *Khan* et al., 14 PPNA 2021, 2901, 2901 ff.; *De Filippi/Wray/Sileno*, 10(2) IPR 2021, 1, 2 ff.

51 *Braegelmann/Kaulartz*, in: Braegelmann/Kaulartz (eds.), Rechtshandbuch Smart Contracts, 2019, p. 10; *Heckelmann*, NJW 2018, 504, 505; *Kollmann*, MMR 2024, 137, 138; *Schawe*, MMR 2019, 218.

52 *Kaulartz/Heckmann*, CR 2016, 618, 621, 624; *Kollmann*, MMR 2024, 137; *Paulus/Matzke*, ZfPW 2018, 431, 433; *Schrey/Thalhofer*, NJW 2017, 1431.

In some cases, the smart contract is referred to as contractual text. Statements describing the smart contract as contract text written in a programming language demonstrate this.[53] An alternative view understands the smart contract as a technical solution for executing a performance promise without any influence on the contractual performance program.[54] At a different level of discussion, some argue that the smart contract is part of the contract because the code is incorporated into the contract.[55] Such statements are somewhat imprecise, as they risk confusing the question of inclusion with the character of the smart contract. However, they are probably based on the understanding of the program code as a contractual text, which can indeed be considered as part of the contract. At the same time, *Möslein* rightly points out that such a contract text can be made part of a contract by reference. These fundamental concepts are obviously not mutually exclusive but describe different forms of the relationship between contract and smart contract.

The underlying question of these concepts concerns the consistency of the content of the contract and the software. This is central from a legal perspective, as deviations can lead to a contract not being implemented correctly by the program. The solution to this fundamental problem represents the central challenge for the use of smart contracts (see 3. below).

3. Challenges of automating contractual relationships through smart contracts

The use of smart contracts, regarded as the automated triggering of services based on predefined conditions, has long been part of everyday life, as the example of vending machines shows.

Depending on the subject matter and the degree of automation, automating contractual relationships through smart contracts can encounter significant challenges, some of which may not be fully resolved. For example, smart contracts for executing agreements with long contract duration and large contract terms are currently difficult to realise. This is because the consideration in the smart contract, such as cryptocurrency, must be held

53 For example, *Durovic/Janssen*, in DiMatteo et al., The Cambridge Handbook of Smart Contracts, Blockchain and Technology and Digital Platforms (fn. 46), p. 68 f.

54 *Mik*, Law, Innovation and Technology 2017, 269, 274.

55 *Möslein*, in: Braegelmann/Kaulartz, Rechtshandbuch Smart Contracts (fn. 51), p. 81, 94 para. 21.

within the smart contract if a service provider is not used for a payment guarantee. However, complete automation of the contractual relationship by eliminating service providers is generally not the primary objective of the parties. In particular when the focus is on the efficiency of contract execution for a large number of uniform contractual relationships, smart contracts are the method of choice.

Smart contracts face two major legal challenges. On the one hand, it is necessary to ensure that the contract and the software match, and on the other, that both the contract and the software match with the facts.

a) The conformity of contract text and software

The goal of matching contracts and software is the fundamental challenge in the design of smart contracts. If the contract is to be fulfilled by automatically triggering contract-relevant actions based on predefined conditions, it is essential that the conditions embodied in the software correspond exactly to the content of the contract.

The content of the contract to be executed by a smart contract is regularly mapped in multiple ways.[56] These include the contractual declarations, such as a text or other expressed agreements, possibly supplemented or even provided for by legal provisions, and the conditions defined in the smart contract, i.e., the code, by which the contract-relevant actions are triggered.[57]

aa) The concept of the smart legal contract

The term smart legal contract describes an interesting approach to clarifying the relationship between contract and software. The basic idea behind this concept is to describe the contractual promise to be executed by the software in natural language text and document it alongside the software. The programmer of the smart contract thus specifies, in a form that is directly usable for the users of the smart contract, which natural language contract text is to be implemented by the software. By referring to the

---

56 *Zheng*, et al., FGCS 2020, 475, 477.

57 Cf. *Allen*, Wrapped and Stacked: 'Smart Contracts' and the Interaction of Natural and Formal Language, in: Allen/Hunn (eds.), Smart Legal Contracts: Computable Law in Theory and Practice, 2022, p. 23, 32 f.

respective natural language performance promise in a contract, a discrepancy between the contract and the natural language text of the smart contract can be avoided. The smart legal contract thus proves not to be an independent category of contract or software, but rather a concept for clarifying a quality requirement for authors and users of a smart contract, who should always specify in natural language which performance promise is to be executed by the software.

This concept is widely used. It underlies the Accord Project,[58] for example, which has developed a detailed concept for ensuring the consistency of contract text and software and aims to build a repository of smart contracts that follow this approach. The Accord Project's approach is used, for example, in the smart contracts of the Industry 4.0 Legal Testbed project.

Ultimately, this approach also highlights the difficulty of ensuring that the agreement between the contracting parties and the content of the contract on which the software was programmed are consistent. This raises the question of how to proceed in the event of discrepancies, specifically whether the contract or the software should be decisive for the fulfilment of overriding obligations. In this regard, different approaches are conceivable and widespread in practice.

bb) Prevalence of the software

The software is prevalent if and insofar as the content of the contract is defined by the processes defined in the software or otherwise in the machine. In this case, the contractual content outside the software is at best described in broad outline in text form and reference is otherwise made to the design of the software or machine. Simple smart contracts often proceed in this way, not least the vending machine. Here, essential content is communicated through context and minimal textual information (e.g., price) or visual information (presence of goods); otherwise, reference is made to the factual design or the content of the contractual declaration is derived from this design. For more complex contracts, however, this approach is not in the interests of the parties.

For more complex contracts, the contract text is typically set out in writing, as in the smart legal contract concept. Here, any discrepancies can only be resolved by the rule of the software's authoritativeness in favour of

58 Accord Project, available at: https://accordproject.org/about (last accessed 23.5.2024).

the software. As there is no legal principle of this effect, it can only arise on the basis of an express or tacit agreement. Such an agreement is possible in principle, but the scope of this possibility has not yet been clarified. This applies in particular if the deviations change the balance of interests. There are likely to be narrow limits here, especially if the deviation was not known or recognisable to the disadvantaged party.

At the same time, deviations raise questions about the obligations of the parties with regard to avoiding such deviations. Such an obligation will probably have to be recognised as a secondary contractual obligation, the culpable breach of which can trigger a claim for damages.

cc) Prevalence of the contract

From a legal perspective, the prevalent nature of the contract is the fundamental solution prescribed by contract law. In practice, however, this leads to legal uncertainty and considerable legal risks. If it is determined, possibly through a court decision, that the software does not accurately represent the contract, the smart contract may fail to execute the agreement correctly. This could result in the general consequences of non-fulfilment of the contractual obligation in question. These legal ramifications can only be avoided if the parties waive warranties and liabilities in this regard, thus accepting the authoritative nature of the software.

In addition, there are the usual means of minimising the negative consequences of non-performance, such as negotiations, which can be supported in the contract by negotiation obligations etc., if necessary. However, these instruments place limits on the automation of contract fulfilment, as they typically require manual intervention.

b) Conclusiveness of the contract

The conformity of the contract with the facts can also be referred to as the "completeness of the contract". This presupposes that the contract fully and conclusively regulates all elements and legal issues relating to the execution of the contract.

In contract law, the completeness of the contract is ensured by various sources, in particular by dispositive law, which may contain rules that are supplemented by elements of gap filling, in particular supplementary interpretation of the contract, etc. In addition, the contracting parties can avoid gaps through general clauses. The problem of legal uncertainty in transactions when gaps are filled can, in principle, be accepted by the parties if the gaps are the rare exception.

With smart contracts, these tried-and-tested instruments reach their limits in several respects. When a contract is implemented in a computer program, the contractual rules are explicitly defined in the program. Therefore, the contractual rules must be explicitly and completely known to the programmer. This is not the case if the relevant content of the contract is determined by recourse to dispositive law, by interpreting general clauses, or even by way of supplementary interpretation of the contract. Therefore, these instruments, which are often extremely important in practice, cannot be used for smart contracts.

The simplest solution to this difficulty is to deviate from automated contract execution by allowing manual intervention in the execution of the contract and to reach an agreement outside of the smart contract if there are gaps in the contract. In this case, of course, automation is restricted. In addition, the smart contract does not contain a final regulation.

Such interventions are envisaged in the smart contracts generated in the Industry 4.0 Legal Testbed project, for example. In particular, these provide for corrections to declarations of fact, which can be used to clarify incorrect information and resolve differences of opinion on facts relevant to the contract. In certain cases, it is also possible to cancel the automated execution of the contract. This ensures that the actual facts take precedence, but the (complete) automation of contract execution is not guaranteed. This arrangement is based on the assumption that the parties to an industrial co-operation seek automation primarily for reasons of efficiency and that the exclusion of manual intervention is not a priority.

An alternative solution is to ensure the completeness of the smart contract by excluding objections. This means that the parties agree that the terms of the contract are determined solely by the conditions set out in the program and that any objections not set out there will not be taken into account. Such an exclusion of objections is permissible in principle. However, there are limits here too, which are not clear in detail.

These considerations show that smart contracts face considerable fundamental challenges in terms of both the software and the design of the underlying contract, which require very different designs depending on the subject matter of the transaction and the intention of the parties.

III. Legal framework for automated data transactions

Against the foregoing background on the fundamental challenges of smart contracts on the one hand and data transactions on the other, it is of particular interest which legal framework conditions exist for the design of autonomous data transactions, not least the significance of the Data Act in this respect.

1. Overview

A specific legal framework for data transactions does not exist yet. However, the currently emerging legal framework for data[59] also contains a number of rules that are directly or indirectly relevant to data transactions. In this respect, a central element of the legal framework are those legal acts that grant rights of access to data and thus create both a need and a legal basis for data transactions.[60]

As data transactions often take place through the involvement of intermediaries, the provisions of the Data Governance Act, in particular, the rules on data service providers,[61] are important. The Data Act also contains regulations on individual elements of data transactions. For example, according to Article 8 para. 1 of the Data Act, a data sharing agreement must be concluded for data transfers that take place on the basis of the access rights under Articles 3 and 4 of the Data Act.[62] In addition, the clause control provision under Article 13 Data Act applies,[63] which extends the in-

59 See, for example, *Apel/Huber*, JuS 2024, 410; *Borges*, in: Borges/Keil, Rechtshandbuch Big Data (fn. 2), § 1 para. 30 ff.; *Hoernig/Ilharco*, Policy Paper 26 – European Data Strategy: Regulatory & Policy Aspects (fn. 23), p. 3 ff.

60 See for example, *Apel/Huber*, JuS 2024, 410; *Borges*, in: Borges/Keil, Rechtshandbuch Big Data (fn. 2), § 1 para. 30 ff.

61 For an overview, see *Borges* in: Borges/Keil, Rechtshandbuch Big Data (fn. 2), § 5 para. 234 ff.

62 For more details, see *Berberich*, in: Borges/Keil, Rechtshandbuch Big Data (fn. 2), § 3 para. 103 ff.

63 See for example *Berberich*, in: Borges/Keil, Rechtshandbuch Big Data (fn. 2), § 3 para. 105 f.; *Borges*, in Borges/Keil, Rechtshandbuch Big Data (fn. 2), § 3 para. 265 ff.

strument of clause control to pre-formulated contracts between companies for the first time under European law.[64]

According to Article 13 para. 1 of the Data Act, clause control applies to provisions on access to data and data use, i.e., to the contractual relationship between the data holder and the data recipient.[65] Accordingly, unfair terms in such contracts are invalid, with unfairness determined through a three-stage procedure akin to the concept of general term control established in the German General Terms and Conditions Act of 1976. In addition to a list of invalid clauses, having the effect enumerated in Article 13 para. 4 of the Data Act, the presumption of unfairness extends to an additional list of contractual terms with effects stipulated in Article 13 para. 5. Furthermore, as a general rule, Article 13 para. 3 of the Data Act classifies a contractual term as unfair if its application constitutes a "gross deviation from good commercial practice" and is "contrary to the principle of good faith".

The term "good commercial practice" (not defined in the Data Act) is, therefore, of considerable importance. This is where the "model contractual terms" to be issued by the Commission under Article 41 of the Data Act come into play. It may be assumed that the Commission intends these to form the benchmark for good commercial practice within the meaning of Article 13 para. 3 of the Data Act.[66] Whether the European legislature has created a gateway for indirect regulation of data transactions will ultimately be determined by the case law of the ECJ. Otherwise, the general rules, particularly contract law, apply to the discussion on the legal framework for data transactions, since special rules for data as the subject of contracts do not exist yet.[67]

In addition, all rules that grant rights to data as an embodiment or information content, such as intellectual property law, or governing its processing, such as data protection law, must be observed insofar as they are affected by data transactions. Such rights and the legal uncertainty regarding their existence are likely to be the main legal obstacles to data transactions.

64 *Beinke/Daute,* RDi 2024, 69, 70; *Borges*, Borges/Keil, Rechtshandbuch Big Data (fn. 2), § 5 para. 265; *Staudenmayer*, in: Janssen/Schulte-Nölke (eds.), Researches in European Private Law and Beyond, 2020, 65, 89.

65 Cf. recital 53 Data Act; see also *Borges,* in: Borges/Keil, Rechtshandbuch Big Data (fn. 2), § 5 para. 268; *Witzel,* CR 2022, 561, 563.

66 *Borges,* in Borges/Keil, Rechtshandbuch Big Data (fn. 2), § 5 para. 272.

67 *Keil,* in: Borges/Keil, Rechtshandbuch Big Data (fn. 2), § 15 para. 35.

In particular, data protection law is considered a major obstacle to data sharing as it often hinders data transfer.[68]

2. The Data Act's regulation of smart contracts

To date, there are no specific legal regulations governing the automation of contract conclusion and execution or the use of smart contracts.[69] Therefore, as shown above, it is of particular interest that the Data Act contains a provision on smart contracts in its Article 36.

a) Overview of Article 36 Data Act

As the title of Article 36 makes clear, the regulation applies to smart contracts (see below) for the execution of "data sharing agreements". Surprisingly, the term "data sharing agreement" is not defined in the Data Act. The term refers to contracts on data sharing, as can be seen from the mention in Article 12 para. 2 of the Data Act and Article 37 para. 6 lit. b). It includes both the mandatory agreements to be concluded under Article 8 Data Act and contracts concluded without a legal obligation.

The main material regulation is contained in Article 36 para. 1 of the Data Act, which in its lit. a) to e) contains five basic requirements for the design of smart contracts for data transactions.

In terms of robustness and access control, the smart contract must offer access control mechanisms and a very high degree of robustness to prevent functions and protect against manipulation by third parties (lit. a). With the requirement of secure termination and interruption, it must be ensured that transactions can be terminated, and the contract can be reset, interrupted, and terminated if necessary (lit. b).

Furthermore, the requirement for data archiving and continuity means that, in the event of interruption or termination, the smart contract must offer the possibility of archiving transactions, logic, and code so that transactions can be verified based on records (lit. c). The requirement of access

68 According to a study commissioned by the European Commission, 49 % of the companies surveyed stated that they do not engage in data sharing for data protection reasons, see *Arnaut/Pont/Scaria/Bergmann/Leconte*, Study on data sharing between companies in Europe (fn. 10), p. 44.

69 For detailed information on the applicable rules, see, *Kipker/Birreck/Niewöhner/Schnorr*, MMR 2020, 509, 510 ff.

control demands that the smart contract is protected by strict access control mechanisms at the governance level, i.e., in monitoring and control, as well as at the level of the contract, i.e., the transactions (lit. d).

Finally, consistency, i.e., the smart contract's conformity with the provisions of the data sharing agreement it executes must be ensured (lit. e).

Compliance with these material requirements is ensured by the concept of conformity assessment and declaration. According to Article 36 para. 2, the vendor of the smart contract must conduct a conformity assessment and issue an EU declaration of conformity if the requirements are met. With the declaration of conformity, the vendor assumes responsibility for fulfilling the requirements in accordance with paragraph 3. Paragraphs 2 and 3 thus introduce the familiar concept of European product safety law for smart contracts in data transactions.

The following paragraphs serve to substantiate the material requirements of Article 36 para. 1. According to para. 5, the Commission mandates European standardisation organisations to prepare drafts for harmonised standards. In addition, the Commission may make the concretisation by means of an implementing act through common specifications. The following paragraphs, 6 to 11, are dedicated to common specifications. Paragraph 6 regulates the conditions under which the Commission may act and the procedure for adopting the implementing act. Paragraphs 7 and 8 regulate the participation of relevant bodies and stakeholders: according to paragraph 7, the Commission must inform the committee referred to in Article 22 of Regulation (EU) No 1025/2012 that the requirements of paragraph 6 are met for its activities before drawing up common specifications. The European Data Innovation Board ("EDIB") and the views of other relevant bodies or expert groups must be considered during the consultation, and the stakeholders must also be consulted.

If a Member State considers that the common specifications do not correctly implement the requirements of paragraph 1, it may notify the Commission in accordance with paragraph 11, and the Commission may then amend the common specification. Where a harmonised standard is proposed for publication after the adoption of an implementing act, the Commission shall repeal the implementing act to the extent that its content is covered by the harmonised standard. It is also noteworthy that, according to Article 36 para. 4 of the Data Act, the vendor of a smart contract is entitled to the presumption that the requirements of para. 1 are met if the harmonised standards are met. The same applies to common specifications in accordance with para. 9.

The overview shows that Article 36 of the Data Act contains the basis for a fairly comprehensive regulation of smart contracts for data transactions. Particularly, paragraph 1 sets the course for essential basic questions regarding the design of smart contracts. Considering the challenges of smart contracts for automated data transactions mentioned above, it is therefore of interest to understand the significance of this standard for smart contracts and data transactions in detail.

b) The term "smart contract" in the Data Act

The term "smart contract" is defined in Article 2 No. 39 Data Act with two half-sentences, the first of which defines the smart contract, in accordance with the widespread definition in the literature,[70] as a computer program for the automated execution of a contract. The second half-sentence appears to refer to blockchain technology, as ensuring the integrity and accuracy of the data records and guaranteeing the sequence are characteristic features of a distributed ledger.

However, this conclusion would be incorrect, as can be seen from recital 104 sentence 3. According to this, the definition should be technology-neutral, but blockchain is mentioned in recital 104 sentence 4 exclusively as an example of implementation ("electronic ledger"). The second half-sentence of Article 2 No. 39 is therefore only intended to distinguish smart contracts from any other software in connection with the performance of contractual acts. The decisive feature of smart contracts, which is rightly at the beginning of the second half-sentence, is the reference to a sequence of electronic data records. This feature is indeed characteristic and central to smart contracts in today's technical understanding, because a smart contract actually works in a predefined sequence of states. This feature is particularly pronounced when using blockchain technology, as the respective states are typically stored in a block.[71]

However, it is also possible to distinguish such states of the algorithm in other designs, in which conditions are formulated and their fulfilment or non-fulfilment is determined in a later step. The characteristics of guaranteeing integrity and the correctness of the sequence appear to be rather

70 See above, II.2.a).

71 *Glarner/Meyer,* Smart Contracts in Escrow-Verhältnissen, available at: https://jusletter.weblaw.ch/juslissues/2017/917/smart-contracts-in-e_6f2f86ebed.html__ONCE&login=false (last accessed 16.5.2024); *Hacker/Thomale,* European Company and Financial Law Review 2018, 645, 649 f.

inappropriate, as they are more likely to be design requirements than suitable demarcation characteristics. The essential requirement of sequencing for a smart contract already results from the feature of sequence.

The term smart contract is, therefore, very broad and covers all applications in which a contractual performance action is carried out automatically using a sequence of states based on predefined conditions.

In the case of data transactions, the provision of data and the issue of a consideration or even just documentation, for example, in the form of a receipt, can be considered as an act of performance in this sense.

c) The significance of Article 36 Data Act for smart contracts

With regard to the regulation of smart contracts, a distinction must be made between three different areas of regulation: regulations on the design of the software, regulations on the contractual significance of the software, not least the relationship between the software and the contract as well as the overall life circumstances, and finally the regulations on the contractual relationship to be executed by means of the smart contract.

aa) Article 36 and design of the software

The material requirements for smart contracts summarised in Article 36 para. 1 of the Data Act address the design of the software and are directly relevant here. Paragraph 1 obliges the vendor of an application that uses smart contracts to comply with the design requirements set out in a) –e). As the term "vendor" used in the Data Act suggests, Article 36 para. 1 of the Data Act is arguably intended to address anyone who places a smart contract on the market, regardless of the basis under civil law.

Only in the absence of a vendor is a person who uses smart contracts as part of their professional activity to execute a data sharing agreement addressed, primarily intermediaries and service providers. Data holders and data recipients are not covered, as Article 36 para. 2 Data Act is only applicable if the smart contract is used "for third parties".

The requirements set out in Article 36 para. 1 lit. a) – e) are not surprising but correspond to the requirements that are generally discussed in relation to smart contracts. However, the provisions of paragraph 1 are very general and provide little concrete guidance. The vagueness of paragraph 1 is, therefore, problematic insofar as the vendor must issue a declaration of conformity in accordance with paragraph 2.

bb) Article 36 and design of the contract

The requirements of Article 36 para. 1 for the design of the software also indirectly affect the contractual relationship between the parties intending to implement an existing contract through smart contracts. This is because the corresponding elements of the software may necessitate a contractual basis or coordination with the contract. For instance, the rules on access control mentioned in Article 36 para. 1 lit d) are typically addressed in a contract between the parties, such as a framework agreement or as part of a one-off contract.

Article 36 of the Data Act does not contain any direct provisions for this accompanying contract. However, Article 36 para. 1 lit. e) contains a standard in the form of the requirement of consistency, which is essential for this contractual relationship and indirectly also for the content of the smart contract agreements.

cc) Smart contracts and the requirement of consistency, Article 36 para. 1 lit. e) Data Act

From a legal perspective, it is of interest whether Article 36 directly or indirectly addresses the fundamental legal challenges of smart contracts. In particular, it is relevant to determine whether the requirement of consistency under paragraph 1 lit. e) sheds light on the issue of conformity between software and facts or between software and the contract.

Article 36 para. 1 lit. e) concerns conformity with the terms of the data sharing agreement implemented by the smart contract, addressing the alignment of software with the contract. The vendor of the smart contract is then obligated to ensure this compliance. It is noteworthy that the vendor of the smart contract cannot fulfil this obligation alone, as the data sharing agreement, the implementation of which is at issue here, is established in the relationship between the data holder and the data recipient. They are not the recipients of the obligation under Article 36 and, as a rule, are also not in the role of the vendor of the smart contract.

Therefore, the obligation of Article 36 can only pertain to ensuring the presence of a (legally permissible) contractual provision that is executed in the smart contract. Additionally, the vendor of the smart contract must specify precisely which contractual provisions are executed by the software.

As a result, Article 36 para. 1 lit. e) is remarkable in several respects and is of fundamental importance in understanding smart contracts. Firstly, it should be noted that this obligation necessitates a genuine legal design. Consistency can only be established through a legal assessment that determines the content of the contractual provision and evaluates the action created in the software in light of this content.

Further, it is fundamental to establish that the responsibility of the vendor of a smart contract extends to the contractual provisions. This clarifies that a smart contract is not just a piece of software designed for the execution of (any) legally permissible actions, but a computer program designed for the fulfilment of a specific contractual provision, which consequently presupposes the existence of this provision, at least conceptually.

Notably, the requirement of consistency quickly reaches its limits here, as the content of a contractual provision always results from the context of the contract as a whole. However, as defined in Art. 2 No. 39 Data Act, a smart contract is a software "used for the automated execution of an agreement or part thereof". Therefore, in principle, smart contracts can be used to implement (only) part of a contract, possibly a single executable action. Accordingly, the requirement of consistency in no way applies to the whole contractual agreement between a data holder and a data recipient but exclusively refers to the "part" of the contract executed by the software.

Therefore, the vendor of the smart contract has the freedom to decide which contractual provisions are executable with the software. In this context, a clear link must be established between the software and the contractual provisions to be executed. Additionally, smart contract users must be made aware of this link so they can take it into account accordingly in their contracts.

The requirement of consistency, therefore, proves to be a complex design task that is only partially addressed in the Data Act with regard to the technical design (of the software). How the vendor is to ensure consistency or, more precisely, enable consistency, is not regulated. In line with the concept of the smart legal contract (see II.3. above), it would make sense to explicitly state the provisions or provisions that are to be implemented by the software.

For the question of whether Art. 36 lit. e) contains a provision regarding the conformity of software and contract, a nuanced response is needed. Conformity is required as a design requirement. Since the contractual relationship between the data holder and the data recipient is not regulated, the exact content of the contract and the legal consequences of any non-conformity between the contract and the software remain unclear. In particular, this ambiguity fails to address whether regulations such as general clauses or undefined legal terms are permissible in data sharing agreements and how they relate to the requirement of consistency.

Ultimately, not even the consistency of the software and the respective contractual provision is regulated, as the specific content of the contractual provision is determined by the contract as a whole (here: the data sharing agreement), which is not determined by the vendor of the smart contract, but by the parties to the contract.

d) Article 36 as product safety law for smart contracts

The analysis of Article 36 of the Data Act shows that the regulation contains design requirements for smart contracts and, in this respect, also legal aspects, particularly regarding the determination of the contractual provisions implemented by the algorithm. However, Article 36 does not regulate the data sharing agreement or other contracts.

If we consider the regulatory concept of Article 36 of the Data Act, we will have to characterise this provision as a product safety law for smart contracts. The regulatory concept corresponds exactly to the concept of product safety law, which obliges the manufacturer of a product to observe certain design requirements for the product. The rule on specification via technical standards is also typical of product safety law.

It is interesting to note that the objectives of Article 36 of the Data Act differ from the typical objectives of product safety law. Product safety law aims to mitigate risks to the legal interests of third parties arising from the use of physical products.[72] Article 36 of the Data Act, however, is not concerned with preventing risks posed by a physical product, nor indirectly with risks arising from transmitted data. Rather, the object of protection is the functioning of data transmission as an efficient and trustworthy element of the infrastructure. Therefore, the standard can be seen as a case

72 See for an overview, *Ruohonen*, International Cybersecurity Law Review 2022 Vol. 3, 345, 346 ff.

of "legal Transplant",[73] which utilises regulatory concepts from product safety law to determine product requirements concerning the efficiency and functional security of data transactions.

From the perspective of vendors and users of smart contracts for data transactions, these provisions raise numerous follow-up questions, particularly regarding the relationship between Article 36 of the Data Act and contractual warranty and liability.

From the perspective of third parties, it is of interest whether the obligations of Article 36 of the Data Act can be used to establish the existence of a product defect within the meaning of product liability law, and whether the obligations of the vendors under Article 36 can be characterised as tortious obligations, so-called duty of care.

e) Data Act and data transactions

Article 36 of the Data Act does not contain any regulation on data transactions. This is in order as smart contracts are not contracts but computer programs for the execution of certain contractually obliged actions. They are merely a tool to support data transactions. Thus, the relevant rules on data transactions are derived, as discussed earlier (above III.1), in the general rules of contract law and other provisions relevant to data transactions. This also applies to the relationship between the computer program and the contract, and to the conclusiveness of the contract.

The impact of the clause control according to Article 13 Data Act is of particular interest in this respect. Pursuant to Article 13 para. 1 of the Data Act, clause control extends to contractual provisions relating to data access or data use. The term "data access," which is not defined in the Act, is to be understood in a broad sense and therefore includes all forms of data sharing. The contractual basis of the data sharing is therefore covered by clause control. Consequently, this also applies to provisions of this contractual basis that concern the relationship between the contract and the execution of the contract through smart contracts. Thus, the central legal challenges of smart contracts are also subject to clause control under Article 13 of the Data Act insofar as they concern data transactions.

As described above (III.1.), such clauses are invalid under Article 13 of the Data Act if they prove to be unfair due to a breach of good commercial

73 The term refers to the process of using legal regulations in another legal system; see, for example, *Watson*, Legal Transplants: an approach to comparative law. University of Georgia Press, 2nd ed. 1993, p. 21.

practice and good faith. It is interesting in this respect that the Commission's mandate under Article 41 of the Data Act is limited to rules on access and cloud computing. Smart contracts are not mentioned, so the Commission probably has no mandate in this respect, not even regarding the relationship between smart contracts and contracts.

It is currently impossible to assess what constitutes good commercial practice regarding the relevant issues; legal discussion and practical use are still in their infancy, as outlined above. Therefore, the central questions of contract law concerning smart contracts remain open.

3. Need for regulation of smart contracts and data transactions

The design requirements of Article 36 of the Data Act concern general questions of smart contracts that do not directly relate to the specifics of data sharing transactions, characterising them as general requirements. At the same time, the scope of the standard is limited; it does not address the specific legal issues of smart contracts. Thus, the relationship between the contract and software is only partially regulated, and its significance for the contract itself and liability is not affected. Furthermore, the relationship between the smart contract and the subject matter, as well as the requirement of completeness of the smart contract and the admissibility of exclusions of objections, are not regulated.

In particular, the responsibility of smart contract manufacturers regarding compliance with the design requirements is not regulated. Given the foreseeable and not insignificant liability risks that arise in contract and tort law, depending on the interpretation of Article 36 of the Data Act, this would certainly be of interest in order to create legal certainty for the benefit of smart contract vendors. Considering that the development of smart contracts for data transactions is an urgent task in the overall context of data sharing, the existing legal uncertainty in this respect is problematic.

Additionally, there is a lack of regulations on the infrastructure of smart contracts. A framework for certification by third parties, which is not regulated by Article 36 of the Data Act, would be interesting here. It is in the interest of product security to have smart contracts tested and certified. While the Data Act does not restrict this, it also does not provide support. Given the legal uncertainty regarding liability risks, a regulation that exempts the vendor from liability in the event of certification would be desirable.

The question of whether there is a need for regulation of data transactions cannot be conclusively answered based on this article. It is evident that data transactions face significant legal challenges, particularly concerning data quality in both syntactic and semantic terms, as well as responsibility for the information content, both at the level of contractual content and tortious liability. Additionally, there is an urgent need for a legal infrastructure for data transactions, encompassing data labelling schemes, verification, and determination of data quality. A legal and organisational framework must be established to facilitate these processes at minimal cost. However, in practice, achieving this goal remains a distant prospect.

IV. Conclusion

The analysis shows that the development of smart contracts for data transactions is essential to ensure the necessary efficiency of data transactions. The legal framework for data transactions, as well as the central aspect of the automation of data transactions, is still in its infancy and is far from complete. Many key issues, such as responsibility for data quality, are still unresolved.

The same applies to the specific questions of the automation of contractual relationships through smart contracts, which primarily concern the relationship between the contractual provision and the algorithm that implements it. These central questions are also not addressed by the Data Act.

It is doubtful whether these issues are currently to be moulded into binding law by the European legislature. The extremely far-reaching activities of the last European legislative period in the area of data law must first be tested in practice, and it takes little imagination to predict the need for corrections and additions. It therefore seems more important to promote research and the development of concepts for data transactions and smart contracts for their efficient implementation.

Cloud-Contracts

Switching of Providers – Mandatory Requirements, important Exception and their Impact on Standard Contractual Clauses for Cloud Computing

*Andreas Sattler**

In order to facilitate a switching of providers the EU legislator imposes mandatory requirements on providers of PaaS, IaaS and SaaS. At the same time the DA is intended to promote competition in an oligopolistic market. In order to achieve these goals, the *EU Commission* will also draw up standard contractual clauses for cloud computing contracts by 12th September 2025. These will initially serve to support the parties in drafting and negotiating such contracts. However, it is predictable that these standard contractual clauses will be declared binding in a second step. This article analyses the mandatory requirements of the DA for the switching of providers, identifies challenges and exceptions for its application and, on this basis, presents an initial proposal for standard contractual clauses.

I. Introduction

For more than a decade, the *EU Commission* has been pursuing the goal of strengthening the use of cloud computing in the EU through accompanying legislative measures. In terms of content, the initial aim was to strengthen confidence in the reliability and security of cloud computing in order to realise presumed welfare-economic efficiency gains.[1] After the growth rates of cloud computing rose rapidly – without the accompanying intervention of the European legislator – it became increasingly clear that three US providers, *AWS* (*Amazon*), *Azure* (*Microsoft*) and *Google Cloud* (*Alphabet*), are particularly successful. Meanwhile their combined market share

---

* Dr., LL.M. (Nottingham), currently representing the chair for Law and Informatics, *Karlsruhe Institute for Technology* (KIT). This publication benefitted from a fellowship of the author at the *Weizenbaum Institute* in March 2024.

1 *EU Commission*, A Digital Single Market Strategy for Europe, 6.5.2015, COM (2015) 192 final, p. 16s.

amounts to approximately 66 %, with AWS alone already having a market share of more than 30 % in key areas.[2] This means that the European and global market for cloud computing currently has an oligopolistic structure.

As a result of this market concentration, it is generally understandable that the focus is currently on facilitating the switching between cloud providers.[3] This led to Chapter VI of the EU Data Act (DA),[4] which is largely independent of the other provisions of the DA and standardises mandatory requirements for switching between data processing services. From the legislator's perspective, these requirements serve not only to protect customers, who are typically structurally inferior,[5] but work primarily as a lever to promote competition on the market for data processing services.[6]

Chapter VI DA was rightly described as a "bombshell" (German: “Paukenschlag”).[7] The mandatory requirements are a further central building block in the foundation of a standardised European contract law for the European data economy, the main features of which are becoming gradual-

2 *Richter*, Amazon Maintains Cloud Lead as Microsoft Edges Closer, 5.2.2024, https://www.statista.com/chart/18819/worldwide-market-share-of-leading-cloud-infrastructure-service-providers/ (last viewed: 10.4.2024); *Armstrong*, Microsoft and Amazon Dominate the Cloud, 26.7.2023, https://www.statista.com/chart/30489/revenue-from-cloud-services-by-cloud-sector-market-leaders/ (last viewed 10.4.2024).

3 While an earlier draft of the planned EU Cybersecurity Certification Scheme (EUCS), would have demanded of U.S. cloud providers to set up a joint venture with an EU-based company and to store and process customer data in the EU in order to qualify for the EU cybersecurity label, the latest draft of EUCS circulated to EU governments no longer contains such requirement. *Foo Yun* Chee, EU drops sovereignty requirements in cybersecurity certification scheme, document shows, Reuters, 3.4.2024, https://www.reuters.com/technology/eu-drops-sovereignty-requirements-cybersecurity-certification-scheme-document-2024-04-03/ (last viewed 10.4.2024).

4 Regulation (EU) 2023/2854 of 13.12.2023 on harmonised rules on fair access to and use of data and amending Regulation (EU) 2017/2394 and Directive (EU) 2020/1828 (Data Act), OJ L, of 22.12.2023, p. 1–71.

5 See the preparatory study: Switching of Cloud Services Providers, Study carried out for the European Commission by IDC and Arthur’s Legal, 2018 (https://publications.europa.eu/resource/cellar/898aeca7-647e-11e8-ab9c-01aa75ed71a1.0001.01/DOC_1).

6 The aim to facilitate the competition between service providers can be found in: Rec. 78 s. 1, Rec. 88 s. 4, Rec. 89 s. 4, Rec. 90 s. 1 and Rec. 94 s. 3 DA. Criticising this approach as only formally neutral, whilst causing asymmetric consequences: *Lagoni*, CR 2024, 91 (para. 31).

7 *Rammos/Wilken* DB 2022, 1241 (1245); *Piltz/Zwerschke*, CR 2024, 153 (para. 7).

ly recognisable.[8] However, Chapter VI DA is also likely to be just an interim regulatory step before the European legislator tightens the thumbscrews even further. This regulatory trend means that Art. 23 et seq. DA and in particular the non-binding standard contractual clauses to be drafted by the *EU Commission* in accordance with Art. 41 DA should not be understood as a mere offer.

The success of these standard contractual clauses will depend less on whether they are "perceived by the market as an attractive means".[9] Rather, these non-mandatory standard contractual clauses are also likely to be used by the *EU Commission* to test the willingness of the three major providers to accept what the *EU Commission* considers to be fair conditions. If these standard contractual clauses are not taken into consideration by *Amazon*, *Alphabet* and *Microsoft* when drafting their general terms and conditions, the European legislator could designate them as a binding legal model (German: "gesetzliches Leitbild") within the meaning of Section 307 para. 2 No. 1 German Civil Code and supplement them with a list of expressly prohibited clauses ("black list").

With the mandatory requirements in Chapter VI DA and the non-mandatory standard contractual clauses pursuant to Art. 41 DA, the EU legislator is entering the second level of regulation after the first level in the form of self-regulation by providers within the framework of the Free-Flow-of-Data-Regulation[10] failed.[11] This step-by-step approach with a progressively mandatory character also enables the legislator to uphold the principle of proportionality (Art. 5 para. 4 TEU). In addition, this tiered approach suggests that the standard contractual clauses[12] to be drafted should

8 A second fundamental building block is Directive (EU) 2019/770 of 20.5.2019 on certain aspects concerning contracts for the supply of digital content and digital services (Digital-Content-Directive), OJ L 136 of 22.5.2019, p. 1–27.

9 *Piltz/Zwerschke*, CR 2024, 153 (para. 42) [translation by the author].

10 Regulation (EU) 2018/1807 of 14.11.2018 on a framework for the free flow of non-personal data in the European Union, OJ L 303 of 28.11.2018, p. 59–68. As far as Chapter VI DA is applicable, the Free-Flow-of-Data-Regulation is substituted according to Art. 44 para. 1 DA and the principle *lex posterior derogat legi priori*. Consequently, there remains only room for self-regulation according to the Free-Flow-of-Data-Regulation in so far as the DA contains no stipulation, see also Art. 1 para. 7 DA.

11 Thus, Rec. 79 s. 2 DA legitimises the need to adopt the DA with „the limited uptake of the self-regulatory frameworks developed in response, and the general unavailability of open standards and interfaces". Therefore, a necessity for a "set of minimum regulatory obligations for providers of data processing services" was assumed.

12 These „standard contractual clauses" have to be distinguished from the non-binding model contractual terms on data access and use according to Art. 41 DA.

not – despite the cautious wording of Art. 41 DA[13] – be misinterpreted as a mere "guidance" by the *EU Commission.*

As a result, it essential for data processing service providers to familiarise with the mandatory requirements and exceptions of Art. 23 ss. DA at an early stage and to closely follow and critically monitor the progress of the *EU Commission*'s drafting of standard contractual clauses. This article is intended to provide an introduction. To this end, the scope of application of Art. 23 et seq. DA (II) is analysed before the main legal challenges are illustrated (III). Finally, on this basis – without claiming to be exhaustive – an initial model for such standard contractual clauses on switching will be presented, which the *EU Commission* is to draw up by 12th September 2025 in accordance with Art. 41 DA (IV).

II. Scope of Application

It is beyond the capacity of this article to provide a clear definition of the scope of Chapter VI DA.[14] Certainly the DA's scope is very extensively. The legislator has moved away from the cloudy marketing term "cloud computing" in time and almost completely,[15] replacing it with the technical term "data processing services". However, this term is rather described and not precisely defined by the DA (1). In addition, the DA provides for important exceptions the parameters of which are not clearly defined. These offer providers a certain amount of leeway in which they can structure their business models and contracts, so that data processing services might not always fall within the scope of Chapter VI DA (2).

13 Art. 41 DA requires that the *EU Commission „shall develop and recommend* [...] non-binding standard contractual clauses for cloud computing contracts to assist parties in drafting and negotiating contracts with fair, reasonable and non-discriminatory contractual rights and obligations“ [emphasis added].

14 In this direction: *Piltz/Zwerschke*, CR 2024, 153 (154/Rn. 2 ff.).

15 Whilst the term „cloud computing“ in Chapter VI DA was replaced by the term „data processing service provider“, this adjustment has – presumably – been forgotten as regards Art. 41 DA. Hereafter, the *EU Commission* will – until 12.9.2025 – explicitly draft and recommend „non-binding standard contractual clauses for cloud-computing contracts“.

1. Central requirement: Provider of Data Processing Services

According to Art. 1 para. 1 lit. d, the Data Act harmonises the provisions on switching between *data processing services providers* (DPSPs) that offer their services to customers in the Union. As the place of establishment of the *DPSP* is not decisive, Art. 1 para. 3 lit. f DA – as known from the GDPR – also focuses on the market place principle in order to cover all *DPSPs* with business relations to customers in the territory of the European Union.

According to Art. 2 para. 8 DA, the term *data processing service* (DPS) means a digital service provided to a customer that enables ubiquitous and on-demand network access to a shared pool of configurable, scalable and elastic computing resources of a centralised, distributed or highly distributed nature that can be rapidly provisioned and released with minimal administrative effort or interaction by the service provider.

It is unusual that Rec. 80 s. 4-9 DA contains supplementary definitions that will be decisive for the scope of application of Chapter VI DA. It remains a mystery why the EU legislator defines the terms "location-independent", "scalable", "elastic", "shared pool", "distributed" and "highly distributed", which are central to the definition of *DPS*, only in the non-binding recitals and not as part of the definition in Art. 2 no. 8 DA. In any case, the consequence is greater flexibility and openness to develop the term, but consequently creates greater legal uncertainty as to which services fall within the scope of Chapter VI DA.

It is helpful that the technically defined concept of *DSP* is supplemented by examples in the recitals. For example, Rec. 78 s. 1 and Rec. 80 s. 10 DA clarify that this definition includes edge services as well as cloud services. It follows from Rec. 81 s. 2 DA that the three models of Infrastructure-as-a-Service (IaaS), Platform-as-a-Service (PaaS) and Software-as-a-Service (SaaS) are certainly such *DPSs* within the meaning of Chapter VI DA. Rec. 81 s. 4 DA adds Storage-as-a-Service and Database-as-a-Service[16] to the scope of application.

Finally, Art. 2 para. 9 DA extends the concept of *DPS* to include so-called "same types of services", which are characterised by the fact that they "have the same main objective and the same service model for data processing

16 Including Database-as-a-Service as *DPS* within Chapter VI DA requires that Art. 43 DA – despite its overarching systematic position at the end of the DA – is interpreted restrictively. This delineation as regards the *sui generis* protection of data bases should not have an impact on the application of Chapter VI DA.

as well as the same main functions".[17] In view of the broad definition and the purpose of preventing a provider lock-in of customers, it would be desirable – at least from the perspective of the European legislator – to also consider more recent offers such as Data-as-a-Service or AI-as-a-Service to fall within the term *DPS*, as these (additional) services are particularly likely to cause lock-in effects for customers. At the same time, the question arises as to whether the rapidly growing business models of Cloud Management & Security-as-a-Service qualify as *DPS* under Art. 2 para. 9 DA. One argument against such classification is that these services regularly require more than a minimal interaction on the part of the *DPSP* as stipulated by Art. 2 no. 8 DA.

2. Exceptions from the Scope of Application

The Data Act recognises several exceptions to the scope of application of the otherwise mandatory requirements for switching between *DPSPs*. The exceptions in Art. 31 DA (a) are obvious and easy to understand. Surprisingly and systematically hidden in an unusual position, another exception can be found in Art. 34 para. 2 DA (b).

a) Exceptions for Testing-Versions and Individual Developments, Art. 31 DA

The most far-reaching exception is contained in Art. 31 para. 2 DA. Accordingly, the entire Chapter VI is not applicable if the *DPSP* does not initially provide its customers with a full version, but only a limited version for testing and evaluation purposes and for a limited period of time. As long as the services either cannot yet be fully developed and offered or as long as a customer is still to be convinced of the services, the provider is not yet burdened with the legal obligations of a future switching of providers. This clarification is reasonable because Chapter IV DA also applies to *DPSs* that a provider makes available to its customers without consideration.[18]

In addition, central obligations pursuant to Art. 31 para. 1 DA do not apply to *DPSs* whose central functions have been customised to the specific needs of the customer or have been developed for the purposes of the

17 See Rec. 81 s. 5–7 DA.
18 Art. 23 lit. c and Rec. 78 s. 1 DA.

customer. The wording of Art. 31 para. 1 DA initially suggests that this exception should be interpreted restrictively. As a result, it would only apply to the provision of services that require individual developments and customisations. This interpretation is supported by the fact that, according to the German language version of Rec. 98 s. 1 DA, this exception should only apply to services where most of the main features are specifically tailored to the concrete requirements of an *individual* (German: "einzelnen") customer or where all components have been developed for the purposes of an *individual* (German: "einzelnen") customer".[19] If one draws a parallel to the distinction between individual software and a parameterisation that is merely adapted for the customer (often also called: "customising"), the exception in Art. 31 para. 1 DA would be limited to genuine individual developments.

However, the English language versions of Art. 31 para. 1 DA and of Rec. 98 s. 1 DA use the term "custom-built". The clarification that the exception in Art. 31 para. 1 DA "should" no longer apply to services that the provider of data processing services offers on a large commercial scale via its catalogue of services[20] also leaves some leeway for services to benefit from the exception in Art. 31 para. 1 DA although these services have merely been adapted to customer needs in the sense of a parameterisation.

However, it is more convincing not to overemploy the term "custom-built", but to interpret Art. 31 para. 1 DA to the effect that it only applies to services that are based on genuine individual developments and genuine individualised adjustments.

If service providers invoke the exception in Art. 31 para. 1 DA to their own benefit, the courts must strictly examine this requirement. Not every contract that refers to "individual developments" for the customer in its title, or that places the term "individualised" in the contract preamble, actually lives up to this promise. However, if there is a genuine individual development, the service provider is not obliged under Art. 23 lit. d in conjunction with Art. 24 DA to remove any obstacles that impair the functionally equivalent use of the new *DPSPs* service, nor do the obligations to gradually withdraw switching charges pursuant to Art. 29 DA apply.[21] Furthermore, providers of individualised developments do not have to take appropriate measures to achieve functional equivalence of the new *DPS*

19 Emphasis added by the author.
20 Rec. 98 s. 1 DA.
21 See below III.3.

(Art. 30 para. 1 DA), nor do they have to ensure compatibility with the *EU Commission's* future specifications for interoperability (Art. 30 para. 3 DA).

b) Exception for so-called Multi-Cloud Strategies, Art. 34 para. 2 DA

Art. 34 para. 2 DA contains a further exception. According to this provision, the providers of such *DPSs* that are used in parallel with another *DPS* may continue to charge data extraction fees, provided that these fees do not exceed the costs incurred by the extraction. Art. 34 para. 2 DA thus provides a well-hidden exception in Chapter VIII DA ("Interoperability") to the gradual withdrawal of *switching charges* in the form of a *data egress charge*[22] as stipulated in Art. 29 DA.

The legislator justifies this exception in Rec. 99 s. 1 DA by stating that the DA aims to improve interoperability for the parallel use of multiple, complementary *DPSs*. According to the legislator, this exception, which systematically should have been included in an additional Art. 29 para. 3 DA, is necessary because it is "important, inter alia, for the successful deployment of multi-cloud strategies, which allow customers to implement future-proof ICT strategies and which decrease dependence on individual providers of data processing services".[23] According to Rec. 99 s. 6 DA, this is intended to facilitate a multi-cloud strategy that also helps to strengthen the operational stability of customers' digital systems. The requirements of the DORA-Regulation[24] in the area of financial services are cited as an example.

As a result, the legislator gives certain *DPSPs* the opportunity to claim *data egress charges* in accordance with Art. 34 para. 2 DA and justifies this exception with the interests of the customers. However, this justification is perplexing because it remains completely unclear what connection exists between these charges and the potentially higher resilience of IT infrastructures that (have to) rely on such a multi-cloud strategy. This could presumably be due to the assessment that ensuring interoperability when switching providers in the context of a multi-cloud strategy is particularly

22 On the definition of *data egress charges*, however, overlooking this hidden exemption in Art. 34 para. 2 DA: *Lagoni*, CR 2024, 91 ff.

23 Rec. 99 s. 5 DA.

24 Regulation (EU) 2022/2554 of 14.12.2022 on digital operational resilience for the financial sector and amending Regulations (EC) No 1060/2009, (EU) No 648/2012, (EU) No 600/2014, (EU) No 909/2014 and (EU) 2016/1011, OJ. L 333, of 27.12.2022, p. 1–79.

time-consuming and complex. However, from the customer's point of view, this challenge regularly leads to a strong lock-in effect anyway. This lock-in is further intensified by the *DPSP's* ability to demand an additional *data egress charge* in the future.

It also remains unclear why these challenges, which are associated with such a (desired) multi-cloud strategy, were only taken into account as an exception in Art. 34 para. 2 DA instead of addressing them in Art. 29 para. 5 DA. According to Art. 29 para. 5 DA, the provider is obliged to provide the customer with information about *DPSs* that make the switching of providers very complicated or costly or require an intervention in the data, the digital assets or the service architecture. Put short: The parallel use of several *DPSPs* as part of a multi-cloud strategy will typically fall within the scope of Art. 29 para. 5 DA, too.

III. Key legal challenges for the drafting of contracts

Obviously, numerous challenges arise in connection with the switching of providers, most of which have been known for decades in the context of IT contract law, especially in the context of complex outsourcing contracts. In the following, this article will therefore only briefly illustrate those challenges that the Data Acts further intensifies.[25]

1. Objects of Switching

In accordance with Art. 2 No. 34 DA, the switching of providers describes a process in which at least the previous *DPSP*, the customer of the *DPS* and, if applicable, an acquiring *DPSP* are involved. In terms of substance, this process is characterised by the fact that the customer switches from using a *DPS* to using another *DPS* of the same service type or another service

25 An additional important challenge follows from the difficult relationship between the customer's claims against the previous *DPSP* (Chapter VI DA) and the user's claims against the data holder pursuant to Art. 4 and Art. 5 DA. With an attempt at delimitation Rec. 16 s. 4 DA: „This Regulation [meant: Chapter III DA?] should also not cover data which was obtained, generated or accessed from the connected product, or which was transmitted to it, for the purpose of storage or other processing operations on behalf of other parties, who are not the user, such as may be the case with regard to servers or cloud infrastructure operated by their owners entirely on behalf of third parties, inter alia for use by an online service."

offered by another *DPSP*. Finally, the transition to the ICT infrastructure on the customer's own premises is also covered (so-called "insourcing"), whereby any form of switching of providers "including through extracting, transforming and uploading the data" takes place. While Rec. 85 s. 1 DA largely repeats the definition in Art. 2 no. 34 DA, Rec. 84 DA states that the customer must be able to transfer its exportable data and digital assets as part of the switching and that – in case of services in the form of IaaS – functionally equivalent services must be made available to it by the new provider.

Although the definition of *exportable data* in Art. 2 para. 38 DA poses complex questions regarding the delimitation of intellectual property rights and the protection of trade secrets in individual cases, it is not unusual.[26] Contrastingly, major challenges are likely to occur based on the concept of *digital assets.*

Pursuant to Art. 2 No. 32 DA, *digital assets* are defined as "elements in digital form, including applications, for which the customer has the right of use, independently from the contractual relationship with the data processing service it intends to switch from". Such a vague term is likely to stimulate different associations by members of various disciplines. While a background in capital market regulation immediately raises the question of whether the legislator is also making a statement on the transferability of so-called crypto-currencies, for intellectual property lawyers the question arises as to why the legislator addresses rights of use in the context of the switching of providers if it otherwise deliberately avoids intellectual property law issues[27] – with the exception of Art. 43 DA.[28] The definition of *digital assets* is particularly unsuccessful because it defines the term by the customer's "right of use, independently from the contractual relationship with the data processing service it intends to switch from". As a result, the

26 According to Art. 2 No. 38 DA exportable data "for the purpose of Articles 23 to 31 and Article 35, means the input and output data, including metadata, directly or indirectly generated, or cogenerated, by the customer's use of the data processing service, excluding any assets or data protected by intellectual property rights, or constituting a trade secret, of providers of data processing services or third parties."

27 According to Art. 1 para. 8 and Rec. 13 the DA is without prejudice to Union and national legal acts providing for the protection of intellectual property rights.

28 Art. 43 DA serves to distinguish it from database protection pursuant to Art. 7 of Directive 96/9/EC (Data-Base-Directive). With criticism as regards Art. 43 DA and its former wording: *Sattler*, in: Borges/Keil, Big Data, 2023, p. 435 (477s.); also, *Wiebe*, GRUR 2023, 227 (228 ss.) and *Wiebe* in Sattler/Zech (eds.), The Data Act – Urgent Need for Synchronisation?, to be published soon.

question arises as to whether the previous *DPSP* can refuse – or is indeed obliged to refuse – to extract *digital assets* if the customer does not provide evidence of its entitlement to use such data that incorporates intellectual property of third parties.

An argument against such an interpretation is that it would not be very plausible if a direct infringement of the rights of third parties by the customer led to the previous *DPSP* having a right to refuse performance *vis-à-vis* its customer. Nevertheless, the answer to this question will probably be left to the *CJEU*, especially since the previous *DPSP* can certainly provide reasons why it does not want to extract digital assets at the customer's request and, meanwhile, reproduce them within the meaning of copyright law,[29] as long as it has not been clarified whether the customer is entitled to rights of use to these digital assets. There are good arguments that the privileges for host providers pursuant to Art. 14 eCommerce Directive[30] intervene in favour of *DPSPs* with regard to such digital assets. However, in the absence of legislative statements on the relationship between the DA and the eCommerce-Directive, considerable legal uncertainties remain – depending on the type of *DPS* offered.

2. Switching Process

Although the switching process is at the centre of Chapter VI DA, important questions remain unanswered or are only rudimentarily regulated. Firstly, it is unclear how this switching of providers can be categorised in terms of contract types, although this classification has significant consequences for the contractual duties (a). In addition, the vague position of the customer, which is only very loosely regulated by Chapter VI DA, will lead to conflicts (b).

29 According to Art. 25 para. 2 lit. g DA a *DPSP* has to make such data available for another 30 calendar days once the switching has been completed. Thus, any reproduction in the context of data extraction cannot be justified by the copyright limitation for transient or incidental reproductions according to Art. 5 para. 1 of the Directive 2001/29/EC on the harmonisation of certain aspects of copyright and related rights in the information society (InfoSoc-Directive), OJ L 167, 22.6.2001, p. 10–19.

30 Directive 2000/31/EC of 8.6.2000 on certain legal aspects of information society services, in particular electronic commerce, in the Internal Market (eCommerce-Directive), OJ L 178, 17.7.2000, p. 1–16.

a) Consequences of a Lack of Typological Classification ("nature of the contract")

The European legislator adheres to its policy of constituting mandatory contract law requirements without deciding on the nature of such contracts.[31] Therefore, the legislator risks creating a dispute as to which performance is contractually owed or when the obligation to perform has been fulfilled. Neither the definition of switching (Art. 2 no. 34 DA) nor the supplementary Rec. 85 DA determine the obligation to be fulfilled by the provider. While Rec. 85 s. 3 DA further diffuses the responsibility by recognising that the "switching process is sometimes managed on behalf of the customer by a third-party entity", s. 5 explains that "providers of data processing services and customers have different levels of responsibilities, depending on the steps of the process referred to." According to s. 6, the current *DPSP* is only responsible for extracting the data to a machine-readable format. In contrast, it remains the responsibility of the customer and the future *DPSP* to upload the data to the new environment. To put it bluntly, one could ask whether the switching model according to Chapter VI DA results in a civil law partnership and thus a legal entity within the meaning of Section 705 para. 2 variant 2 German Civil Code, which is made up of the customer, the previous *DPSP* and the future *DPSP*.

Instead, it would be reasonable and in comformity with the purpose of Chapter VI DA to interpret the obligations of the previous *DPSP* – in case of doubt – as a contractual obligation to deliver a specific result within the meaning of Sections 631 et seq. German Civil Code (German: Werkvertrag). Such an interpretation is suggested by the fact that the previous *DPSP* is obliged to delete the data "providing that the switching process has been completed *successfully*"[32] (Art. 25 para. 2 lit. h DA) and to ensure that, in the case of IaaS, functionally equivalent services are available to the customer after the switching (Art. 30 para. 1 DA). As a result, the provider undoubtedly bears a significant part of the responsibility for the success of the switching. Nevertheless, even the concept of functional equivalence in Art. 2 para. 37 DA remains very vague because it suffices to "re-establishing [...] a minimum level of functionality in the environment of a new data processing service of the same service type".

As a result, Chapter VI DA leaves the question open of when such a success and thus the fulfilment of the performance obligation has occurred.

31 See also: Art. 3 para. 10 and Rec. 12 s. 2 Digital-Content-Directive.

32 Emphasis added by the author.

If the previous *DPSP* assumes that it has fulfilled its switching obligations, it will cease its services – at least after the expiry of the subsequent minimum period for data retrieval in accordance with Art. 25 para. 2 lit. g DA – and refuse further activities. That this option is available for the previous *DPSP* is supported by the fact that no clear criteria for the success of the service are defined and that the DA does not provide for a corresponding obligation of the customer to declare an acceptance.

b) Rights and Duties of the Customer

As the legislator assumes a strong market position of few providers, the focus on the obligations of the providers is essentially consistent. Nevertheless, the – at best – fragmentary regulation of the customer's rights and obligations will very likely lead to conflicts. The "rights and *obligations of the customer* established by this Regulation, including the obligation to cooperate in good faith [...]"[33] are only mentioned in Rec. 85 s. 4 DA.

As Chapter VI DA does not constitute any explicit obligations of the customer, the customer's right to extend the switching process could easily lead to disputes. According to Art. 25 para. 5 DA, the contract must include clauses according to which the customer is entitled to extend the transition period once by the period it deems more appropriate for its own purposes. It is true that the previous *DPSP* retains the right to payment of the agreed standard-service-fee for the *DPS* during this extended transitional period (Rec. 87 s. 6 DA). However, this extension makes it considerably more difficult for the provider – depending on the service provided – to dispose of its own employees and resources. As a result, it remains the task of the courts and eventually the *CJEU* to specify the essential rights and obligations of providers and customers on the basis of the obligation to act in good faith (Art. 27 DA).

3. Gradual Withdrawal of Switching Charges

According to Art. 29 DA, *switching charges* are to be largely withdrawn in two stages. According to Art. 29 para. 2 DA, *reduced switching charges* may be charged – in a surprising deviation from the general applicability date

33 Emphasis added by the author.

of the DA from 12th September 2025 – from 11th January 2024 and until 12th January 2027[34] provided that these do not exceed the costs actually incurred by the provider (a). However, the DA contains several exceptions that allow the previous *DPSPs* to demand the payment of *switching charges* beyond 12th January 2027 (b).

a) Gradual Withdrawal of Data Egress Charges

The European legislator has decided on the gradual, albeit not complete, withdrawal of *switching charges* in accordance with Art. 34 para. 2 DA. According to Art. 2 No. 36 DA, *switching charges* are defined as charges levied by a *DPSP* "on a customer for the actions mandated by [the DA] for switching to the system of a different provider or to on-premises ICT infrastructure, including data egress charges".

This stipulation, which is crucial to facilitating switching has – as expected – already triggered a backlash from the industry which aims at limiting the scope of the term *switching charges.*[35] However, an attempt to teleologically reduce the wording of Art. 2 No. 36 DA so that it *only* covers the levying of *data egress charges* is not convincing for four reasons.

Firstly, such a restrictive interpretation is not compatible with the wording of the definition. According to Art. 2 No. 36 DA, *switching charges* are defined as "*including* data egress charges".[36] This wording cannot be reinterpreted as a withdrawal of data egress charges *exclusively*.[37]

Secondly, such a restrictive interpretation is not compatible with the system of the DA. If the term "*switching charges*" and "*data egress charges*" were actually congruent, the separate definition of the *data egress charge* in Art. 2 No. 35 DA would be superfluous.

Thirdly, the European legislator assumes a multi-leveled concept of switching. According to Rec. 85 s. 1 DA, this consists of "of several steps, including data extraction", but it also might require the transformation of the data and in any case the uploading of the data onto a new destination location. If the legislator is therefore speaking about the withdrawal of *switching charges* and if such a switching is typically not completed with the

34 Art. 50 DA.
35 *Lagoni*, CR 2024, 91 ff.
36 Emphasis added by the author.
37 However, with such argument: *Lagoni*, CR 2024, 91 (para. 4 ss./22).

extraction of data,[38] it must also be possible for such costs to fall under the term of *switching charges* that only arise as a result of a transformation or the uploading of data that has already been extracted.

Fourthly, the European legislator has expressly provided for costs that are not to be covered by the withdrawal of *switching charges*. While this systematic argument does not allow the reverse argument that all other costs arising from switching should be excluded in accordance with Art. 29 para. DA, it follows from this regulatory structure that the term of *switching charges* and that of *data egress charges* are not identical. Furthermore, as Art. 34 para. 2 DA makes clear, not all *data egress charges* will be withdrawn according to Art. 29 DA. If the customer uses several complementary *DPSPs* in parallel (so-called multi-cloud strategy), the existing *DPSPs* can also demand *data egress charges* beyond 12th January 2027.[39]

Put short: The term *switching charges* is to be interpreted broadly and includes all charges that are to be demanded on the occasion of the switching of providers for such actions to which the previous *DPSP* is already legally obliged under Chapter VI DA. As a result, the term *switching charges* does not cover only those charges that the DA continues to permit expressively or at least impliedly.

b) Permissibility of Charges in the Context of a Switching of Providers

If the concept of *switching charges* and, above all, the scope of the gradual withdrawal of *switching charges* is to be determined, this can be done negatively by identifying all charges that the legislator has excluded expressively (aa) or at least impliedly (bb) from the gradual withdrawal of *switching charges* in accordance with Art. 29 DA.

aa) Expressive Exception

Firstly, standard service charges are expressively excluded from the term "*switching charges*" (Art. 2 para. 36 DA) and consequently also from the

38 However, such a data extraction does not suffice the requirements of any of the stipulations according to Art. 25 para. 3 DA. Whilst it is not sufficient as regards a switching of providers (lit. a) nor as regards the switching to an on-premises ICT infrastructure (lit. b), it is superfluous as regards the request for erasure (lit. c).

39 See above II.2.b.

scope of application of Art. 29 DA, cf. Art. 29 para. 4 DA.[40] As a result, the previous *DPSP* may continue to charge the agreed standard service charge for all *DPSs* after the customer's request to switch. This applies during the ongoing switching procedure, which may be extended by the customer,[41] and it applies also to the 30-day retrieval period following the switching.[42]

Secondly, the legislator allows the demanding of *data egress charges* beyond 12th January 2027 in the amount of the costs actually incurred, provided that these either concern individual developments for a customer (Art. 31 para. 1 DA) or are made in connection with a switching of providers in the case of parallel use of several *DPSs* (multi-cloud strategy). The latter is clearly stated in Art. 34 para. 2 DA, although the underlying reasons for this exception remain vague.[43]

Thirdly, the previous *DPSP* may – if switching takes place at a time before the expiry of the agreed minimum contract term – continue to demand a charge as a "sanction". However, such a sanction will – at least according to Section 309 No. 6 German Civil Code – be void in B2C contracts.[44] This exception follows directly from the definition of the switching charge in Art. 2 para. 36 DA and indirectly from Art. 29 para. 4 DA.

However, it should be noted that this charge is expressly linked only to the *time of termination*. According to the unambiguous wording in this respect, the previous *DPSP* shall not be entitled to claim such a contractual penalty in the event of a reduction in the *quantity* of services obtained.[45]

---

40 Also Rec. 89 s. 5 DA.

41 Art. 25 para. 5; Rec. 87 s. 6 DA.

42 Art. 25 para. 2 lit. g DA.

43 Rec. 99 DA.

44 Arguably not void in B2C contracts according to Art. 3 para. 3 Annex No. 1 lit. e Council Directive 93/13/EEC of 5.4.1993 on unfair terms in consumer contracts, OJ L 95, 21.4.1993, p. 29–34.

45 Whilst Art. 2 No. 36, Art. 29 para. 4 and Rec. 89 DA clearly only provide for a remaining obligation of the customer to pay a contractual penalty "in the event of *early* termination" [emphasis added by the author] of a contract, this provision should, in the opinion of *Lagoni* (CR 2024, 91 (para. 21)), also be extended to agreements in which the customer has undertaken "to purchase a certain *amount* of computing power per year (so-called commitment model)" [translation and emphasis added by the author]. However, such an analogy, firstly requires proof that the legislator has missed a loophole and that the agreement on minimum purchase quantities creates – in the event of a switching of providers – a situation of comparable interest to a situation in which a minimum contract term as been agreed.

bb) Potential Implied Exceptions

Two further points of reference can be found in the DA that do not contain any explicit exceptions to Art. 29 para. 1 DA, but at least impliedly suggest such an exception.

(1) Additional Services at Customer's Prior Request

Rec. 89 s. 2 DA clarifies that although the previous *DPSP* can outsource services to third parties, the customer does not have to bear these "costs arising from the outsourcing of services concluded by the source provider of data processing services during the switching process". An exception should exist insofar as it relates to services that the previous *DPSP* provides – possibly by commissioning third parties – at the request of the customer and that go beyond the obligations of the previous *DPSP* constituted by the DA. The previous *DPSP* should be able to charge for such services if "the customer agrees to the price of those services in advance", Rec. 89 s. 8 DA.

It does not take any power of clairvoyance to predict that Rec. 89 DA will lead to disputes between providers and customers. This is because it initially presupposes that there is certainty on all obligations that Chapter VI DA establishes for the previous *DPSP*. Additional and chargeable services can only be agreed upon if they lie beyond the mandatory statutory obligations. The undefined legal concept of the provision of functionally equivalent services (Art. 2 No. 37; Art. 30 para. 1 s. 1 DA) as well as the – as far as can be seen – first Union-autonomous general clause of good faith in Art. 27 DA are predestined for such a dispute about the legal obligations of the previous *DPSP*. Indeed, it may never be possible to determine the duties of the previous *DPSP* conclusively and with legal certainty.

The door opened by Rec. 89 DA for additional claims for remuneration certainly incentivises *DPSPs* to offer customers additional services for remuneration as soon as there is an initial uncertainty about the legal scope of the duties of the previous *DPSP* under the DA. Such claims for remuneration are justified if the customer demands the extraction of switching objects in a special format that is neither part of the harmonised standards for interoperability pursuant to Art. 30 para. 3 DA nor – in the absence of such standards – corresponds to the commonly used and machine-readable format within the meaning of Art. 30 para. 5 DA.

(2) Additional Charge for Highly Costly Switching?

According to Art. 29 para. 5 DA, *DPSPs* must provide information about *DPSs* that make switching (very) costly. The starting point of Art. 29 para. 5 DA is merely an obligation to provide information. However, since the *switching charges* payable by the customer are to be withdrawn from 12th January 2027 onwards (Art. 29 para. 1 DA), the question arises as to why these high switching costs should be communicated to a customer if he will no longer have to bear them in the future anyway. There are two possible interpretations.

Either it is merely the purpose of Art. 29 para. 5 DA to ensure that those customers are informed in advance, who will have to bear the switching costs until 12th January 2027 in accordance with Art. 29 para. 2 DA or beyond this date in accordance with Art. 34 para. 2 DA. In this case, Art. 29 para. 5 DA – at least with regard to the costs – has a very narrow temporal and material scope of application.

Alternatively, it could be argued that it should also be possible for *DPSPs* to pass on such – actually incurred – costs to their customers beyond 12th January 2027 if the switching turns out to be highly complex or costly due to the *DPS* being provided and for which it is impossible to switch without significant interference in the data, digital assets or service architecture.

This second interpretation is firstly supported by the fact that such an exception to Art. 29 para. 1 DA seems objectively more justified than the vague perpetual exception in Art. 34 para. 2 DA for multi-cloud-strategies. The DA leaves unanswered why the switching of providers in the context of a parallel use of several *DPSs* should justify *switching charges* in the future, but not the objectively more obvious reason that it is a highly complex and costly switching due to the services being provided.

However, the wording and the systematic structure of Art. 29 para. 5 DA suggest that the legislator's intention with this provision was – with a high degree of probability – merely to provide customers with information in order to make them aware of the risks of switching providers in such a scenario. In this case, no basis could be derived from Art. 29 para. 5 DA for continuing to request payment of *switching charges* after 12th January 2027. However, because this interpretation is not unambiguous, the option of *switching charges* in the event of a highly complex and costly switching is still taken into account in the following standard contractual clauses, although such contractual stipulations are overwhelmingly likely to be void.

IV. Standard Contractual Clauses pursuant to Art. 41 DA

Duties to inform customers can – especially in B2B-contracts – be a proportionate means of reducing existing information asymmetries and protecting customers from being taken advantage of by providers.[46] Nevertheless, the benefit of information is very limited, even in the B2B-contracts, if the vast majority of customers are faced with a small number of providers which can always enforce their GTCs due to their negotiating power on an oligopolistic market. For this reason, the European legislator has not only opted for information duties (1), but instead, isets out mandatory requirements for *DPSPs* in Art. 25 and Art. 29 DA, which according to Art. 41 DA must also be implemented in the – for the time being non-mandatory – standard contractual clauses for cloud computing (2).

1. Pre-Contractual Information Duties

A brief discussion of the pre-contractual information duties contained in Chapter VI DA is important because certain clauses provided for in the following standard contractual clauses can only be validly agreed if the customer has been informed of their content prior to concluding a contract.[47] Therefore, from 12th September 2025, *DPSPs* must inform their customers before concluding a contract of the following:

- Offer does not provide data processing services as a non-production version for testing and evaluation purposes and for a limited period of time (Art. 31 para. 2 and para. 3 DA)
- limited applicability of the contractual clauses to *DPSs* that make switching highly complex or costly or impossible without significant intervention in the data, digital assets or service architecture, Art. 29 para. 5 DA.

---

46 *Louis Brandeis* (1914), "What Publicity Can Do", in Other People's Money and How the Bankers Use It: "Publicity is justly commended as a remedy for social and industrial diseases. Sunlight is said to be the best of disinfectants; electric light the most efficient policeman."

47 According to Art. 25 para. 1 lit. a (iii) DA upon the customer's request for switching the provider has to inform the customer of known risks to continuity in the provision of the functions or services on the part of the source provider of data processing services.

In addition, according to Art. 29 para. 4 DA, the provider is obliged to inform the customer of any costs incurred during the term of the contract before the contract is concluded. This includes the

- Standard-Service-Charges
- Contractual penalty for early termination of a contract with a fixed minimum term (likely such a penalty is only available as regards B2B contracts)
- Reduced Switching Charges (applicable since 11th January 2024 and until 12th January 2027, Art. 29 para. 2 DA)

2. Standard Contractual Clauses

Finally, the complex requirements of Chapter VI DA will result in standard contractual clauses. The following options can provide initial guidance on how the DA's requirements for a switching of providers could be structured. As Art. 25 para. 1 DA stipulates, the contractual clauses on switching must be unambiguous, in writing and provided by the *DPSP* before the contract is signed in such a way that the customer can save and reproduce them. As the following clauses already take into account the inconsistencies and exceptions to Chapter VI DA, the clauses tend to be drafted from the perspective of the previous *DPSP*. However, this perspective is not intended to further consolidate the current oligopolistic market. Rather, it is precisely this perspective that reveals the potentially remaining alternative paths for *DPSPs* and thus enable a better observation of the market in order to provide insights for any revisions of the DA.

The drafted clauses are supplemented by references to the respective provisions of the DA, whereby in individual cases it may also be merely a recital that seems to be supportive of such a clause. These references also contain brief explanatory notes. Of course, these standard contractual clauses are only for exemplary purposes and must be adapted to the respective type of contract. Furthermore, this guidance does not constitute a statement on their validity in the event of a GTC review. In particular, Art. 27 DA hangs like the sword of Damocles over all future clauses. It expressly obliges all parties – presumably for the first time at the level of Union law – to act in good faith.

Switching Process

§ 1 – Initiation of Switching Process

(1) *The Customer shall notify the Provider of its decision to perform one or more of the following actions upon termination of the Contract* [Art. 25 para. 3 DA]:
 (a) *Switch to a different provider of data processing services, in which case the Customer shall provide the necessary details of that provider;*
 (b) *Switch to an on-premises ICT infrastructure;*
 (c) *Erase the Customer's exportable data and digital assets.*

(2) *Upon the request by the Customer (hereafter „Switching Request")* [Art. 25 para. 2 lit. a DA] *and no later than two months after such Switching Request* [Art. 25 para. 2 lit. d DA], *the Provider shall initiate the switching of the exportable data and the digital assets as listed in Schedule 2 (hereafter "Switching Objects")* [Art. 2 No. 32; No. 37 DA].

(3) *The switching request, including the contact details of the new provider, should be declared via the following contact point: (contact option)* [Art. 25 para. 2 lit. a DA].

§ 2 – Switching Process

(1) *Switching generally includes the extracting, transforming and uploading of the Switching Objects (hereafter "Switching Process") whereby the Customer changes from the Provider to a different provider of data processing services, or to an on-premises ICT infrastructure.* [Art. 2 No. 34 DA].

(2) *During the Switching Process the Contract remains applicable.* [Rec. 87 s. 6; Rec. 89 s. 5/6]

(3) *During the Switching Process the Provider shall:* [Art. 25 para. 2 lit. a (i)–(iv) DA]
 (a) *provide reasonable assistance to the Customer and third parties authorised by the Customer*
 (b) *act with due care to maintain business continuity, and continue the provision of the functions or services under the Contract;*
 (c) *provide clear information concerning known risks to continuity in the provision of the functions or services on his part of the data processing services;*
 (d) *ensure that a high level of security is maintained throughout the Switching Process and the Retrieval Period (as defined in § 5 (1)).*

(4) *The Provider is obliged to support the Customer's exit strategy relevant to the contracted services, including by providing all relevant information.* [Art. 25 para. 2 lit. b DA]

(5) *The Switching process is completed when [depending on the customer's request pursuant to § 1 (1) a-c]. If the Provider provides Infrastructure-as-a-Service under this Agreement, the Switching Process is completed once the Customer, having switched to a service of the same service type, is provided with functionally equivalent data processing services when using the acquiring Provider. The Provider shall facilitate the switching process by providing capabilities, adequate information, documentation, technical support and, where appropriate, the necessary tools.* [Art. 30 para. 1 DA]

§ 3 – Switching Period and Extension

(1) *The initiated switching will be proceeded without undue delay and shall generally be completed within a maximum transitional period of 30 calendar days (hereafter "Standard Switching Period").* [Art. 25 para. 2 lit. a DA; Art. 25 para. 2 and para. 4 call it "mandatory maximum transitional period".]

(2) *Where the Standard Switching Period is technically unfeasible, the Provider shall notify the Customer hereof within 14 working days after receival of the Switching Request.* [Art. 25 para. 4 DA stipulates "within 14 days of the making of the switching request"]. *In such notification the Provider shall duly justify the technical unfeasibility and indicate an alternative transitional period, which shall not exceed seven months ("Extended Switching Period (Provider)").* [Art. 25 para. 4 DA; Valid in B2C-Contracts: No "automatic" prolonging of contract (§ 309 Nr. 9b) German Civil Code / Art. 3 para. 3; Annex No. 1 lit. h) Council Directive 93/13/EEC of 5.4.1993 on unfair terms in consumer contracts, as transitional (switching) period is no "automatic" prolonging of the contract]

(3) *Without prejudice to paragraph 2, the Customer has the right to extend the transitional period once for a period that the Customer considers more appropriate for its purposes ("Extended Switching Period (Customer)").* [Art. 25 para. 5 DA; Rec. 87 s. 4/5 DA]

§ 4 – Switching Charges

(1) *Until completion of the (Extended) Switching Process and completion of the Retrieval Period the Customer shall continue to pay the Standard Charges according to Schedule 1 (1).* [Rec. 89 s. 5/6 DA].

(2) *From 11.1.2024 to 12.1.2027 the Customer shall additionally pay the Provider the Switching Charges according to Schedule 1 (2)* [Art. 29 para. 2 DA], *which shall not exceed the costs incurred by the Provider that are directly linked to the Switching Process.* [Art. 29 para. 3 DA]

(3) *Insofar as the Provider's data processing service is used in parallel with the data processing service of a third party, the Provider shall be entitled to payment of the data egress charge for a multi-cloud strategy in accordance with Schedule 1 (3) if the Customer requests a change; however, the amount of this charge shall be limited by the costs actually incurred by the Provider.* [Art. 34 para. 2 DA; Rec. 99 DA]

(4) *Once initiated by the Provider according to § 3 (2) or by the Customer according to § 3 (3), the Customer shall continue to pay the Provider the Standard Charges according to Schedule 1 (1).*[Art. 25 para. 5 DA; Rec. 89 s. 5/6 DA]

(5) *If the Customer is not a consumer* [Potentially invalid in B2C-Contracts according to § 309 Nr. 6 German Civil Code. Arguably not invalid according to Art. 3 para. 3 Annex No. 1 lit. e) Council Directive 93/13/EEC of 5.4.1993 on unfair terms in consumer contracts] *and terminates the Contract prior to the agreed Standard Contract Period, such Customer shall pay the Provider the Early Termination Penalty Charge according to Schedule 1 (4).* [Art. 29 para. 4 DA; Rec. 89 s. 3 DA]

(6) *If the switching is highly complex or costly, the Customer shall pay the Provider the Additional Switching Charge for "Highly Complex Data Processing Services" according to Schedule 1 (5)* [However, unlikely that Art. 29 para. 5 provides a legal basis for such charges]. *If the Switching Objects were generated as individual development for the customer, the Customer shall pay the Provider the Switching Charges for „Custom-Built Data Processing Services" according to Schedule 1 (6).* [Art. 31 para. 1 DA; Rec. 98 s. 1 DA]

(7) *Insofar as the Customer requests additional services from the Provider that are beyond the Provider's binding duties constituted by the DA, the Customer shall pay the Provider the Additional Service Charges for additional services requested by the Customer according to Schedule 1 (7).* [Rec. 89 s. 7/8 DA]

(8) *Insofar as the Customer – mediated by the Provider – requests services from third parties, the Customer shall reimburse the Provider for the costs incurred by the Provider in accordance with Schedule 1*

(8) as a result of the commissioning of third parties on behalf of the Customer. [Rec. 89 s. 2/3 DA]

§ 5 – Right to Erasure

(1) *The Provider is obliged to continue to make all switching objects (Schedule 2) that are generated directly by the Customer or relate directly to the Customer available for retrieval for at least 30 calendar days after the end of the Switching Period ("Retrieval Period"). The Retrieval Period begins at the end of the Switching Period in accordance with § 3 (1-3) and provided that the Switching Procedure has been successfully completed at this time.*[Art. 25 para. 2 lit. g DA]

(2) *The Provider reserves the right to retain a copy of the Exportable Data (Schedule 2 (1)) and to use it for its own purposes, which was generated indirectly through the use of the data processing service by the Customer or jointly and insofar as this Exportable Data relates only indirectly to the Customer.* [Clarification: Provider can continue to use derived data (i.e. as training data). Consequence: Both, Customer and Provider, receive/remain a copy of such data generated indirectly by the Customer or relating indirectly to the Customer. Challenge: Conflict with GDPR / ePrivacy-Directive and potentially trade secrets as regards data indirectly relating to the Customer]

§ 6 – Switching and Termination of Contract

The contract shall be considered to be terminated and the Customer shall be notified of such termination by the Provider, in one of the following cases: [Art. 25 para. 2 lit. c DA]

(a) *upon the successful completion of the Switching Process;*

(b) *at the end of the maximum two months' notice period for initiating the switching process, where the Customer does not wish to switch but to erase the Switching Objects upon service termination.*

Schedule 1
(Charges)

(1) *Standard Service Charges*

(2) *Reduced Switching Charge: 11.1.2024 – 12.1.2027* [Art. 29 para. 2 DA]

(3) *Data Egress Charge for In-Parallel-Use* [Art. 34 para. 2 DA; Rec. 99 DA]

(4) *Early Termination Penalty* [Art. 2 No. 36; Art. 29 para. 4 DA; Rec. 89 s. 3 DA]

(5) *Switching Charge "Highly Complex & Costly"* [Art. 29 para. 5 DA]
(6) *Switching Charge „Custom-Built"* [Art. 31 para. 1 DA; Rec. 98 DA]
(7) *Additional Service Charge at request of Customer* [Rec. 89 s. 7/8 DA]
(8) *Third-Party-Costs at request of Customer* [Rec. 89 s. 3 DA]

Schedule 2
(Switching Objects)

(1) *List of Exportable Data* [Art. 2 No. 38 DA; Art. 25 para. 2 lit. e DA]
(2) *List of Digital Assets* [Art. 2 No. 32 DA]
(3) *List of Non-Exportable Data, for reasons of Trade Secret Protection* [Art. 25 para. 2 lit. f DA]
(4) *List of IP-Rights (Software/Data Base)*
(5) *List of Custom-Built Services*

Schedule 3
(Technical Acknowledgements)

(1) *Methods of Switching* [Art. 26 lit. a DA]
(2) *Available/Supported Formats* [Art. 26 lit. a DA]
(3) *Technical Limitations and Restrictions due to* [Art. 30 DA]
 (a) *Trade Secrets Protection*
 (b) *IP-Rights (Software/Data Base)*
 (c) *Custom-Built-Services*
 (d) *Compatibility & Interoperability*

Discussion Panel

The Data Act as a design for (non-personal) industrial data markets

Damian Boeselager and Johannes Jaenicke[1]

I. Introduction

The famous adage about the legislative process being akin to sausage making seems particularly relevant in the case of the Data Act ("DA"). Up until the very last trilogues in July 2023, the Commission's 2022 proposal was the only concrete basis of discussion for an academic debate on the future European data regime. When, at the end of a relatively fast-paced legislative process, the finally agreed text emerged in November 2023 it included notable conceptional changes to the Commission proposal – in particular with regards to the data sharing regime for IoT products in Chapters II and III of the DA. These have since been critically reviewed[2], including during the 2024 Münster Colloquium on 'Private Law and the Data Act' to which the authors were very grateful to be invited.

During the trilogue phase the co-legislators introduced, among others, (a) a distinction between product data and related service data, (b) an exclusive sharing and marketing right for users with respect to non-personal product data and (c) separate information requirements for the sale of an IoT product and the offering of a related service. In this commentary, the

1 Damian Boeselager (Volt Europa) is a Member of the European Parliament and one of the EP's lead negotiators for the Data Act. Johannes Jaenicke was at the time Damian's legislative advisor, in charge of the Data Act.

2 Contributions since the adoption of the final text with a particular emphasis on Chapters II and III include Hennemann/Steinrötter: Der Data Act, NJW 2024, 1; Bomhard/Schmidt-Kessel: EU-Datengesetz ante portas, MMR 2024, 69; Schmidt-Kessel: Heraus- und Weitergabe von IoT-Gerätedaten, MMR 2024, 75; Eckardt/Kerber: Property rights theory, bundles of rights on IoT data, and the EU Data Act. Eur J Law Econ (2024); Antoine: Datenzugangsrechte im finalen Data Act - Fortschritt, Rückschritt, neue Fragen? — Schlüssel zur Förderung datengetriebener Geschäftsmodelle?" Computer und Recht, vol. 40, no. 1, 2024, pp. 1–8; Etzkorn: (Vertragliche) Datenzugangsansprüche nach dem Data Act, Recht Digital 2024, 116; Kim/Kwok: Data Usability as a Parameter of Rights and Obligations under the EU Data Act (February 1, 2024).

authors, as participants in the legislative process, will attempt to contribute the perspective of the co-legislators to the ongoing academic debate. We believe that this perspective is important in interpreting the final Data Act – after all, any law is a collection of suboptimal compromises established during messy negotiations. In addition, as Metzger points out, there are few national or international precedents for the DA's data sharing regime, which in the absence of established legal practices, means that the DA is Europe's big leap into the unknown.[3]

This article is structured as follows:

(a) it lays out our reasoning for the newly introduced market design for non-personal product data (for ease referred to as "industrial data" in this article),
(b) it then provides our interpretation of the various options for sharing non-personal data open to the user under the regime in the final DA text, and
(c) it puts forward our recommendations for further action on the side of public policy makers and businesses.

The authors will argue that the DA does not create data ownership per se, but instead introduces an exclusive marketing right for the user to industrial data generated in the user's IoT product. As we will try to demonstrate, users have ample choices how to plan and arrange the access to and sharing of data. The resulting market design provides incentives for users, data holders (DHs) and data intermediaries to engage in data sharing in primary and secondary data markets. We will argue that the public sector can be a key beneficiary from such markets, both as a user of IoT products, and through additional tax revenue.

II. A market design for non-personal (industrial) data

The advent of artificial intelligence (AI) on the global main stage has put an additional emphasis on the availability of high-quality data to train the algorithms that drive the AI expansion. Unlike images, string text or open-source code, which could be scraped from the internet to train

3 Metzger: Dateninhaber verlieren ihre Machtposition, Frankfurter Allgemeine Zeitung, 23.11.2023, retrieved from Dateninhaber verlieren ihre Machtposition (faz.net).

large language models[4], industrial data (i.e., data recorded by machines in manufacturing processes, energy production and transmission, civil infrastructure, etc.) is not easily available in a curated and centralized manner. Those who hold those data therefore need incentives to make it available in useable form. The co-legislators shared the Commission's objective for the DA to increase the amount of available data. They also supported the Commission's intention to distribute the value-creation in the data economy more fairly between users, manufacturers and related service providers of IoT products. However, from the co-legislators' perspective, the Commission proposal did not succeed in creating and clearly allocating monetary incentives for the making available, sharing and secondary trading of non-personal data among owners, users, manufacturers and service providers of IoT products.[5]

1. The user's exclusive marketing rights over industrial data

The new Art. 4(14), added to the legal text late during the trilogues and originally put forward in an amendment by the authors[6], is at the centre of a market design for industrial data. This design is built on contract law. The other changes referred above (distinction between product and related service data, separation of information requirements for sale of IoT product and offer of the related service) were included to operationalise the market design. Art. 4(14) forbids DHs to *"make available non-personal product data to third parties for commercial or non-commercial purposes other than the fulfilment of their contract with the user"* and forces them to *"contractually bind third parties not to further share data received from them"*. It thus attributes to the user[7] the exclusive right to determine who can access, use and share non-personal data and for what purposes. It allows users to control the diffusion of data from their product and to be compensated

4 The authors will refrain from commenting on the legality of such scraping.

5 There was broad agreement among the co-legislators that the question of monetization of personal data was not to be addressed in the DA, which left the GDPR's remit over the processing of personal data untouched.

6 ITRE Committee amendment 597 by Damian Boeselager on behalf of the Verts/ALE Group can be retrieved under https://www.europarl.europa.eu/doceo/document/ITRE-AM-738548_EN.pdf.

7 The user is the owner of the IoT product, or one or more legal persons who have been transferred this right by the owner.

for allowing access or transferring use rights. Importantly, this right only applies to non-personal product data, i.e., the data which is collected by the product's sensors and available from the product without the additional involvement of another legal person, different from the owner. In contrast, in the case of related service data, which is co-generated by the user's product's sensors and the service provision of the related service provider, the DA does not create exclusive marketing rights for either the data holder or the user. As a consequence, the DA does not create data ownership per se, but instead introduces a variant of Zech's data producer right[8] by importing a basic consequence of the property of the IoT product (usus fructus) into this previously unregulated space.

2. Competition between users and DHs in offering data products

At the same time data holders may use, aggregate and also monetize product data and data from related services in aggregated form as part of a contract with the user. Recital 25 of the DA clarifies the co-legislators' intention that DHs should be able to take advantage of a contractually granted access right under Art. 4(13) for purposes including *"improving the functioning of the connected product or related services, developing new products or services, or aggregating data with the aim of making available the resulting derived data to third parties"*.[9]

This division of rights introduces an important question; Why should a single data point from a given IoT product be worth anything, given that data tend to develop their value only when available in aggregated form? The answer, in our view, lies in the power of intermediaries. In drafting the amendment, we were inspired by Zech's argument that "data as a tradeable commodity"[10] requires not just the attribution of a right to commercializa-

8 Zech: A Legal Framework for a Data Economy in the European Digital Single Market: Rights to Use Data (November 20, 2016). Journal of Intellectual Property Law & Practice, 2016, Vol. 11, 460–470.

9 This clarification was initially suggested to be included in the legal text in the authors' amendments (see amendment 598, retrievable under https://www.europarl.europa.eu/doceo/document/ITRE-AM-738548_EN.pdf) but was relegated to the recitals during the trilogue negotiations.

10 Zech: Data as a Tradeable Commodity – Implications for Contract Law (September 2017) in: Drexl (ed.): Proceedings of the 18th EIPIN Congress: The New Data Economy between Data Ownership, Privacy and Safeguarding Competition, Edward Elgar Publishing, 2017.

tion, but also the existence of a secondary market for access or use of this data. A user should be able to market single data points to data aggregators (i.e., data intermediaries), who collect, structure and combine individual data from different sources into valuable data products. A single product owner could never match a DH's access to data from multiple products and its power to aggregate and market that data. A competing offer by the data holder at the individual data level would eliminate the incentive to make such data available in the first place.[11]

Interestingly, an analysis of complex data clauses in non-personal data contracts by Deloitte, referenced in the Commission 2017 Communication[12], found that "in most cases, one party was prevented from using the data for any purpose other than fulfilling the contract". Where data is not directly accessible from the product under Art. 3(1), the marginal costs of accessing data will by design be higher for the user than for the data holder, whose marginal costs in this case will often be close to zero, given that it collects the data for the purpose of providing a related service. Therefore, in order to introduce the possibility of competing aggregated data products, a user's exclusive ability to share data with an aggregator, or invest itself in the aggregation has to be protected. Crucially, in doing so the DA does not undermine the ability of the data holder to offer aggregated data sets in data markets.

3. The role of data markets

While the 2017 Commission communication[13] did reference the role of data markets to match demand from companies to "obtain data like any other (physical) resource" with companies seeking to "monetise certain data they hold", the Commission's DA proposal did not address data markets or data

11 We believe the explanation we gave when introducing amendment 597 still holds: *"In order for a market price for a given individual dataset or data product to emerge, only one market participant can have the right to share this dataset. Otherwise, another market participant who holds the same data can destroy the market simply by offering the identical dataset on the same market. This would lead to the situation where a data holder can at any time destroy the business case for the user to monetize data, and vice versa. The resulting commercial insecurity will prevent the sharing of data."*

12 Communication from the Commission to the European Parliament, the Council, the European economic and social Committee and the Committee of the Regions "Building a European Data Economy", COM (2017).

13 See note 12.

monetization. The co-legislators have strengthened the incentives for the monetization of industrial data (see above), including by removing prohibitions for business users to market data to third parties on an exclusive basis.[14]

Users can licence or transfer rights to data access and use to third parties, subject to certain conditions by means of data exchanges[15]. The DA explicitly provides that a third party can further market those rights in secondary markets, if agreed with the user.[16] Functioning data markets would allow for various new data-related business models to emerge. On the one hand, aggregators can help users to access, process and market data in a value-generating way. On the other hand, brokers and market places can link users offering data with third parties demanding data, for example to train AI-based applications or models. The DA also introduced explicit links to the Data Governance Act (DGA), which regulates data intermediaries of various kinds (i.e., data exchanges, aggregators, data brokers, etc.).

III. The mechanics of data access and sharing in Ch. II & III

With the market design in place, users will need to understand how they can actually receive data to share with third parties. In the following section the authors provide their interpretation of the DA's data sharing regime, which includes numerous options for a user seeking to share data with a third party. From the pre-purchase information provisions, up until the re-sale of data by a third party on a data market, users have ample opportunities to structure their data access and sharing according to their needs and capabilities. A user, who is a small company without IT-trained staff may opt for a one-stop-shop solution offered by a manufacturer who will at the same time be the related service provider/DH and may even arrange the monetization of non-personal product data on behalf of the user. On the other hand, a large business may have enough bargaining power to force a manufacturer to grant direct Art. 3(1) access to the desired

14 Art. 6(2h).

15 Zabelin/Tomonori/Nakanishi: The world is drowning in data. Why don't we trade it like on a stock exchange? (2022).

16 See Art. 6(1), which regulates among others the erasure of data by the third party and Art. 6(2c), which forces the third party to protect trade secrets, where relevant, when further sharing data with the permission of the user. Art. 6(2h) prevents the exclusive sale of data by a consumer to a third party, but leaves open that option in business to business transactions.

product data. It may choose to invest into its own data management and sharing infrastructure. The ability of the DA to reflect a wide amount of data sharing models is one of its strengths as a horizonal regulation.

1. Pre-sale information obligations in Art. 3(2&3)

The DA's final text allows those prospective users, who are able and willing to anticipate the economic value of industrial data produced by an IoT-product they buy, to take informed decisions about the modalities of accessing and monetizing data *in advance* of the purchase.[17] The information obligations in Art. 3(2) and Art. 3(3) provide for ample information to construct a business plan for utilizing and monetizing data generated during the use of the product and related services. A prospective user seeking to purchase a certain IoT product, can learn about the nature and volume of data that the desired product is able to make available. It can compare products from different providers as well as the related service offered with them. Data production and access modalities thus become a potential differentiating factor in a manufacturer's product offer. Prospective users can decide, based on competing product offerings, which degree of data availability they prefer and which price they are willing to pay for the additional data availability. Already at this pre-purchase stage, a prospective user will know whether it can access data directly from the product (i.e., whether it can use the Art. 3(1) provisions in the DA), or whether data access involves requesting data from a DH[18], which would mean that Art. 4(1) would apply. Furthermore, the prospective user could – at this pre-purchase stage – plan on whether a data sharing regime

17 A frequent criticism is that consumers might not be able or willing to think through these consequences. We assumed that non-personal data sharing is predominantly a B2B-activity, however do not exclude the possibility that consumers utilize the economic potential of the non-personal data generated by their devices. As far as personal data is concerned, GDPR is unaffected and continues to apply, as do consumer protection laws.

18 As mentioned above, a consequence of the DH definition in Art. 2(13) is that, for the purposes of Chapter II, a data holder is equivalent to a related service provider, which implies that multiple data holders can exist in the context of a given connected product. As an example, a machine could have the related service of 'remote control', provided for by the manufacturer and another related service for 'predictive maintenance' provided by a third party. Both parties are data holders for the purpose of the data which they can access in the context of their service provision.

under Art. 5(1) with the DH as intermediary is preferential to receiving the data from the DH and sharing it directly with third parties. Insofar as the data produced by the product have a positive economic value for the user, the DA introduces a significant choice for users and hence a competitive incentive for innovative offers by manufacturers with respect to making data available. One can easily imagine a situation, where some product offerings in the market make a certain data point available directly from a product, while some competing offerings require a DH (i.e., a related service provider) to access data from the product.[19]

The utility of owning an IoT product is a function of its performance, the value received from related services *and* a potential sharing and/or monetization of the generated data. In turn, the combined utility determines the decisions with regards to (1) the choice of product and the price to pay for it, (2) whether or not to receive one or more related services and what to pay for it, and (3) what modalities for data access and sharing to choose.

2. Options for accessing and sharing data

Depending on the product capabilities and availability of related services there are four scenarios under which a user can access and share data in the DA (see Table 1). These scenarios and their implication for data sharing will be discussed in more detail below.

Scenario	**Description**	**Data sharing modalities / Comment**
Product data directly available / No related service in place	User receives data directly from product but does not receive a related service	User can share product data directly with third parties*
Product data directly available / Related service(s) in place	User can choose to receive product data directly OR request those product data which DH accessed and can access	User can*: - share accessed product data directly, **or** - under Art 4(1) request DH-accessed product or related

19 Data collection may be a primary function of the connected product (a simple example would be a scale or a thermostat). Insofar as these are being operated by a legal person, who is not the user, via a related service this legal person is a DH.

Scenario	Description	Data sharing modalities / Comment
	related service data from DH	service data from DH to share it directly with third party, **or** - under Art 5(1) request DH to share DH-accessed product or related service data with third party. DH receives compensation for making data available
No product data directly available / Related service(s) in place	User can access those product data, which DH accessed, as well as related service data via DH	User can*: - under Art 4(1) request DH-accessed product or related service data from DH to share it directly with third party, **or** - under Art 5(1) request DH to share DH-accessed product or related service data with third party. DH receives compensation for making data available*
No product data directly available / No related service in place	No data available as product can only make data available via DH but user does not receive a related service	No data available and no sharing possible. Could happen when related service is not available on the market or user voluntarily chooses not to receive a related service

* GDPR applies to personal data sharing regardless of the access modalities

Scenario 1: In a first instance, imagine a user, who buys a product which makes data available directly and decides not to receive any additional related services or cannot agree a contract with a related service provider. Scenario 1 applies and the remainder of the data sharing regime in Chapters II and III is not necessary because there is no related service and thus no

DH. The user can make data available to a third party on whichever terms they agree.

Scenario 2: In this most advantageous scenario for the user, product data is available to the user from the product directly *and, at the same time,* a related service provider has access to the same data while providing a service.[20] The addition of a DH (the service provider) creates a distinction between product data, generated by the product's sensors and related service data, generated during the provision of that service.[21] As discussed above, the user has an exclusive right to determine whether and how its *product data* is shared or monetized, however for *related service data* such restriction of the DHs ability to share or monetize does not exist. With respect to the monetization of the product data, the user has four choices:

1. Share the data directly with a third party. The DH is not involved in this transaction and can be bound through the user's exclusive monetization right in Art. 4(14) not to share the data in a competing offer.
2. Request and download the data from the DH under Art. 4(1) onto its own servers and subsequentially make the data available to a third party directly.[22] The user needs to have a technical interface with the DH and has to have the technical infrastructure in place to receive the data and share it with the third party. The DH may not charge the user and needs to make the data available in the same quality as is available to itself.

---

20 To use the example of a wind turbine: a remote-control function provided by a related service provider uses wind speed and direction data, collected in sensors atop the product, as an input in an algorithm to remotely change the rotation of the blades, while the user can obtain the same wind speed and direction data from the on-site computer. The service provider is the DH for the data it accessed, while the user can access the same data.

21 In this example, wind speed and direction data would be "product data" while the rotation angle of the blades would be "related service data". It is easy to see from this example how the remote command to change blade rotation is "co-generated" using the user's product data and the service providers algorithm, whereas the product data is generated only by a single legal person – the user.

22 Eckart/Kerber (see note 2) appear to have failed to recognize this ability to circumvent Art. 5(1) and the related compensation mechanism in their remarkably confident critique of the data sharing regime in the Data Act. In contrast Etzkorn (see note 2) points out that thanks to this circumvention of Art. 5(1) "third parties have the ability to get access via the user to data that the DH had no intention to share".

As in the previous case, the user has the exclusive right to decide over sharing / monetization and does not have to fear competing offers.[23]

3. Request the DH under Art. 5(1) to share the data with a third party. Compared to the previous option this may be preferable to users who do not have the technical infrastructure for data sharing in place or in cases where the DH can share data more cost efficiently.[24] In this case a contract between the DH and the third party (a data recipient in the nomenclature of the DA) is necessary. The DH can demand compensation. Importantly, the threat of conducting the data sharing directly via the Art. 4(1)-mechanism can be helpful in keeping the DH's compensation in check.
4. Finally, under Art. 4(14) the user could contractually mandate the DH to monetize non-personal product data on its behalf. Multiple models for the economic compensation of the user in this case could be contemplated, for example a commission of the data proceeds, a reduction in service fees, or, where the manufacturer is a related service provider, a reduction in the product purchase price.[25]

Scenario 3: Product data is not directly accessible from the product for the user under Art. 3(1), however the user can request access to product and related service data from the DH under Art. 4(1). While the first of the four abovementioned choices under Scenario 2 is not available to the user, the remaining three are open to it in this scenario. As was pointed out earlier, perceptive users are aware of this modality already before the purchase of the product. This scenario is the most favourable from the perspective of a DH, who is able to protect its interests through the various provisions under Art. 4, including the restriction of data sharing for security reasons under Art. 4(2), the protection of trade secrets under Art. 4(6,7,8) and the prohibition to use the data to develop a competing product under Art. 4(10). Nonetheless, significant economic agency for the user remains with regards to the options of data sharing. Importantly, a user is not bound to use the data sharing mechanism under Art. 5(1) but can request data

23 This is not the case for related service data, which the DH is allowed to share / monetize without the agreement of the user within the boundaries set by Chapters II. / III.

24 In general, a doubling of the computing power, storage capacity and latency needed for data sharing at the user and the DH is likely to be economically inefficient. This could be particularly relevant for real-time data sharing.

25 Recital 25 explicitly includes such a scenario, including self-restricting access and use rights by the user "in exchange for being compensated appropriately".

from the DH and share it directly with a third party. A "de-facto" control[26] therefore can be circumvented.

Scenario 4: In this scenario a user has no direct access to data from a product and does not receive a related service. Reasons for this situation could be that no related service provider was willing to enter into a contract with the user or that a user chose voluntarily not to receive such services. In such case no data will become available from owning the product. The user's ownership of the product implies that the user bears the burden or at least the opportunity costs of not receiving any data from it. The functionality of the product without related services may be enough for the user to warrant the purchase. In addition, a user is not prevented from seeking related services for the product at a later stage, should none be available at the point of purchase.

The above discussion has shown that the pre-purchase information requirements in Art. 3(2&3), as well as the various modalities of data access and sharing, provide the user with substantial economic agency vis-à-vis a prospective product seller. In cases where no direct access to product data is possible under Art. 3(1), the ability to circumvent Art. 5(1) via Art. 4(1) provides leverage to the user to negotiate attractive terms with a DH.

IV. Recommendations for further action to public policy makers and businesses

1. Non-personal data exists. Yes, really!

The authors can remember countless occasions, especially in Germany, in which some discussion participant challenged the notion that non-personal data exists. Because non-personal data does not exist – the argument goes – and because the DA only really changes things for non-personal data, the DA is useless and will in reality only affect a meaninglessly small part of social and economic life, if at all.[27]

We would like to say it loud and clear: non-personal data does really exist![28] Fixating on personal data and their anonymization conceals the

26 As stipulated by Eckart/Kerber (see note 2).

27 This argument was not put forward during the 2024 Münster Colloquium, of course.

28 E.g., heat data from a thermostat at the bottom of an offshore windmill, voltage data from an energy grid, etc.

enormous economic potential of marketing non-personal industrial data. Data policy initiatives should provide more and better information to the wider business community about the fact that there are large volumes of machine-generated data that, from the outset, do not contain any *"information relating to an identified or identifiable natural person"*[29] and are therefore not dependent on anonymization to become non-personal data. A focus of the legal and business discussion on non-personal industrial data is slowly emerging post the adoption of the DA and should be speedily expanded ahead of the entry into force of the DA's provisions in September 2025.

Of course, we recognize the enormous grey area between personal data and non-personal data as a consequence of the technical difficulty anonymising personal data irreversibly. We would encourage authorities to develop guidelines and assistance to help delineate at least the subset of non-personal industrial data that has never been personal data (i.e., did not need to be anonymised). The fact that the market design in Art. 4 (13&14) is explicitly limited to non-personal data may also give users and DHs market-based incentives to invest in distinguishing non-personal data from personal data in a legally secure manner.

2. The public sector can be a trailblazer in monetizing non-personal data

The public sector is in a very advantageous position to benefit economically from the new data sharing regime and market design. Public enterprises, municipalities and cities own a very large amount of IoT products[30]. The DA grants the public sector, in its role of a user, the ability to exploit a very sizeable economic potential from the commercial utilisation of industrial data, to the benefit of innovative products, services and scientific results. At the same time, the public sector can raise much-needed funds from turnover and business tax from data transactions by private companies. Such tax revenue is generated where the data was generated or where the user is resident for tax purposes. Thereby the economic welfare from data collection is distributed locally to where the data has been generated.

29 Art. 4(1), GDPR.
30 Think about all the data produced by civil infrastructure equipment (e.g., energy production facilities, energy grids, transport infrastructure, sewers, the military, etc.).

3. The DA will lead to a decentralisation of economic value creation from data.

Indeed, the decentralization of economic value creation from the DA is an important consequence that warrants further study. Thanks to the contract-led nature of the DA's data sharing regime, both additional turnover and additional tax revenue from data transactions will be generated in a decentralised manner at the user's location. This is a stark contrast to the pre-DA situation, where value creation has previously been centralised and taxed at the manufacturers' headquarters. For energy infrastructure (wind turbines, transformers, etc.), for example, this could lead to a boost in business income and municipal tax revenue in rural and coastal communities.

V. Conclusion

The DA is a game changer for the data economy. It has the potential to completely redraw the power relations between buyers and manufacturers of IoT products and to decentralize the gains from data generation. One of the co-legislators' central objective in Chapters II/III was to provide a market design for industrial data markets which would create incentives for users of IoT products to make data available, including via data intermediaries addressed in the Data Governance Act (DGA). As this commentary has argued, this market design has been further strengthened by the addition of Art. 4(14) in the final text of the DA. The co-legislators thus opted for what Schweitzer and Metzger[31] called a "market-shaping approach".

From the authors' perspective, the DA's data sharing regime is by no means perfect. Its complexity and the ability of DHs to restrict data access in Articles 4 and 5 provide ample room for legal uncertainty, which will have to be interpreted by the various data coordinators and, ultimately, the courts. Indeed, the practical application of the DA will show, whether users are able to extract significant economic value vis-à-vis the DHs, who in many cases will be the manufacturers. As Bomhard and Schmidt-Kessel[32] point out, getting ahead of the Data Act implementation may be a source of competitive advantage as much as ignoring it may endanger a company's business model.

31 Metzger/Schweitzer: Shaping Markets: A Critical Evaluation of the Data Act, ZEuP 2023, 42.

32 Bomhard/Schmidt-Kessel: EU-Datengesetz ante portas, MMR 2024, 69.

The development of aggregators, secondary data market places and other intermediaries will be crucial, as will be the innovation of contractual designs, that distribute value amongst the participants along the value chain. Financial marketplaces (e.g., commodity exchanges) and intermediaries can serve as role models and illustrative examples for future business models. It will be a vital task for regulators, in particular the Commission and the European Data Innovation Board to support the emergence of data intermediaries via funding programs, information provision and conferences. In any case, the bold claim by Eckart and Kerber[33] that the DA "will not lead to much more unlocking of IoT data for innovation and competition" seems premature at best. The authors lean more towards Hennemann and Steinrötter's assessment that the DA is an "innovative law" and that "it remains to be seen whether it will itself foster innovation".[34]

33 See note 2.
34 See note 2.

EU Data Act: Where we are and where to go ...

*Wolfgang Kerber**

I. Introduction

What are the problems that should be solved by the provisions of ch. II of the Data Act (DA)?[1] Manufacturers of smart IoT devices can get through their own technical design exclusive de facto control over all data that are generated by the IoT devices, which usually have been sold to their users, both in B2C and B2B contexts. The DA claims that this leads to not enough access to this data (1) for the users of these devices, which are seen as co-generators of this IoT data, and (2) for many other firms who would like to offer complementary services to the IoT device users (e.g. repair services) or develop new services and products with the help of this IoT data (data-driven innovation). This lack of access to and sharing of IoT data would lead to negative effects on innovation and competition on IoT-related secondary markets and an under-utilization of this IoT data for innovative activities and research in the entire data economy. The exclusive control of the manufacturers over the IoT data can also lead to negative effects on the choice of users, e.g., regarding service providers, and an unfair sharing of the value of data that are generated through the use of the IoT devices.

The DA intends to solve these problems primarily through the introduction of two instruments: (1) New rights for the users of IoT devices to access, use, and share the IoT data with third parties (Art. 4 and 5 DA), and (2) a new mandatory contract between the data holders and the users about the use of the generated non-personal IoT data by the data holders (Art. 4(13) DA).[2] In addition, all IoT devices have to be designed in such a way that the IoT data are easily accessible to the users and to third parties with whom the users want to share the data (Art. 3 DA). Can these two

---

1 Regulation (EU) 2023/2854 of the European Parliament and of the Council of 13 December 2023 on harmonised rules on fair access to and use of data and amending Regulation (EU) 2017/2394 and Directive (EU) 2020/1828 (Data Act).

2 The processing, use, and sharing of personal IoT data is subject to EU data protection law.

instruments be expected to be sufficiently effective to solve the above-mentioned problems?

In a first assessment of the initial DA proposal of the EU Commission from an economic perspective, I was very skeptical that the proposed provisions would be sufficient for breaking up the entrenched powerful positions of the manufacturers (and data holders) over the IoT data in order to achieve better the objectives of the DA.[3] The main reason is that the DA proposal favored too much the interests of the data holders instead of focusing primarily on the manifold benefits of sharing more IoT data for innovation and competition. However, through important initiatives by the European Parliament in the Trilogue process, substantial changes have been achieved in the final version of the DA which might help to change the basic approach of the DA and offer also new opportunities for improving its effectiveness. Most important is that the final version strengthened a user-centric interpretation of the DA which assigns the bundle of rights on non-personal data primarily to the users. This rejects in a much clearer way the underlying notion in the initial DA proposal that the data holders should primarily benefit from the extraction of value from the IoT data. Since, however, many other provisions of the initial DA proposal have not been changed, the contradictions between different concepts inherent in the DA have increased in the final version. In the following, I will briefly summarize the results of an analysis of the final version of the DA, explain some unsolved problems, and suggest some policy conclusions.[4]

II. Key instrument I: Effectiveness of the data sharing mechanism

The data sharing mechanism of Art. 5 DA is most important for better achieving the objectives of more innovation, competition on secondary markets, and more choice of users between service providers. However, the DA (in both its initial and in its final version) has made this path for third parties to get access to this IoT data difficult and expensive due to too many hurdles, restrictions, unresolved legal issues as well as often

3 Kerber, Governance of IoT data: Why the EU Data Act will not fulfill its objectives (2023), GRURInt, 120, 133.

4 For the following, see in more detail, Eckardt/Kerber, Property Rights Theory, Bundles of Rights on IoT Data, and the EU Data Act (2024), European Journal of Law & Economics, https://link.springer.com/content/pdf/10.1007/s10657-023-09791-8.pdf.

high transaction costs. The need for bilateral negotiations about "reasonable compensation", technical protection measures, trade secret protection, compliance with data protection law, as well as the (for many services and innovations too) narrow scope of the shared data can make this data sharing mechanism weak and ineffective. If the data holders do not want to share the data, they have many options to make it hard and unattractive for third parties to get IoT data through these user rights. A specific important question is whether making data accessible implies that the users and third parties have a right to get a copy of the accessible IoT data, or whether access and use of this data only means that they can get access on a server under the (direct or indirect) control of the data holder ("in-situ" access).[5] Also the lack of solutions for technical interoperability with the IoT device (e.g., access to proprietary software) for providing, e.g., repair services, shows the limitations of effective solutions in the DA.[6]

However, in the final version of the DA a big step has been done regarding this data sharing mechanism by clarifying that the IoT data that are shared by the users with data recipients can be used as input for new emerging markets for non-personal data. Moreover, the new recital 26 states that only the users are allowed to monetize the IoT product data. The main argument is that such an exclusive assignment of the right to monetize the non-personal IoT product data might give users larger incentives to share the data. This can enable the emergence of "liquid, fair and efficient" data markets which, in turn, could have positive effects on innovation and competition.[7] Whereas the DA proposal of the Commission was very unclear whether it wanted to open a path to such data markets,[8] the final version of the DA now clearly states that it wants such data markets via these user rights (including an active role for data intermediaries as defined and regulated in the Data Governance Act). On the one hand, this clarification offers important opportunities for more effective data sharing, e.g. by enabling aggregated data sets be used by innovating firms; on the other hand, it is not clear to what extent the otherwise still very complex

5 For the problem of "in-situ" access see Kerber (fn.3), 124, and Wiebe, Der Data Act–Innovation oder Illusion? (2023), GRUR 1569, 1571.

6 Although the latter solution would enable the users and data recipients to analyze and use the data, the data holders would never lose exclusive de facto control over the IoT data. This also implies that the option that users share directly the data with third parties without using the data sharing mechanism of Art. 5 DA would not be possible.

7 Recital 33 DA; important is that Art. 6(2)(c) DA of the final version now explicitly allows that data recipients can resell the non-personal data to other firms if users agree.

8 See Kerber (fn.3), 125.

rules of the DA (regarding trade secrets, technical protection measures, "reasonable compensation", "in-situ" access etc.) can lead to big problems and impediments for such markets for non-personal data. This is an issue that is in urgent need to be further clarified during the implementation process of the DA.

III. Key instrument II: Data use contract between data holders and users

The second new key instrument is the requirement that data holders need a contract with the users of the IoT device for being allowed to use the non-personal IoT data. This is conceptually and legally a far-reaching change of the bundle of rights on non-personal data. Whereas so far the data holders were free to use, share, and monetize the generated non-personal IoT data which are under their de facto control, Art. 4(13) DA eliminates this property-like position of the data holders and assigns the bundle of rights on the non-personal IoT data to the users.[9] Without the users' consent, the data holders cannot use this data, i.e. it is the users who are licensing the data to the data holders.[10] Therefore, this new data use contract seems to give the users a very strong position for empowering them to get meaningful control over their non-personal IoT data and to get a fairer share of the value of this IoT data. However, the question arises whether this key instrument can increase the empowerment of users, lead to a fairer distribution of the value of IoT data and have positive effects on innovation and competition. We will see that it is particularly important that manufacturers (data holders) have the option to make the sale of the IoT device to the users conditional on the conclusion of the data use contract on non-personal data.[11] Such a bundling of contracts limits the choice of users regarding the licensing of their non-personal IoT data, with far-reaching implications for the effectiveness of this second key instrument of the DA. In the following analysis, we will distinguish between B2B and B2C situations.

9 See Eckardt/Kerber (fn.4), section 4.2.

10 See already Hennemann/Steinrötter, Data Act – Fundament des neuen Datenwirtschaftsrechts (2022), NJW, 1481, 1483; Specht-Riemenschneider, Der Entwurf des Data Act (2022), MMR, 809. The already mentioned clarification that only the users are allowed to monetize the IoT product data has further strengthened this interpretation. See Eckardt/Kerber (fn.4), section 4.2.

11 It is similar for the data use contract regarding personal data (according to EU data protection law).

1. B2B situations

In the discussion about the DA, it was never clear whether in B2B situations a general market failure exists which justifies the mandatory rules of the DA, in particular, the mandatory introduction of the user rights of Art. 4 and 5. Usually, economists would assume that firms can solve their problems best through free negotiations and freedom of contract. This implies that if business users want to have access to the data of their IoT devices (and want to share this data, e.g., with independent providers of repair services), then they can negotiate access and sharing rights to this IoT data in their negotiations with the manufacturers of the IoT devices. There might be cases of unequal negotiation power between manufacturers and users, which can be interpreted as a market failure, but it is very unclear whether such a limited number of cases justifies the mandatory introduction of these user rights and the data use contract for non-personal data in all B2B situations. From that perspective, it can be seen as an improvement that in the final version of the DA business users can waive their user rights and can also "sell" them to other parties (including the data holders). This can avoid unnecessary over-regulation.[12]

However, this undifferentiated elimination of the non-waivability of these user rights might also have problematic effects. It leads back to a solution in which the allocation of rights regarding who can use, share, and monetize the IoT data is based on free negotiations between the firms. Since the manufacturers can bundle the sales contract with a data use contract which gives them far-reaching rights to use, share, and monetize the IoT data (according to Art. 4(13) DA) and an (additional?) contract about the waiving of the user rights of Art. 4 and 5 DA, the manufacturer can keep exclusive control over all IoT data. Through the bundling strategy, the business users can neither use the data use contract for getting some control over their IoT data nor the user rights of Art. 4 and 5, which are contracted away in this situation of free negotiations between the manufacturers and the business users who buy the IoT devices. In most cases, the manufacturers will not be in such a strong position that business users have to accept that, i.e., they can negotiate much better solutions. However, in those cases such negotiations are already possible right now before the enactment of the DA. And in the other case of unequal bargaining power,

12 See DA, recital 25. For this issue with a more cautious proposal, see Metzger/Schweitzer, Shaping markets: A critical evaluation of the draft Data Act (2023), Zeitschrift für europäisches Privatrecht, 42, 56–58.

the DA does not seem to be able to help the business users (due to the waivability that enables the contracting away of these rights).

If this argumentation is correct, then it is not clear why the DA can be expected to lead to much more sharing of data by the business users, because before and after the enactment of the DA everything depends on free negotiations between the firms. It can be asked, however, whether the new "Unfair Terms Control" (Art. 13 DA) or the new instrument of "model contract terms" (Art. 41 DA) can help in cases of unequal bargaining power to some extent or facilitate otherwise the sharing of IoT data by the business users.[13]

2. B2C situations

For the governance of IoT data in B2C situations, the problems with the data use contracts are very different.[14] Due to the serious market failure problems regarding information asymmetries and behavioral problems, which are well-known in the discussion about "consent" to the processing of personal data in EU data protection law (and which are so far not solved),[15] it can be assumed that the consumers will have the same problems with the data use contract for non-personal IoT data. In B2C situations, it can be generally expected that the manufacturers will tie the sale of the IoT devices to a far-reaching ("take-it-or-leave-it") buy-out contract about the use, sharing, and monetizing of the non-personal data by the data holders. This implies that the bundle of rights that the DA assigns to the consumers is contracted away to the data holders who then can extract most of the value from this IoT data. Since the data holders are allowed to bundle these contracts, even for the entire life-time of the IoT device,[16] the consumers are left only with the user rights of Art. 4 and 5, which in B2C situations (in contrast to B2B situations) cannot be contracted away due to their

13 See, e.g., Hennemann, A Fair Share? – Data Contracts and Unfair Terms Control (2024), in this volume.

14 See, in more detail, Kerber (fn.3), 131–133; Eckardt/Kerber (fn.4), section 4.2.

15 See Metzger/Schweitzer/Wagner, Datenschutz und Datenmarkt: Grundzüge einer Marktordnung für die europäische Datenwirtschaft (2023), ZfPW, 227, 236–242.

16 Since the data holders seem to be allowed to brick, i.e. disable, the IoT device if the consumers terminate the data use contract, such buy-out contracts are de facto concluded for the entire life-time of the IoT device. For the problem of "bricking", see Specht-Riemenschneider/El-Rifaai/Bodemann/Mehnert, IoT-Data sharing in B2C: How to better serve the consumer (2024), in this volume.

non-waivability. Due to the information problems of consumers regarding the processing, use, and value of the non-personal IoT data, it also cannot be assumed that competition between the manufacturers of IoT devices would lead to effective competition regarding the terms of this data use contract.[17]

Therefore, in B2C situations it cannot be expected that this data use contract will empower the consumers to make meaningful decisions about the use and sharing of their non-personal IoT data, and it might also not lead to a fairer allocation of the value of this data. What are possible future policy solutions for this problem?

(1) One option is to require that the data holders have to compensate the consumers directly for the value of the IoT data, which they can use on the basis of such a contract with the consumers. This can be done both for non-personal and personal data.
(2) Another policy option is to focus on additional regulatory solutions for ensuring that the consumers have more choice about the terms of this data use contract, e.g. by limiting the extent of the bundling of the sales contract with the data use contract by the data holders.

In the following, both options will be briefly discussed.

Compensation: The basic idea of a 'compensation' solution is that the consumers should get a fair share of the value of the consumer data which they are licensing to the data holders through such data use contracts about non-personal and personal IoT data. Does this imply that the data holders have to pay direct monetary compensation to the consumers? This is not clear from an economic perspective, even in the case of such buy-out contracts. Economists would make the argument that if the manufacturers would get through these data use contracts significant direct and indirect benefits from the data, which would lower the costs for the firms (e.g. through additional revenues from data monetization), then competition between the IoT device manufacturers can lead to lower prices of the IoT devices. Therefore, the consumers might be indirectly compensated through these lower product prices for allowing the data holders to use their IoT data. It is, however, unclear, how well price competition on markets for IoT devices works, and whether this effect can be seen as sufficient for giving the consumers a fair share of the value of their consumer data. This issue

---

17 This is different in B2B situations where the business users do not have such large information problems, and where competition regarding the terms of the data use contract can work much better.

needs much more research, also with respect to the question what the value of this consumer IoT data means and how to measure it.

More choice of consumers: Even if the consumers were to receive a fair share of the value of their IoT data, such buy-out data use contracts do not allow the consumers to make meaningful decisions according to their own preferences about whether and to what extent they want to grant data holders their rights to use, share, and monetize their IoT data. Since IoT devices are simultaneously surveillance instruments, consumers might want to have a genuine choice about when and where what types of data are generated and collected with their devices, how they are used for what purposes, and with whom these IoT data are shared. In order to achieve more consumer sovereignty (or consumer autonomy), it could be very important to protect a minimum standard of choice for consumers with regard to their IoT data. The problem is that the DA relies only on freedom of contract for the data use contract. This does not protect consumers sufficiently against the negative effects of the market failure problems on this market.

It cannot be discussed in detail here how such regulatory solutions, which might be very similar to consumer protection measures, might look like. Possible examples are (1) that data holders are not allowed to tie the use of the IoT device to terms in the data use contract for collecting and using of data which are not necessary for the functionality of the device, (2) that consumers have a right to terminate the data use contract after a certain period of time without losing the right to use the IoT device (i.e. data holders cannot brick the device), or (3) that consumers get more granular rights to decide freely about the collection, use, and sharing of their non-personal data.[18] A much more fundamental question is whether consumers should also have a say about who the holder of their IoT data is, and whether it should be possible for the consumer to switch the data holder.[19] The problem of how to ensure that consumers are better empowered to make meaningful choices about their non-personal and personal data is

18 See also Specht-Riemenschneider/El-Rifaai/Bodemann/Mehnert (fn.16), Eckardt/Kerber (fn.4), section 4.2.

19 So far, the DA does not give the user of an IoT device the right to choose the data holder. These decisions are unilaterally made by the manufacturers of IoT devices. This does not fit well to an interpretation of the DA which views the bundle of rights on IoT data assigned to the users of these devices. The data portability right of Art. 20 GDPR has always be seen as an instrument for facilitating switching between digital platforms, which again would support competition between platforms. This question of a possible competition between data holders as service providers for the users is missing in the DA. See also Schmidt-Kessel, Heraus- und Weitergabe von

a complex issue, which, however, is increasingly discussed, e.g. also in data protection law.

IV. Some policy conclusions

With regard to the governance of IoT data the Data Act is an ambitious, complex, and fascinating new legislative act which raises also new fundamental questions for the general policy discussion about the governance of data. However, also in its enacted version, it still suffers from the lack of a clear legal and economic concept which leads to serious contradictions, inconsistencies, many open questions, and also widely different interpretations of the rules of the DA. Therefore, much more clarifications and additional concrete rules will be necessary for its successful implementation. So far, it is still very unclear whether its rules are capable of helping to achieve the objectives of the DA, especially with respect to unlock more IoT data for innovation, enable more competition on secondary markets, and lead to more empowerment of the users, especially the consumers. A necessary precondition for any further proposals to improve the DA, either during the implementation process (e.g., model contracts) or through additional regulations beyond the DA, is a much better understanding of the markets for IoT devices and IoT data, the market failures in B2B and B2C contexts, as well as the role of technology.

Based upon the results of our brief analysis, the following policy conclusions can be suggested:

(1) It is particularly important to make the data sharing mechanism of Art. 5 DA much more effective by finding pragmatic solutions on how to deal with the many hurdles, restrictions, and impediments to this mechanism and how to reduce transaction costs for the sharing and use of IoT data, including enabling new markets for non-personal data.

(2) Since the strategy of bundling the sales contract of an IoT device with far-reaching buy-out contracts about the use of non-personal data can significantly impede the achievement of the objectives of the DA, it is important to develop pragmatic solutions for limiting such bundling strategies. Especially in B2C contexts, additional regulatory solutions

IoT-Gerätedaten (2024), MMR, 75, 81 for an interpretation of the legal relationship between data holder and user as “Geschäftsbesorgung”.

which better protect consumers, e.g. regarding more choice or better compensation for their data, are necessary.

(3) A very interesting feature of the DA is that the new user rights refer also to personal IoT data. One view is that the DA is irrelevant for personal data due to the GDPR. But since the rules of the GDPR do not work well in protecting the privacy of IoT users, we should also think about the potential of the DA (e.g., through its more far-reaching rights about access to and sharing of personal IoT data) to empower the consumers also with regard to their personal data. This would also mean that EU data protection law could better achieve its objectives. Therefore, policy discussions about the potential positive effects of the DA should focus also much more on the issue of personal IoT data.

(4) Despite these options to make the DA more effective, it should be kept in mind that the basic approach of the DA with its exclusive focus on an user-initiated data sharing mechanism might not be a sufficiently suitable approach for unlocking much more IoT data for innovation and competition. Additional approaches, like, in particular, sectoral regulations for much more targeted and effective solutions regarding competition and innovation on secondary markets, might be necessary. These additional solutions might also include direct data access rights for firms (e.g., for training AI and algorithms), data trustee solutions, and regulations regarding technology and standardization.[20]

20 See also Wiebe (fn.5), 1578.